ROMANIAN
VOCABULARY

FOR ENGLISH SPEAKERS

ENGLISH-ROMANIAN

The most useful words
To expand your lexicon and sharpen
your language skills

9000 words

Romanian vocabulary for English speakers - 9000 words
By Andrey Taranov

T&P Books vocabularies are intended for helping you learn, memorize and review foreign words. The dictionary is divided into themes, covering all major spheres of everyday activities, business, science, culture, etc.

The process of learning words using T&P Books' theme-based dictionaries gives you the following advantages:

- Correctly grouped source information predetermines success at subsequent stages of word memorization
- Availability of words derived from the same root allowing memorization of word units (rather than separate words)
- Small units of words facilitate the process of establishing associative links needed for consolidation of vocabulary
- Level of language knowledge can be estimated by the number of learned words

T&P Books Publishing
www.tpbooks.com

ISBN: 978-1-78071-684-8

This book is also available in E-book formats.
Please visit www.tpbooks.com or the major online bookstores.

ROMANIAN VOCABULARY
for English speakers

T&P Books vocabularies are intended to help you learn, memorize, and review foreign words. The vocabulary contains over 9000 commonly used words arranged thematically.

- Vocabulary contains the most commonly used words
- Recommended as an addition to any language course
- Meets the needs of beginners and advanced learners of foreign languages
- Convenient for daily use, revision sessions, and self-testing activities
- Allows you to assess your vocabulary

Special features of the vocabulary

- Words are organized according to their meaning, not alphabetically
- Words are presented in three columns to facilitate the reviewing and self-testing processes
- Words in groups are divided into small blocks to facilitate the learning process
- The vocabulary offers a convenient and simple transcription of each foreign word

The vocabulary has 256 topics including:

Basic Concepts, Numbers, Colors, Months, Seasons, Units of Measurement, Clothing & Accessories, Food & Nutrition, Restaurant, Family Members, Relatives, Character, Feelings, Emotions, Diseases, City, Town, Sightseeing, Shopping, Money, House, Home, Office, Working in the Office, Import & Export, Marketing, Job Search, Sports, Education, Computer, Internet, Tools, Nature, Countries, Nationalities and more ...

T&P BOOKS' THEME-BASED DICTIONARIES

The Correct System for Memorizing Foreign Words

Acquiring vocabulary is one of the most important elements of learning a foreign language, because words allow us to express our thoughts, ask questions, and provide answers. An inadequate vocabulary can impede communication with a foreigner and make it difficult to understand a book or movie well.

The pace of activity in all spheres of modern life, including the learning of modern languages, has increased. Today, we need to memorize large amounts of information (grammar rules, foreign words, etc.) within a short period. However, this does not need to be difficult. All you need to do is to choose the right training materials, learn a few special techniques, and develop your individual training system.

Having a system is critical to the process of language learning. Many people fail to succeed in this regard; they cannot master a foreign language because they fail to follow a system comprised of selecting materials, organizing lessons, arranging new words to be learned, and so on. The lack of a system causes confusion and eventually, lowers self-confidence.

T&P Books' theme-based dictionaries can be included in the list of elements needed for creating an effective system for learning foreign words. These dictionaries were specially developed for learning purposes and are meant to help students effectively memorize words and expand their vocabulary.

Generally speaking, the process of learning words consists of three main elements:

- Reception (creation or acquisition) of a training material, such as a word list
- Work aimed at memorizing new words
- Work aimed at reviewing the learned words, such as self-testing

All three elements are equally important since they determine the quality of work and the final result. All three processes require certain skills and a well-thought-out approach.

New words are often encountered quite randomly when learning a foreign language and it may be difficult to include them all in a unified list. As a result, these words remain written on scraps of paper, in book margins, textbooks, and so on. In order to systematize such words, we have to create and continually update a "book of new words." A paper notebook, a netbook, or a tablet PC can be used for these purposes.

This "book of new words" will be your personal, unique list of words. However, it will only contain the words that you came across during the learning process. For example, you might have written down the words "Sunday," "Tuesday," and "Friday." However, there are additional words for days of the week, for example, "Saturday," that are missing, and your list of words would be incomplete. Using a theme dictionary, in addition to the "book of new words," is a reasonable solution to this problem.

The theme-based dictionary may serve as the basis for expanding your vocabulary.

It will be your big "book of new words" containing the most frequently used words of a foreign language already included. There are quite a few theme-based dictionaries available, and you should ensure that you make the right choice in order to get the maximum benefit from your purchase.

Therefore, we suggest using theme-based dictionaries from T&P Books Publishing as an aid to learning foreign words. Our books are specially developed for effective use in the sphere of vocabulary systematization, expansion and review.

Theme-based dictionaries are not a magical solution to learning new words. However, they can serve as your main database to aid foreign-language acquisition. Apart from theme dictionaries, you can have copybooks for writing down new words, flash cards, glossaries for various texts, as well as other resources; however, a good theme dictionary will always remain your primary collection of words.

T&P Books' theme-based dictionaries are specialty books that contain the most frequently used words in a language.

The main characteristic of such dictionaries is the division of words into themes. For example, the *City* theme contains the words "street," "crossroads," "square," "fountain," and so on. The *Talking* theme might contain words like "to talk," "to ask," "question," and "answer".

All the words in a theme are divided into smaller units, each comprising 3–5 words. Such an arrangement improves the perception of words and makes the learning process less tiresome. Each unit contains a selection of words with similar meanings or identical roots. This allows you to learn words in small groups and establish other associative links that have a positive effect on memorization.

The words on each page are placed in three columns: a word in your native language, its translation, and its transcription. Such positioning allows for the use of techniques for effective memorization. After closing the translation column, you can flip through and review foreign words, and vice versa. "This is an easy and convenient method of review – one that we recommend you do often."

Our theme-based dictionaries contain transcriptions for all the foreign words. Unfortunately, none of the existing transcriptions are able to convey the exact nuances of foreign pronunciation. That is why we recommend using the transcriptions only as a supplementary learning aid. Correct pronunciation can only be acquired with the help of sound. Therefore our collection includes audio theme-based dictionaries.

The process of learning words using T&P Books' theme-based dictionaries gives you the following advantages:

- You have correctly grouped source information, which predetermines your success at subsequent stages of word memorization
- Availability of words derived from the same root (lazy, lazily, lazybones), allowing you to memorize word units instead of separate words
- Small units of words facilitate the process of establishing associative links needed for consolidation of vocabulary
- You can estimate the number of learned words and hence your level of language knowledge
- The dictionary allows for the creation of an effective and high-quality revision process
- You can revise certain themes several times, modifying the revision methods and techniques
- Audio versions of the dictionaries help you to work out the pronunciation of words and develop your skills of auditory word perception

The T&P Books' theme-based dictionaries are offered in several variants differing in the number of words: 1.500, 3.000, 5.000, 7.000, and 9.000 words. There are also dictionaries containing 15,000 words for some language combinations. Your choice of dictionary will depend on your knowledge level and goals.

We sincerely believe that our dictionaries will become your trusty assistant in learning foreign languages and will allow you to easily acquire the necessary vocabulary.

TABLE OF CONTENTS

PRONUNCIATION GUIDE

T&P phonetic alphabet	Romanian example	English example
[a]	**arbust** [ar'bust]	shorter than in ask
[e]	**a merge** [a 'merdʒe]	elm, medal
[ə]	**brățară** [brə'tsarə]	Schwa, rediced 'e'
[i]	**impozit** [im'pozit]	shorter than in feet
[ɨ]	**cuvânt** [ku'vɨnt]	big, America
[o]	**avocat** [avo'kat]	pod, John
[u]	**fluture** ['fluture]	book
[b]	**bancă** ['bankə]	baby, book
[d]	**durabil** [du'rabil]	day, doctor
[dʒ]	**gemeni** ['dʒemenʲ]	joke, general
[f]	**frizer** [fri'zer]	face, food
[g]	**gladiolă** [gladi'olə]	game, gold
[ʒ]	**jucător** [ʒukə'tor]	forge, pleasure
[h]	**pahar** [pa'har]	home, have
[k]	**actor** [ak'tor]	clock, kiss
[l]	**clopot** ['klopot]	lace, people
[m]	**mobilă** ['mobilə]	magic, milk
[n]	**nuntă** ['nuntə]	name, normal
[p]	**profet** [pro'fet]	pencil, private
[r]	**roată** [ro'atə]	rice, radio
[s]	**salată** [sa'latə]	city, boss
[ʃ]	**cleştişor** [kleʃti'ʃor]	machine, shark
[t]	**statuie** [sta'tue]	tourist, trip
[ts]	**forță** ['fortsə]	cats, tsetse fly
[tʃ]	**optzeci** [opt'zetʃi]	church, French
[v]	**valiză** [va'lizə]	very, river
[z]	**zmeură** ['zmeurə]	zebra, please
[j]	**foios** [fo'jos]	yes, New York
[ʲ]	**zori** [zorʲ]	palatalization sign

ABBREVIATIONS used in the vocabulary

English abbreviations

ab.	-	about
adj	-	adjective
adv	-	adverb
anim.	-	animate
as adj	-	attributive noun used as adjective
e.g.	-	for example
etc.	-	et cetera
fam.	-	familiar
fem.	-	feminine
form.	-	formal
inanim.	-	inanimate
masc.	-	masculine
math	-	mathematics
mil.	-	military
n	-	noun
pl	-	plural
pron.	-	pronoun
sb	-	somebody
sing.	-	singular
sth	-	something
v aux	-	auxiliary verb
vi	-	intransitive verb
vi, vt	-	intransitive, transitive verb
vt	-	transitive verb

Romanian abbreviations

f	-	feminine noun
f pl	-	feminine plural
m	-	masculine noun
m pl	-	masculine plural
n	-	neuter
n pl	-	neuter plural
pl	-	plural

BASIC CONCEPTS

Basic concepts. Part 1

1. Pronouns

I, me	**eu**	[eu]
you	**tu**	[tu]
he	**el**	[el]
she	**ea**	[ʲa]
we	**noi**	[noj]
you (to a group)	**voi**	['voj]
they (masc.)	**ei**	['ej]
they (fem.)	**ele**	['ele]

2. Greetings. Salutations. Farewells

Hello! (fam.)	**Bună ziua!**	['bunə 'ziwa]
Hello! (form.)	**Bună ziua!**	['bunə 'ziwa]
Good morning!	**Bună dimineața!**	['bunə dimi'nʲatsa]
Good afternoon!	**Bună ziua!**	['bunə 'ziwa]
Good evening!	**Bună seara!**	['bunə 'sʲara]
to say hello	**a se saluta**	[a se salu'ta]
Hi! (hello)	**Salut!**	[sa'lut]
greeting (n)	**salut** (n)	[sa'lut]
to greet (vt)	**a saluta**	[a salu'ta]
How are you?	**Ce mai faci?**	[ʧie maj 'faʧi]
What's new?	**Ce mai e nou?**	[ʧe maj e 'nou]
Bye-Bye! Goodbye!	**La revedere!**	[la reve'dere]
See you soon!	**Pe curând!**	[pe ku'rɨnd]
Farewell! (to a friend)	**Rămâi cu bine!**	[rə'mɨj ku 'bine]
Farewell! (form.)	**Rămâneți cu bine!**	[rəmɨ'nets ku 'bine]
to say goodbye	**a-şi lua rămas bun**	[aʃ lu'a rə'mas bun]
So long!	**Pa!**	[pa]
Thank you!	**Mulțumesc!**	[multsu'mesk]
Thank you very much!	**Mulțumesc mult!**	[multsu'mesk mult]
You're welcome	**Cu plăcere**	[ku plə'ʧere]
Don't mention it!	**Pentru puțin**	['pentru pu'tsin]

It was nothing	**Pentru puțin**	['pentru pu'tsin]
Excuse me! (fam.)	**Scuză-mă!**	['skuzəmə]
Excuse me! (form.)	**Scuzați-mă!**	[sku'zatsimə]
to excuse (forgive)	**a scuza**	[a sku'za]
to apologize (vi)	**a cere scuze**	[a 'tʃere 'skuze]
My apologies	**Cer scuze**	[tʃer 'skuze]
I'm sorry!	**Lertați-mă!**	[er'tatsimə]
to forgive (vt)	**a ierta**	[a er'ta]
please (adv)	**vă rog**	[və rog]
Don't forget!	**Nu uitați!**	[nu uj'tatsʲ]
Certainly!	**Desigur!**	[de'sigur]
Of course not!	**Desigur ca nu!**	[de'sigur kə nu]
Okay! (I agree)	**Sunt de acord!**	[sunt de a'kord]
That's enough!	**Ajunge!**	[a'ʒundʒe]

3. How to address

mister, sir	**Domnule**	['domnule]
ma'am	**Doamnă**	[do'amnə]
miss	**Domnişoară**	[domniʃo'arə]
young man	**Tinere**	['tinere]
young man (little boy, kid)	**Băiatule**	[bə'jatule]
miss (little girl)	**Fetițo**	[fe'titso]

4. Cardinal numbers. Part 1

0 zero	**zero**	['zero]
1 one	**unu**	['unu]
2 two	**doi**	[doj]
3 three	**trei**	[trej]
4 four	**patru**	['patru]
5 five	**cinci**	[tʃintʃ]
6 six	**şase**	['ʃase]
7 seven	**şapte**	['ʃapte]
8 eight	**opt**	[opt]
9 nine	**nouă**	['nowə]
10 ten	**zece**	['zetʃe]
11 eleven	**unsprezece**	['unsprezetʃe]
12 twelve	**doisprezece**	['dojsprezetʃe]
13 thirteen	**treisprezece**	['trejsprezetʃe]
14 fourteen	**paisprezece**	['pajsprezetʃe]
15 fifteen	**cincisprezece**	['tʃintʃsprezetʃe]
16 sixteen	**şaisprezece**	['ʃajsprezetʃe]

17 seventeen	**şaptesprezece**	['ʃaptesprezetʃe]
18 eighteen	**optsprezece**	['optsprezetʃe]
19 nineteen	**nouăsprezece**	['nowəsprezetʃe]
20 twenty	**douăzeci**	[dowə'zetʃi]
21 twenty-one	**douăzeci şi unu**	[dowə'zetʃi ʃi 'unu]
22 twenty-two	**douăzeci şi doi**	[dowə'zetʃi ʃi doj]
23 twenty-three	**douăzeci şi trei**	[dowə'zetʃi ʃi trej]
30 thirty	**treizeci**	[trej'zetʃi]
31 thirty-one	**treizeci şi unu**	[trej'zetʃi ʃi 'unu]
32 thirty-two	**treizeci şi doi**	[trej'zetʃi ʃi doj]
33 thirty-three	**treizeci şi trei**	[trej'zetʃi ʃi trej]
40 forty	**patruzeci**	[patru'zetʃi]
41 forty-one	**patruzeci şi unu**	[patru'zetʃi ʃi 'unu]
42 forty-two	**patruzeci şi doi**	[patru'zetʃi ʃi doj]
43 forty-three	**patruzeci şi trei**	[patru'zetʃi ʃi trej]
50 fifty	**cincizeci**	[tʃintʃ'zetʃ]
51 fifty-one	**cincizeci şi unu**	[tʃintʃ'zetʃ ʃi 'unu]
52 fifty-two	**cincizeci şi doi**	[tʃintʃ'zetʃ ʃi doj]
53 fifty-three	**cincizeci şi trei**	[tʃintʃ'zetʃ ʃi trej]
60 sixty	**şaizeci**	[ʃaj'zetʃi]
61 sixty-one	**şaizeci şi unu**	[ʃaj'zetʃi ʃi 'unu]
62 sixty-two	**şaizeci şi doi**	[ʃaj'zetʃi ʃi doj]
63 sixty-three	**şaizeci şi trei**	[ʃaj'zetʃi ʃi trej]
70 seventy	**şaptezeci**	[ʃapte'zetʃi]
71 seventy-one	**şaptezeci şi unu**	[ʃapte'zetʃi ʃi 'unu]
72 seventy-two	**şaptezeci şi doi**	[ʃapte'zetʃi ʃi doj]
73 seventy-three	**şaptezeci şi trei**	[ʃapte'zetʃi ʃi trej]
80 eighty	**optzeci**	[opt'zetʃi]
81 eighty-one	**optzeci şi unu**	[opt'zetʃi ʃi 'unu]
82 eighty-two	**optzeci şi doi**	[opt'zetʃi ʃi doj]
83 eighty-three	**optzeci şi trei**	[opt'zetʃi ʃi trej]
90 ninety	**nouăzeci**	[nowə'zetʃi]
91 ninety-one	**nouăzeci şi unu**	[nowə'zetʃi ʃi 'unu]
92 ninety-two	**nouăzeci şi doi**	[nowə'zetʃi ʃi doj]
93 ninety-three	**nouăzeci şi trei**	[nowə'zetʃi ʃi trej]

5. Cardinal numbers. Part 2

100 one hundred	**o sută**	[o 'sutə]
200 two hundred	**două sute**	['dowə 'sute]
300 three hundred	**trei sute**	[trej 'sute]
400 four hundred	**patru sute**	['patru 'sute]

500 five hundred	**cinci sute**	[ʧinʧ 'sute]
600 six hundred	**şase sute**	['ʃase 'sute]
700 seven hundred	**şapte sute**	['ʃapte 'sute]
800 eight hundred	**opt sute**	[opt 'sute]
900 nine hundred	**nouă sute**	['nowə 'sute]
1000 one thousand	**o mie**	[o 'mie]
2000 two thousand	**două mii**	['dowə mij]
3000 three thousand	**trei mii**	[trej mij]
10000 ten thousand	**zece mii**	['zeʧe mij]
one hundred thousand	**o sută de mii**	[o 'sutə de mij]
million	**milion** (n)	[mi'ljon]
billion	**miliard** (n)	[mi'ljard]

6. Ordinal numbers

first (adj)	**primul**	['primul]
second (adj)	**al doilea**	[al 'dojlʲa]
third (adj)	**al treilea**	[al 'trejlʲa]
fourth (adj)	**al patrulea**	[al 'patrulʲa]
fifth (adj)	**al cincilea**	[al 'ʧinʧilʲa]
sixth (adj)	**al şaselea**	[al 'ʃaselʲa]
seventh (adj)	**al şaptelea**	[al 'ʃaptelʲa]
eighth (adj)	**al optulea**	[al 'optulʲa]
ninth (adj)	**al nouălea**	[al 'nowəlʲa]
tenth (adj)	**al zecelea**	[al 'zeʧelʲa]

7. Numbers. Fractions

fraction	**fracţie** (f)	['fraktsie]
one half	**o doime**	[o 'doime]
one third	**o treime**	[o 'treime]
one quarter	**o pătrime**	[o pə'trime]
one eighth	**o optime**	[o op'time]
one tenth	**o zecime**	[o ze'ʧime]
two thirds	**două treimi**	['dowə 'treimʲ]
three quarters	**trei pătrimi**	[trej pə'trimʲ]

8. Numbers. Basic operations

subtraction	**scădere** (f)	[skə'dere]
to subtract (vi, vt)	**a scădea**	[a skə'dʲa]
division	**împărţire** (f)	[ɨmpər'tsire]
to divide (vt)	**a împărţi**	[a ɨmpər'tsi]

addition	**adunare** (f)	[adu'nare]
to add up (vt)	**a aduna**	[a adu'na]
to add (vi, vt)	**a adăuga**	[a adəu'ga]
multiplication	**înmulțire** (f)	[ɨnmul'tsire]
to multiply (vt)	**a înmulți**	[a ɨnmul'tsi]

9. Numbers. Miscellaneous

digit, figure	**cifră** (f)	['tʃifrə]
number	**număr** (n)	['numər]
numeral	**numeral** (n)	[nume'ral]
minus sign	**minus** (n)	['minus]
plus sign	**plus** (n)	[plus]
formula	**formulă** (f)	[for'mulə]
calculation	**calcul** (n)	['kalkul]
to count (vi, vt)	**a calcula**	[a kalku'la]
to count up	**a socoti**	[a soko'ti]
to compare (vt)	**a compara**	[a kompa'ra]
How much?	**Cât?**	[kɨt]
How many?	**Câți? Câte?**	[kɨts], ['kɨte]
sum, total	**sumă** (f)	['sumə]
result	**rezultat** (n)	[rezul'tat]
remainder	**rest** (n)	[rest]
a few (e.g., ~ years ago)	**câțiva, câteva**	[kɨts'va], [kɨte'va]
little (I had ~ time)	**puțin**	[pu'tsin]
few (I have ~ friends)	**puțini**	[pu'tsin^j]
a little (~ water)	**puțin**	[pu'tsin]
the rest	**rest** (n)	[rest]
one and a half	**unu şi jumătate**	['unu ʃi ʒumə'tate]
dozen	**duzină** (f)	[du'zinə]
in half (adv)	**în două**	[ɨn 'dowə]
equally (evenly)	**în părți egale**	[ɨn pərts^j e'gale]
half	**jumătate** (f)	[ʒumə'tate]
time (three ~s)	**dată** (f)	['datə]

10. The most important verbs. Part 1

to advise (vt)	**a sfătui**	[a sfətu'i]
to agree (say yes)	**a fi de acord**	[a fi de a'kord]
to answer (vi, vt)	**a răspunde**	[a rəs'punde]
to apologize (vi)	**a cere scuze**	[a 'tʃere 'skuze]
to arrive (vi)	**a sosi**	[a so'si]
to ask (~ oneself)	**a întreba**	[a ɨntre'ba]
to ask (~ sb to do sth)	**a cere**	[a 'tʃere]

to be (vi)	**a fi**	[a fi]
to be afraid	**a se teme**	[a se 'teme]
to be hungry	**a fi foame**	[a fi fo'ame]
to be interested in ...	**a se interesa**	[a se intere'sa]
to be needed	**a fi necesar**	[a fi netʃe'sar]
to be surprised	**a se mira**	[a se mi'ra]
to be thirsty	**a fi sete**	[a fi 'sete]
to begin (vt)	**a începe**	[a in'tʃepe]
to belong to ...	**a aparține**	[a apar'tsine]
to boast (vi)	**a se lăuda**	[a se ləu'da]
to break (split into pieces)	**a rupe**	[a 'rupe]
to call (~ for help)	**a chema**	[a ke'ma]
can (v aux)	**a putea**	[a pu'tʲa]
to catch (vt)	**a prinde**	[a 'prinde]
to change (vt)	**a schimba**	[a skim'ba]
to choose (select)	**a alege**	[a a'ledʒe]
to come down (the stairs)	**a coborî**	[a kobo'rɨ]
to compare (vt)	**a compara**	[a kompa'ra]
to complain (vi, vt)	**a se plânge**	[a se 'plɨndʒe]
to confuse (mix up)	**a încurca**	[a ɨnkur'ka]
to continue (vt)	**a continua**	[a kontinu'a]
to control (vt)	**a controla**	[a kontro'la]
to cook (dinner)	**a găti**	[a gə'ti]
to cost (vt)	**a costa**	[a kos'ta]
to count (add up)	**a calcula**	[a kalku'la]
to count on ...	**a conta pe ...**	[a kon'ta pe]
to create (vt)	**a crea**	[a 'krʲa]
to cry (weep)	**a plânge**	[a 'plɨndʒe]

11. The most important verbs. Part 2

to deceive (vi, vt)	**a minți**	[a min'tsi]
to decorate (tree, street)	**a împodobi**	[a ɨmpodo'bi]
to defend (a country, etc.)	**a apăra**	[a apə'ra]
to demand (request firmly)	**a cere**	[a 'tʃere]
to dig (vt)	**a săpa**	[a sə'pa]
to discuss (vt)	**a discuta**	[a disku'ta]
to do (vt)	**a face**	[a 'fatʃe]
to doubt (have doubts)	**a se îndoi**	[a se ɨndo'i]
to drop (let fall)	**a scăpa**	[a skə'pa]
to enter (room, house, etc.)	**a intra**	[a in'tra]
to excuse (forgive)	**a scuza**	[a sku'za]
to exist (vi)	**a exista**	[a ekzis'ta]

to expect (foresee)	**a prevedea**	[a preve'dʲa]
to explain (vt)	**a explica**	[a ekspli'ka]
to fall (vi)	**a cădea**	[a kə'dʲa]
to find (vt)	**a găsi**	[a gə'si]
to finish (vt)	**a termina**	[a termi'na]
to fly (vi)	**a zbura**	[a zbu'ra]
to follow ... (come after)	**a urma**	[a ur'ma]
to forget (vi, vt)	**a uita**	[a uj'ta]
to forgive (vt)	**a ierta**	[a er'ta]
to give (vt)	**a da**	[a da]
to give a hint	**a face aluzie**	[a 'fatʃe a'luzie]
to go (on foot)	**a merge**	[a 'merdʒe]
to go for a swim	**a se scălda**	[a se skəl'da]
to go out (for dinner, etc.)	**a ieşi**	[a e'ʃi]
to guess (the answer)	**a ghici**	[a gi'tʃi]
to have (vt)	**a avea**	[a a'vʲa]
to have breakfast	**a lua micul dejun**	[a lu'a 'mikul de'ʒun]
to have dinner	**a cina**	[a tʃi'na]
to have lunch	**a lua prânzul**	[a lu'a 'prɨnzul]
to hear (vt)	**a auzi**	[a au'zi]
to help (vt)	**a ajuta**	[a aʒu'ta]
to hide (vt)	**a ascunde**	[a as'kunde]
to hope (vi, vt)	**a spera**	[a spe'ra]
to hunt (vi, vt)	**a vâna**	[a vɨ'na]
to hurry (vi)	**a se grăbi**	[a se grə'bi]

12. The most important verbs. Part 3

to inform (vt)	**a informa**	[a infor'ma]
to insist (vi, vt)	**a insista**	[a insis'ta]
to insult (vt)	**a jigni**	[a ʒig'ni]
to invite (vt)	**a invita**	[a invi'ta]
to joke (vi)	**a glumi**	[a glu'mi]
to keep (vt)	**a păstra**	[a pəs'tra]
to keep silent, to hush	**a tăcea**	[a tə'tʃa]
to kill (vt)	**a omorî**	[a omo'rɨ]
to know (sb)	**a cunoaşte**	[a kuno'aʃte]
to know (sth)	**a şti**	[a ʃti]
to laugh (vi)	**a râde**	[a 'rɨde]
to liberate (city, etc.)	**a elibera**	[a elibe'ra]
to like (I like ...)	**a plăcea**	[a plə'tʃa]
to look for ... (search)	**a căuta**	[a kəu'ta]
to love (sb)	**a iubi**	[a ju'bi]

to make a mistake	**a greşi**	[a gre'ʃi]
to manage, to run	**a conduce**	[a kon'dutʃe]
to mean (signify)	**a însemna**	[a ɨnsem'na]
to mention (talk about)	**a menţiona**	[a mentsio'na]
to miss (school, etc.)	**a lipsi**	[a lip'si]
to notice (see)	**a observa**	[a obser'va]
to object (vi, vt)	**a contrazice**	[a kontra'zitʃe]
to observe (see)	**a observa**	[a obser'va]
to open (vt)	**a deschide**	[a des'kide]
to order (meal, etc.)	**a comanda**	[a koman'da]
to order (mil.)	**a ordona**	[a ordo'na]
to own (possess)	**a poseda**	[a pose'da]
to participate (vi)	**a participa**	[a partitʃi'pa]
to pay (vi, vt)	**a plăti**	[a plə'ti]
to permit (vt)	**a permite**	[a per'mite]
to plan (vt)	**a planifica**	[a planifi'ka]
to play (children)	**a juca**	[a ʒu'ka]
to pray (vi, vt)	**a se ruga**	[a se ru'ga]
to prefer (vt)	**a prefera**	[a prefe'ra]
to promise (vt)	**a promite**	[a pro'mite]
to pronounce (vt)	**a pronunţa**	[a pronun'tsa]
to propose (vt)	**a propune**	[a pro'pune]
to punish (vt)	**a pedepsi**	[a pedep'si]

13. The most important verbs. Part 4

to read (vi, vt)	**a citi**	[a tʃi'ti]
to recommend (vt)	**a recomanda**	[a rekoman'da]
to refuse (vi, vt)	**a refuza**	[a refu'za]
to regret (be sorry)	**a regreta**	[a regre'ta]
to rent (sth from sb)	**a închiria**	[a ɨnkiri'ja]
to repeat (say again)	**a repeta**	[a repe'ta]
to reserve, to book	**a rezerva**	[a rezer'va]
to run (vi)	**a alerga**	[a aler'ga]
to save (rescue)	**a salva**	[a sal'va]
to say (~ thank you)	**a spune**	[a 'spune]
to scold (vt)	**a certa**	[a tʃer'ta]
to see (vt)	**a vedea**	[a ve'dʲa]
to sell (vt)	**a vinde**	[a 'vinde]
to send (vt)	**a trimite**	[a tri'mite]
to shoot (vi)	**a trage**	[a 'tradʒə]
to shout (vi)	**a striga**	[a stri'ga]
to show (vt)	**a arăta**	[a arə'ta]
to sign (document)	**a semna**	[a sem'na]

to sit down (vi)	**a se aşeza**	[a se aʃə'za]
to smile (vi)	**a zâmbi**	[a zɨm'bi]
to speak (vi, vt)	**a vorbi**	[a vor'bi]
to steal (money, etc.)	**a fura**	[a fu'ra]
to stop (for pause, etc.)	**a se opri**	[a se o'pri]
to stop (please ~ calling me)	**a înceta**	[a antʃe'ta]
to study (vt)	**a studia**	[a studi'a]
to swim (vi)	**a înota**	[a ɨno'ta]
to take (vt)	**a lua**	[a lu'a]
to think (vi, vt)	**a se gândi**	[a se gɨn'di]
to threaten (vt)	**a amenința**	[a amenin'tsa]
to touch (with hands)	**a atinge**	[a a'tindʒe]
to translate (vt)	**a traduce**	[a tra'dutʃe]
to trust (vt)	**a avea încredere**	[a a'vʲa ɨn'kredere]
to try (attempt)	**a încerca**	[a ɨntʃer'ka]
to turn (e.g., ~ left)	**a întoarce**	[a ɨnto'artʃe]
to underestimate (vt)	**a subaprecia**	[a subapretʃi'a]
to understand (vt)	**a înțelege**	[a ɨntse'ledʒe]
to unite (vt)	**a uni**	[a u'ni]
to wait (vt)	**a aştepta**	[a aʃtep'ta]
to want (wish, desire)	**a vrea**	[a vrʲa]
to warn (vt)	**a avertiza**	[a averti'za]
to work (vi)	**a lucra**	[a lu'kra]
to write (vt)	**a scrie**	[a 'skrie]
to write down	**a nota**	[a no'ta]

14. Colors

color	**culoare** (f)	[kulo'are]
shade (tint)	**nuanță** (f)	[nu'antsə]
hue	**ton** (n)	[ton]
rainbow	**curcubeu** (n)	[kurku'beu]
white (adj)	**alb**	[alb]
black (adj)	**negru**	['negru]
gray (adj)	**sur**	['sur]
green (adj)	**verde**	['verde]
yellow (adj)	**galben**	['galben]
red (adj)	**roşu**	['roʃu]
blue (adj)	**albastru închis**	[al'bastru ɨ'nkis]
light blue (adj)	**albastru deschis**	[al'bastru des'kis]
pink (adj)	**roz**	['roz]
orange (adj)	**portocaliu**	[portoka'lju]

violet (adj)	**violet**	[vio'let]
brown (adj)	**cafeniu**	[kafe'nju]
golden (adj)	**de culoarea aurului**	[de kulo'arʲa 'auruluj]
silvery (adj)	**argintiu**	[arʤin'tju]
beige (adj)	**bej**	[beʒ]
cream (adj)	**crem**	[krem]
turquoise (adj)	**turcoaz**	[turko'az]
cherry red (adj)	**vişiniu**	[viʃi'nju]
lilac (adj)	**lila**	[li'la]
crimson (adj)	**de culoarea zmeurei**	[de kulo'arʲa 'zmeurej]
light (adj)	**de culoare deschisă**	[de kulo'are des'kisə]
dark (adj)	**de culoare închisă**	[de kulo'are ɨ'nkisə]
bright, vivid (adj)	**aprins**	[a'prins]
colored (pencils)	**colorat**	[kolo'rat]
color (e.g., ~ film)	**color**	[ko'lor]
black-and-white (adj)	**alb-negru**	[alb 'negru]
plain (one-colored)	**monocrom**	[mono'krom]
multicolored (adj)	**multicolor**	[multiko'lor]

15. Questions

Who?	**Cine?**	['ʧine]
What?	**Ce?**	[ʧe]
Where? (at, in)	**Unde?**	['unde]
Where (to)?	**Unde?**	['unde]
From where?	**De unde?**	[de 'unde]
When?	**Când?**	[kɨnd]
Why? (What for?)	**Pentru ce?**	['pentru ʧe]
Why? (~ are you crying?)	**De ce?**	[de ʧe]
What for?	**Pentru ce?**	['pentru ʧe]
How? (in what way)	**Cum?**	[kum]
What? (What kind of ...?)	**Care?**	['kare]
Which?	**Care?**	['kare]
To whom?	**Cui?**	[kuj]
About whom?	**Despre cine?**	['despre 'ʧine]
About what?	**Despre ce?**	['despre ʧe]
With whom?	**Cu cine?**	[ku 'ʧine]
How many?	**Cât? Câtă?**	[kɨt], ['kɨtə]
How much?	**Câţi? Câte?**	[kɨʦ], ['kɨte]
Whose?	**Al cui?**	['al kuj]
Whose? (fem.)	**A cui?**	[a kuj]
Whose? (pl)	**Ai cui?, Ale cui?**	[aj kuj], ['ale kuj]

16. Prepositions

with (accompanied by)	**cu**	[ku]
without	**fără**	[fərə]
to (indicating direction)	**la**	[la]
about (talking ~ ...)	**despre**	['despre]
before (in time)	**înainte de**	[ɨna'inte de]
in front of ...	**înaintea**	[ɨna'intʲa]
under (beneath, below)	**sub**	[sub]
above (over)	**deasupra**	[dʲa'supra]
on (atop)	**pe**	[pe]
from (off, out of)	**din**	[din]
of (made from)	**din**	[din]
in (e.g., ~ ten minutes)	**peste**	['peste]
over (across the top of)	**prin**	[prin]

17. Function words. Adverbs. Part 1

Where? (at, in)	**Unde?**	['unde]
here (adv)	**aici**	[a'iʧi]
there (adv)	**acolo**	[a'kolo]
somewhere (to be)	**undeva**	[unde'va]
nowhere (not in any place)	**nicăieri**	[nikə'erʲ]
by (near, beside)	**lângă ...**	['lɨngə]
by the window	**lângă fereastră**	['lɨngə fe'rʲastrə]
Where (to)?	**Unde?**	['unde]
here (e.g., come ~!)	**aici**	[a'iʧi]
there (e.g., to go ~)	**acolo**	[a'kolo]
from here (adv)	**de aici**	[de a'iʧi]
from there (adv)	**de acolo**	[de a'kolo]
close (adv)	**aproape**	[apro'ape]
far (adv)	**departe**	[de'parte]
near (e.g., ~ Paris)	**alături**	[a'ləturʲ]
nearby (adv)	**alături**	[a'ləturʲ]
not far (adv)	**aproape**	[apro'ape]
left (adj)	**stâng**	[stɨng]
on the left	**din stânga**	[din 'stɨnga]
to the left	**în stânga**	[ɨn 'stɨnga]
right (adj)	**drept**	[drept]
on the right	**din dreapta**	[din 'drʲapta]

to the right	**în dreapta**	[ɨn 'drʲapta]
in front (adv)	**în faţă**	[ɨn 'fatsə]
front (as adj)	**din faţă**	[din 'fatsə]
ahead (the kids ran ~)	**înainte**	[ɨna'inte]
behind (adv)	**în urmă**	[ɨn 'urmə]
from behind	**din spate**	[din 'spate]
back (towards the rear)	**înapoi**	[ɨna'poj]
middle	**mijloc** (n)	['miʒlok]
in the middle	**la mijloc**	[la 'miʒlok]
at the side	**dintr-o parte**	['dintro 'parte]
everywhere (adv)	**peste tot**	['peste tot]
around (in all directions)	**în jur**	[ɨn ʒur]
from inside	**dinăuntru**	[dinə'untru]
somewhere (to go)	**undeva**	[unde'va]
straight (directly)	**direct**	[di'rekt]
back (e.g., come ~)	**înapoi**	[ɨna'poj]
from anywhere	**de undeva**	[de unde'va]
from somewhere	**de undeva**	[de unde'va]
firstly (adv)	**în primul rând**	[ɨn 'primul rɨnd]
secondly (adv)	**în al doilea rând**	[ɨn al 'dojlʲa rɨnd]
thirdly (adv)	**în al treilea rând**	[ɨn al 'trejlʲa rɨnd]
suddenly (adv)	**deodată**	[deo'datə]
at first (in the beginning)	**la început**	[la ɨntʃe'put]
for the first time	**prima dată**	['prima 'datə]
long before ...	**cu mult timp înainte de ...**	[ku mult timp ɨna'inte de]
anew (over again)	**din nou**	[din 'nou]
for good (adv)	**pentru totdeauna**	['pentru totdʲa'una]
never (adv)	**niciodată**	[nitʃio'datə]
again (adv)	**iarăşi**	['jarəʃ]
now (at present)	**acum**	[a'kum]
often (adv)	**des**	[des]
then (adv)	**atunci**	[a'tuntʃi]
urgently (quickly)	**urgent**	[ur'dʒent]
usually (adv)	**de obicei**	[de obi'tʃej]
by the way, ...	**apropo**	[apro'po]
possibly	**posibil**	[po'sibil]
probably (adv)	**probabil**	[pro'babil]
maybe (adv)	**poate**	[po'ate]
besides ...	**în afară de aceasta, ...**	[ɨn a'farə de a'tʃasta]
that's why ...	**de aceea**	[de a'tʃeja]
in spite of ...	**deşi ...**	[de'ʃi]
thanks to ...	**datorită ...**	[dato'ritə]

what (pron.)	**ce**	[ʧe]
that (conj.)	**că**	[kə]
something	**ceva**	[ʧe'va]
anything (something)	**ceva**	[ʧe'va]
nothing	**nimic**	[ni'mik]
who (pron.)	**cine**	['ʧine]
someone	**cineva**	[ʧine'va]
somebody	**cineva**	[ʧine'va]
nobody	**nimeni**	['nimenʲ]
nowhere (a voyage to ~)	**nicăieri**	[nikə'erʲ]
nobody's	**al nimănui**	[al nimə'nuj]
somebody's	**al cuiva**	[al kuj'va]
so (I'm ~ glad)	**aşa**	[a'ʃa]
also (as well)	**de asemenea**	[de a'semenʲa]
too (as well)	**la fel**	[la fel]

18. Function words. Adverbs. Part 2

Why?	**De ce?**	[de ʧe]
for some reason	**nu se ştie de ce**	[nu se 'ʃtie de ʧe]
because ...	**pentru că ...**	['pentru kə]
for some purpose	**cine ştie pentru ce**	['ʧine 'ʃtie 'pentru ʧe]
and	**şi**	[ʃi]
or	**sau**	['sau]
but	**dar**	[dar]
for (e.g., ~ me)	**pentru**	['pentru]
too (~ many people)	**prea**	[prʲa]
only (exclusively)	**numai**	['numaj]
exactly (adv)	**exact**	[e'gzakt]
about (more or less)	**vreo**	['vrəo]
approximately (adv)	**aproximativ**	[aproksima'tiv]
approximate (adj)	**aproximativ**	[aproksima'tiv]
almost (adv)	**aproape**	[apro'ape]
the rest	**restul**	['restul]
each (adj)	**fiecare**	[fie'kare]
any (no matter which)	**oricare**	[ori'kare]
many, much (a lot of)	**mult**	[mult]
many people	**mulți**	[mulʦ]
all (everyone)	**toți**	[toʦ]
in return for ...	**în schimb la ...**	[ɨn 'skimb la]
in exchange (adv)	**în schimbul**	[ɨn 'skimbul]
by hand (made)	**manual**	[manu'al]

hardly (negative opinion)	**puțin probabil**	[pu'tsin pro'babil]
probably (adv)	**probabil**	[pro'babil]
on purpose (intentionally)	**intenționat**	[intentsio'nat]
by accident (adv)	**întâmplător**	[ɨntɨmplə'tor]
very (adv)	**foarte**	[fo'arte]
for example (adv)	**de exemplu**	[de e'gzemplu]
between	**între**	['ɨntre]
among	**printre**	['printre]
so much (such a lot)	**atât**	[a'tɨt]
especially (adv)	**mai ales**	[maj a'les]

Basic concepts. Part 2

19. Weekdays

Monday	**luni** (f)	[lunʲ]
Tuesday	**marți** (f)	['martsʲ]
Wednesday	**miercuri** (f)	['merkurʲ]
Thursday	**joi** (f)	[ʒoj]
Friday	**vineri** (f)	['vinerʲ]
Saturday	**sâmbătă** (f)	['sɨmbətə]
Sunday	**duminică** (f)	[du'minikə]
today (adv)	**astăzi**	['astəzʲ]
tomorrow (adv)	**mâine**	['mɨjne]
the day after tomorrow	**poimâine**	[poj'mɨne]
yesterday (adv)	**ieri**	[jerʲ]
the day before yesterday	**alaltăieri**	[a'laltəerʲ]
day	**zi** (f)	[zi]
working day	**zi** (f) **de lucru**	[zi de 'lukru]
public holiday	**zi** (f) **de sărbătoare**	[zi de sərbəto'are]
day off	**zi** (f) **liberă**	[zi 'liberə]
weekend	**zile** (f pl) **de odihnă**	['zile de o'dihnə]
all day long	**toată ziua**	[to'atə 'ziwa]
the next day (adv)	**a doua zi**	['dowa zi]
two days ago	**cu două zile în urmă**	[ku 'dowə 'zile ɨn 'urmə]
the day before	**în ajun**	[ɨn a'ʒun]
daily (adj)	**zilnic**	['zilnik]
every day (adv)	**în fiecare zi**	[ɨn fie'kare zi]
week	**săptămână** (f)	[səptə'mɨnə]
last week (adv)	**săptămâna trecută**	[səptə'mɨna tre'kutə]
next week (adv)	**săptămâna viitoare**	[səptə'mɨna viito'are]
weekly (adj)	**săptămânal**	[səptəmɨ'nal]
every week (adv)	**în fiecare săptămână**	[ɨn fie'kare səptə'mɨnə]
twice a week	**de două ori pe săptămână**	[de 'dowə orʲ pe səptə'mɨnə]
every Tuesday	**în fiecare marți**	[ɨn fie'kare 'marts]

20. Hours. Day and night

morning	**dimineață** (f)	[dimi'nʲatsə]
in the morning	**dimineața**	[dimi'nʲatsa]

noon, midday	**amiază** (f)	[a'mjazə]
in the afternoon	**după masă**	['dupə 'masə]
evening	**seară** (f)	['sʲarə]
in the evening	**seara**	['sʲara]
night	**noapte** (f)	[no'apte]
at night	**noaptea**	[no'aptʲa]
midnight	**miezul** (n) **nopții**	['mezul 'noptsij]
second	**secundă** (f)	[se'kundə]
minute	**minut** (n)	[mi'nut]
hour	**oră** (f)	['orə]
half an hour	**jumătate de oră**	[ʒumə'tate de 'orə]
a quarter-hour	**un sfert de oră**	[un sfert de 'orə]
fifteen minutes	**cincisprezece minute**	['ʧinʧsprezeʧe mi'nute]
24 hours	**o zi** (f)	[o zi]
sunrise	**răsărit** (n)	[rəsə'rit]
dawn	**zori** (m pl)	[zorʲ]
early morning	**zori** (m pl) **de zi**	[zorʲ de zi]
sunset	**apus** (n)	[a'pus]
early in the morning	**dimineața devreme**	[dimi'nʲatsa de'vreme]
this morning	**azi dimineață**	[azʲ dimi'nʲatsə]
tomorrow morning	**mâine dimineață**	['mɨjne dimi'nʲatsə]
this afternoon	**această după-amiază**	[a'ʧastə 'dupa ami'azə]
in the afternoon	**după masă**	['dupə 'masə]
tomorrow afternoon	**mâine după-masă**	['mɨjne 'dupə 'masə]
tonight (this evening)	**astă-seară**	['astə 'sʲarə]
tomorrow night	**mâine seară**	['mɨjne 'sʲarə]
at 3 o'clock sharp	**la ora trei fix**	[la 'ora trej fiks]
about 4 o'clock	**în jur de ora patru**	[ɨn ʒur de 'ora 'patru]
by 12 o'clock	**pe la ora douăsprezece**	[pe la 'ora 'dowəsprezeʧe]
in 20 minutes	**peste douăzeci de minute**	['peste dowə'zeʧi de mi'nute]
in an hour	**peste o oră**	['peste o 'orə]
on time (adv)	**la timp**	[la timp]
a quarter to ...	**fără un sfert**	['fərə un sfert]
within an hour	**în decurs de o oră**	[ɨn de'kurs de o 'orə]
every 15 minutes	**la fiecare cincisprezece minute**	[la fie'kare 'ʧinʧsprezeʧe mi'nute]
round the clock	**zi şi noapte**	[zi ʃi no'apte]

21. Months. Seasons

January	**ianuarie** (m)	[janu'arie]
February	**februarie** (m)	[febru'arie]

March	**martie** (m)	['martie]
April	**aprilie** (m)	[a'prilie]
May	**mai** (m)	[maj]
June	**iunie** (m)	['junie]

July	**iulie** (m)	['julie]
August	**august** (m)	['august]
September	**septembrie** (m)	[sep'tembrie]
October	**octombrie** (m)	[ok'tombrie]
November	**noiembrie** (m)	[no'embrie]
December	**decembrie** (m)	[de'ʧembrie]

spring	**primăvară** (f)	[primə'varə]
in spring	**primăvara**	[primə'vara]
spring (as adj)	**de primăvară**	[de primə'varə]

summer	**vară** (f)	['varə]
in summer	**vara**	['vara]
summer (as adj)	**de vară**	[de 'varə]

fall	**toamnă** (f)	[to'amnə]
in fall	**toamna**	[to'amna]
fall (as adj)	**de toamnă**	[de to'amnə]

winter	**iarnă** (f)	['jarnə]
in winter	**iarna**	['jarna]
winter (as adj)	**de iarnă**	[de 'jarnə]

month	**lună** (f)	['lunə]
this month	**în luna curentă**	[ɨn 'luna ku'rentə]
next month	**în luna următoare**	[ɨn 'luna urməto'are]
last month	**în luna trecută**	[ɨn 'luna tre'kutə]

a month ago	**o lună în urmă**	[o 'lunə ɨn 'urmə]
in a month (a month later)	**peste o lună**	['peste o 'lunə]
in 2 months (2 months later)	**peste două luni**	['peste 'dowə lunʲ]
the whole month	**luna întreagă**	['luna ɨn'trʲagə]
all month long	**o lună întreagă**	[o 'lunə ɨn'trʲagə]

monthly (~ magazine)	**lunar**	[lu'nar]
monthly (adv)	**în fiecare lună**	[ɨn fie'kare 'lunə]
every month	**fiecare lună**	[fie'kare 'lunə]
twice a month	**de două ori pe lună**	[de 'dowə orʲ pe 'lunə]

year	**an** (m)	[an]
this year	**anul acesta**	['anul a'ʧesta]
next year	**anul viitor**	['anul vii'tor]
last year	**anul trecut**	['anul tre'kut]

a year ago	**acum un an**	[a'kum un an]
in a year	**peste un an**	['peste un an]

in two years	**peste doi ani**	['peste doj anʲ]
the whole year	**tot anul**	[tot 'anul]
all year long	**un an întreg**	[un an ɨn'treg]
every year	**în fiecare an**	[ɨn fie'kare an]
annual (adj)	**anual**	[anu'al]
annually (adv)	**în fiecare an**	[ɨn fie'kare an]
4 times a year	**de patru ori pe an**	[de 'patru orʲ pe an]
date (e.g., today's ~)	**dată** (f)	['datə]
date (e.g., ~ of birth)	**dată** (f)	['datə]
calendar	**calendar** (n)	[kalen'dar]
half a year	**jumătate** (f) **de an**	[ʒumə'tate de an]
six months	**jumătate** (f) **de an**	[ʒumə'tate de an]
season (summer, etc.)	**sezon** (n)	[se'zon]
century	**veac** (n)	[vʲak]

22. Time. Miscellaneous

time	**timp** (m)	[timp]
moment	**clipă** (f)	['klipə]
instant (n)	**moment** (n)	[mo'mənt]
instant (adj)	**momentan**	[momen'tan]
lapse (of time)	**perioadă** (f)	[perio'adə]
life	**viață** (f)	['vjatsə]
eternity	**veşnicie** (f)	[veʃni'tʃie]
epoch	**epocă** (f)	[e'pokə]
era	**eră** (f)	['erə]
cycle	**ciclu** (n)	['tʃiklu]
period	**perioadă** (f)	[perio'adə]
term (short-~)	**termen** (n)	['termen]
the future	**viitor** (n)	[vii'tor]
future (as adj)	**viitor**	[vii'tor]
next time	**data următoare**	['data urməto'are]
the past	**trecut** (n)	[tre'kut]
past (recent)	**trecut**	[tre'kut]
last time	**data trecută**	['data tre'kutə]
later (adv)	**mai târziu**	[maj tɨr'zju]
after (prep.)	**după**	['dupə]
nowadays (adv)	**acum**	[a'kum]
now (at this moment)	**acum**	[a'kum]
immediately (adv)	**imediat**	[imedi'at]
soon (adv)	**în curând**	[ɨn ku'rɨnd]
in advance (beforehand)	**în prealabil**	[ɨn prʲa'labil]
a long time ago	**demult**	[de'mult]
recently (adv)	**recent**	[re'tʃent]

destiny	**soartă** (f)	[so'artə]
memories (childhood ~)	**memorie** (f)	[me'morie]
archives	**arhivă** (f)	[ar'hivə]
during ...	**în timpul ...**	[ɨn 'timpul]
long, a long time (adv)	**îndelung**	[ɨnde'lung]
not long (adv)	**puțin timp**	[pu'tsin 'timp]
early (in the morning)	**devreme**	[de'vreme]
late (not early)	**târziu**	[tɨr'zju]
forever (for good)	**pentru totdeauna**	['pentru totdʲa'una]
to start (begin)	**a începe**	[a ɨn'tʃepe]
to postpone (vt)	**a amâna**	[a amɨ'na]
at the same time	**concomitent**	[konkomi'tent]
permanently (adv)	**mereu**	[me'reu]
constant (noise, pain)	**permanent**	[perma'nent]
temporary (adj)	**temporar**	[tempo'rar]
sometimes (adv)	**uneori**	[une'orʲ]
rarely (adv)	**rar**	[rar]
often (adv)	**adesea**	[a'desʲa]

23. Opposites

rich (adj)	**bogat**	[bo'gat]
poor (adj)	**sărac**	[sə'rak]
ill, sick (adj)	**bolnav**	[bol'nav]
well (not sick)	**sănătos**	[sənə'tos]
big (adj)	**mare**	['mare]
small (adj)	**mic**	[mik]
quickly (adv)	**repede**	['repede]
slowly (adv)	**încet**	[ɨn'tʃet]
fast (adj)	**rapid**	[ra'pid]
slow (adj)	**lent**	[lent]
glad (adj)	**vesel**	['vesel]
sad (adj)	**trist**	[trist]
together (adv)	**împreună**	[ɨmpre'unə]
separately (adv)	**separat**	[sepa'rat]
aloud (to read)	**cu voce tare**	[ku 'votʃe 'tare]
silently (to oneself)	**în gând**	[ɨn gɨnd]
tall (adj)	**înalt**	[ɨ'nalt]
low (adj)	**scund**	[skund]

deep (adj)	**adânc**	[a'dɨnk]
shallow (adj)	**de adâncime mică**	[de adɨn'ʧime 'mikə]
yes	**da**	[da]
no	**nu**	[nu]
distant (in space)	**îndepărtat**	[ɨndepər'tat]
nearby (adj)	**apropiat**	[apropi'jat]
far (adv)	**departe**	[de'parte]
nearby (adv)	**aproape**	[apro'ape]
long (adj)	**lung**	[lung]
short (adj)	**scurt**	[skurt]
good (kindhearted)	**bun**	[bun]
evil (adj)	**rău**	['rəu]
married (adj)	**căsătorit**	[kəsəto'rit]
single (adj)	**celibatar** (m)	[ʧeliba'tar]
to forbid (vt)	**a interzice**	[a inter'ziʧe]
to permit (vt)	**a permite**	[a per'mite]
end	**sfârşit** (n)	[sfɨr'ʃit]
beginning	**început** (n)	[ɨnʧe'put]
left (adj)	**stâng**	[stɨng]
right (adj)	**drept**	[drept]
first (adj)	**primul**	['primul]
last (adj)	**ultimul**	['ultimul]
crime	**crimă** (f)	['krimə]
punishment	**pedeapsă** (f)	[pe'dʲapsə]
to order (vt)	**a ordona**	[a ordo'na]
to obey (vi, vt)	**a se supune**	[a se su'pune]
straight (adj)	**drept**	[drept]
curved (adj)	**strâmb**	[strɨmb]
paradise	**rai** (n)	[raj]
hell	**iad** (n)	[jad]
to be born	**a se naşte**	[a se 'naʃte]
to die (vi)	**a muri**	[a mu'ri]
strong (adj)	**puternic**	[pu'ternik]
weak (adj)	**slab**	[slab]
old (adj)	**bătrân**	[bə'trɨn]
young (adj)	**tânăr**	['tɨnər]

old (adj)	**vechi**	[vekʲ]
new (adj)	**nou**	['nou]
hard (adj)	**tare**	['tare]
soft (adj)	**moale**	[mo'ale]
warm (tepid)	**cald**	[kald]
cold (adj)	**rece**	['retʃe]
fat (adj)	**gras**	[gras]
thin (adj)	**slab**	[slab]
narrow (adj)	**îngust**	[ɨn'gust]
wide (adj)	**lat**	[lat]
good (adj)	**bun**	[bun]
bad (adj)	**rău**	['rəu]
brave (adj)	**curajos**	[kura'ʒos]
cowardly (adj)	**fricos**	[fri'kos]

24. Lines and shapes

square	**pătrat** (n)	[pə'trat]
square (as adj)	**pătrat**	[pə'trat]
circle	**cerc** (n)	[tʃerk]
round (adj)	**rotund**	[ro'tund]
triangle	**triunghi** (n)	[tri'ungʲ]
triangular (adj)	**triunghiular**	[trjungju'lar]
oval	**oval** (n)	[o'val]
oval (as adj)	**oval**	[o'val]
rectangle	**dreptunghi** (n)	[drep'tungʲ]
rectangular (adj)	**dreptunghiular**	[dreptungju'lar]
pyramid	**piramidă** (f)	[pira'midə]
rhombus	**romb** (n)	[romb]
trapezoid	**trapez** (n)	[tra'pez]
cube	**cub** (n)	[kub]
prism	**prismă** (f)	['prizmə]
circumference	**circumferință** (f)	[tʃirkumfe'rintsə]
sphere	**sferă** (f)	['sferə]
ball (solid sphere)	**sferă** (f)	['sferə]
diameter	**diametru** (n)	[di'ametru]
radius	**rază** (f)	['razə]
perimeter (circle's ~)	**perimetru** (n)	[peri'metru]
center	**centru** (n)	['tʃentru]
horizontal (adj)	**orizontal**	[orizon'tal]
vertical (adj)	**vertical**	[verti'kal]

parallel (n)	**paralelă** (f)	[para'lelə]
parallel (as adj)	**paralel**	[para'lel]
line	**linie** (f)	['linie]
stroke	**linie** (f)	['linie]
straight line	**dreaptă** (f)	['drʲaptə]
curve (curved line)	**curbă** (f)	['kurbə]
thin (line, etc.)	**subțire**	[sub'ʦire]
contour (outline)	**contur** (n)	[kon'tur]
intersection	**intersecție** (f)	[inter'sekʦie]
right angle	**unghi** (n) **drept**	[ungʲ drept]
segment	**segment** (n)	[seg'ment]
sector (circular ~)	**sector** (n)	[sek'tor]
side (of triangle)	**latură** (f)	['laturə]
angle	**unghi** (n)	[ungʲ]

25. Units of measurement

weight	**greutate** (f)	[greu'tate]
length	**lungime** (f)	[lun'ʤime]
width	**lățime** (f)	[lə'ʦime]
height	**înălțime** (f)	[ɨnəl'ʦime]
depth	**adâncime** (f)	[adɨn'ʧime]
volume	**volum** (n)	[vo'lum]
area	**suprafață** (f)	[supra'faʦə]
gram	**gram** (n)	[gram]
milligram	**miligram** (n)	[mili'gram]
kilogram	**kilogram** (n)	[kilo'gram]
ton	**tonă** (f)	['tonə]
pound	**funt** (m)	[funt]
ounce	**uncie** (f)	['unʧie]
meter	**metru** (m)	['metru]
millimeter	**milimetru** (m)	[mili'metru]
centimeter	**centimetru** (m)	[ʧenti'metru]
kilometer	**kilometru** (m)	[kilo'metru]
mile	**milă** (f)	['milə]
inch	**țol** (m)	[ʦol]
foot	**picior** (m)	[pi'ʧior]
yard	**yard** (m)	[jard]
square meter	**metru** (m) **pătrat**	['metru pə'trat]
hectare	**hectar** (n)	[hek'tar]
liter	**litru** (m)	['litru]
degree	**grad** (n)	[grad]
volt	**volt** (m)	[volt]

ampere	**amper** (m)	[am'per]
horsepower	**cal-putere** (m)	[kal pu'tere]
quantity	**cantitate** (f)	[kanti'tate]
a little bit of ...	**puțin ...**	[pu'tsin]
half	**jumătate** (f)	[ʒumə'tate]
dozen	**duzină** (f)	[du'zinə]
piece (item)	**bucată** (f)	[bu'katə]
size	**dimensiune** (f)	[dimensi'une]
scale (map ~)	**proporție** (f)	[pro'portsie]
minimal (adj)	**minim**	['minim]
the smallest (adj)	**cel mai mic**	[tʃel maj mik]
medium (adj)	**de, din mijloc**	[de, din 'miʒlok]
maximal (adj)	**maxim**	['maksim]
the largest (adj)	**cel mai mare**	[tʃel maj 'mare]

26. Containers

canning jar (glass ~)	**borcan** (n)	[bor'kan]
can	**cutie** (f)	[ku'tie]
bucket	**găleată** (f)	[gə'lʲatə]
barrel	**butoi** (n)	[bu'toj]
wash basin (e.g., plastic ~)	**lighean** (n)	[li'gʲan]
tank (100L water ~)	**rezervor** (n)	[rezer'vor]
hip flask	**damigeană** (f)	[dami'dʒanə]
jerrycan	**canistră** (f)	[ka'nistrə]
tank (e.g., tank car)	**cisternă** (f)	[tʃis'ternə]
mug	**cană** (f)	['kanə]
cup (of coffee, etc.)	**ceașcă** (f)	['tʃaʃkə]
saucer	**farfurioară** (f)	[farfurio'arə]
glass (tumbler)	**pahar** (n)	[pa'har]
wine glass	**cupă** (f)	['kupə]
stock pot (soup pot)	**cratiță** (f)	['kratitsə]
bottle (~ of wine)	**sticlă** (f)	['stiklə]
neck (of the bottle, etc.)	**gâtul** (n) **sticlei**	['gitul 'stiklej]
carafe (decanter)	**garafă** (f)	[ga'rafə]
pitcher	**ulcior** (n)	[ul'tʃior]
vessel (container)	**vas** (n)	[vas]
pot (crock, stoneware ~)	**oală** (f)	[o'alə]
vase	**vază** (f)	['vazə]
flacon, bottle (perfume ~)	**flacon** (n)	[fla'kon]
vial, small bottle	**sticluță** (f)	[sti'klutsə]

tube (of toothpaste)	**tub** (n)	[tub]
sack (bag)	**sac** (m)	[sak]
bag (paper ~, plastic ~)	**pachet** (n)	[pa'ket]
pack (of cigarettes, etc.)	**pachet** (n)	[pa'ket]
box (e.g., shoebox)	**cutie** (f)	[ku'tie]
crate	**ladă** (f)	['ladə]
basket	**coş** (n)	[koʃ]

27. Materials

material	**material** (n)	[materi'al]
wood (n)	**lemn** (n)	[lemn]
wood-, wooden (adj)	**de, din lemn**	[de, din lemn]
glass (n)	**sticlă** (f)	['stiklə]
glass (as adj)	**de, din sticlă**	[de, din 'stiklə]
stone (n)	**piatră** (f)	['pjatrə]
stone (as adj)	**de, din piatră**	[de, din 'pjatrə]
plastic (n)	**masă** (f) **plastică**	['masə 'plastikə]
plastic (as adj)	**de, din masă plastică**	[de, din 'masə 'plastikə]
rubber (n)	**cauciuc** (n)	[kau'ʧuk]
rubber (as adj)	**de, din cauciuc**	[de, din kau'ʧiuk]
cloth, fabric (n)	**ţesătură** (f)	[ʦesə'turə]
fabric (as adj)	**de, din ţesătură**	[de, din ʦesə'turə]
paper (n)	**hârtie** (f)	[hir'tie]
paper (as adj)	**de, din hârtie**	[de, din hɨr'tie]
cardboard (n)	**carton** (n)	[kar'ton]
cardboard (as adj)	**de, din carton**	[de, din kar'ton]
polyethylene	**polietilenă** (f)	[polieti'lenə]
cellophane	**celofan** (n)	[ʧelo'fan]
linoleum	**linoleum** (n)	[linoleum]
plywood	**furnir** (n)	[fur'nir]
porcelain (n)	**porţelan** (n)	[porʦe'lan]
porcelain (as adj)	**de, din porţelan**	[de, din porʦe'lan]
clay (n)	**argilă** (f)	[ar'ʤilə]
clay (as adj)	**de lut**	[de 'lut]
ceramic (n)	**ceramică** (f)	[ʧe'ramikə]
ceramic (as adj)	**de, din ceramică**	[de, din ʧe'ramikə]

28. Metals

metal (n)	**metal** (n)	[me'tal]
metal (as adj)	**de, din metal**	[de, din me'tal]
alloy (n)	**aliaj** (n)	[a'ljaʒ]
gold (n)	**aur** (n)	['aur]
gold, golden (adj)	**de, din aur**	[de, din 'aur]
silver (n)	**argint** (n)	[ar'ʤint]
silver (as adj)	**de, din argint**	[de, din ar'ʤint]
iron (n)	**fier** (n)	[fier]
iron-, made of iron (adj)	**de, din fier**	[de, din 'fjer]
steel (n)	**oțel** (n)	[o'ʦel]
steel (as adj)	**de, din oțel**	[de, din o'ʦel]
copper (n)	**cupru** (n)	['kupru]
copper (as adj)	**de, din cupru**	[de, din 'kupru]
aluminum (n)	**aluminiu** (n)	[alu'miniu]
aluminum (as adj)	**de, din aluminiu**	[de, din alu'miniu]
bronze (n)	**bronz** (n)	[bronz]
bronze (as adj)	**de, din bronz**	[de, din bronz]
brass	**alamă** (f)	[a'lamə]
nickel	**nichel** (n)	['nikel]
platinum	**platină** (f)	['platinə]
mercury	**mercur** (n)	[mer'kur]
tin	**cositor** (n)	[kosi'tor]
lead	**plumb** (n)	[plumb]
zinc	**zinc** (n)	[zink]

HUMAN BEING

Human being. The body

29. Humans. Basic concepts

human being	**om** (m)	[om]
man (adult male)	**bărbat** (m)	[bər'bat]
woman	**femeie** (f)	[fe'meje]
child	**copil** (m)	[ko'pil]
girl	**fată** (f)	['fatə]
boy	**băiat** (m)	[bə'jat]
teenager	**adolescent** (m)	[adoles'ʧent]
old man	**bătrân** (m)	[bə'trin]
old woman	**bătrână** (f)	[bə'trinə]

30. Human anatomy

organism (body)	**organism** (n)	[orga'nizm]
heart	**inimă** (f)	['inimə]
blood	**sânge** (n)	['sinʤe]
artery	**arteră** (f)	[ar'terə]
vein	**venă** (f)	['venə]
brain	**creier** (m)	['krejer]
nerve	**nerv** (m)	[nerv]
nerves	**nervi** (m pl)	[nervʲ]
vertebra	**vertebră** (f)	[ver'tebrə]
spine (backbone)	**coloană** (f) **vertebrală**	[kolo'anə verte'bralə]
stomach (organ)	**stomac** (n)	[sto'mak]
intestines, bowels	**intestin** (n)	[intes'tin]
intestine (e.g., large ~)	**intestin** (n)	[intes'tin]
liver	**ficat** (m)	[fi'kat]
kidney	**rinichi** (m)	[ri'nikʲ]
bone	**os** (n)	[os]
skeleton	**schelet** (n)	[ske'let]
rib	**coastă** (f)	[ko'astə]
skull	**craniu** (n)	['kranju]
muscle	**muşchi** (m)	[muʃkʲ]
biceps	**biceps** (m)	['biʧeps]

triceps	**triceps** (m)	['tritʃeps]
tendon	**tendon** (n)	[ten'don]
joint	**încheietură** (f)	[ɨnkeje'turə]
lungs	**plămâni** (m pl)	[plə'mɨnʲ]
genitals	**organe** (n pl) **genitale**	[or'gane dʒeni'tale]
skin	**piele** (f)	['pjele]

31. Head

head	**cap** (n)	[kap]
face	**față** (f)	['fatsə]
nose	**nas** (n)	[nas]
mouth	**gură** (f)	['gurə]
eye	**ochi** (m)	[okʲ]
eyes	**ochi** (m pl)	[okʲ]
pupil	**pupilă** (f)	[pu'pilə]
eyebrow	**sprânceană** (f)	[sprɨn'tʃanə]
eyelash	**geană** (f)	['dʒanə]
eyelid	**pleoapă** (f)	[pleo'apə]
tongue	**limbă** (f)	['limbə]
tooth	**dinte** (m)	['dinte]
lips	**buze** (f pl)	['buze]
cheekbones	**pomeți** (m pl)	[po'metsʲ]
gum	**gingie** (f)	[dʒin'dʒie]
palate	**palat** (n)	[pa'lat]
nostrils	**nări** (f pl)	[nərʲ]
chin	**bărbie** (f)	[bər'bie]
jaw	**maxilar** (n)	[maksi'lar]
cheek	**obraz** (m)	[o'braz]
forehead	**frunte** (f)	['frunte]
temple	**tâmplă** (f)	['tɨmplə]
ear	**ureche** (f)	[u'reke]
back of the head	**ceafă** (f)	['tʃafə]
neck	**gât** (n)	[gɨt]
throat	**gât** (n)	[gɨt]
hair	**păr** (m)	[pər]
hairstyle	**coafură** (f)	[koa'furə]
haircut	**tunsoare** (f)	[tunso'are]
wig	**perucă** (f)	[pe'rukə]
mustache	**mustăți** (f pl)	[mus'tətsʲ]
beard	**barbă** (f)	['barbə]
to have (a beard, etc.)	**a purta**	[a pur'ta]
braid	**cosiță** (f)	[ko'sitsə]
sideburns	**favoriți** (m pl)	[favo'ritsʲ]

red-haired (adj)	**roşcat**	[roʃ'kat]
gray (hair)	**cărunt**	[kə'runt]
bald (adj)	**chel**	[kel]
bald patch	**chelie** (f)	[ke'lie]
ponytail	**coadă** (f)	[ko'adə]
bangs	**breton** (n)	[bre'ton]

32. Human body

hand	**mână** (f)	['mɨnə]
arm	**braț** (n)	[braʦ]
finger	**deget** (n)	['deʤet]
toe	**deget** (n) **de la picior**	['deʤet de la pi'ʧior]
thumb	**degetul** (n) **mare**	['deʤetul 'mare]
little finger	**degetul** (n) **mic**	['deʤetul mik]
nail	**unghie** (f)	['ungie]
fist	**pumn** (m)	[pumn]
palm	**palmă** (f)	['palmə]
wrist	**încheietura** (f) **mâinii**	[inkeje'tura 'mɨnij]
forearm	**antebraț** (n)	[ante'braʦ]
elbow	**cot** (n)	[kot]
shoulder	**umăr** (m)	['umər]
leg	**picior** (n)	[pi'ʧior]
foot	**talpă** (f)	['talpə]
knee	**genunchi** (n)	[ʤe'nunkʲ]
calf (part of leg)	**pulpă** (f)	['pulpə]
hip	**coapsă** (f)	[ko'apsə]
heel	**călcâi** (n)	[kəl'kɨj]
body	**corp** (n)	[korp]
stomach	**burtă** (f)	['burtə]
chest	**piept** (n)	[pjept]
breast	**sân** (m)	[sɨn]
flank	**coastă** (f)	[ko'astə]
back	**spate** (n)	['spate]
lower back	**regiune** (f) **lombară**	[reʤi'une lom'barə]
waist	**talie** (f)	['talie]
navel (belly button)	**buric** (n)	[bu'rik]
buttocks	**fese** (f pl)	['fese]
bottom	**şezut** (n)	[ʃə'zut]
beauty mark	**aluniță** (f)	[alu'niʦə]
birthmark (café au lait spot)	**semn** (n) **din naştere**	[semn din 'naʃtere]
tattoo	**tatuaj** (n)	[tatu'aʒ]
scar	**cicatrice** (f)	[ʧika'triʧe]

Clothing & Accessories

33. Outerwear. Coats

clothes	**îmbrăcăminte** (f)	[ɨmbrəkə'minte]
outerwear	**haină** (f)	['hajnə]
winter clothing	**îmbrăcăminte** (f) **de iarnă**	[ɨmbrəkə'minte de 'jarnə]
coat (overcoat)	**palton** (n)	[pal'ton]
fur coat	**şubă** (f)	['ʃubə]
fur jacket	**scurtă** (f) **îmblănită**	['skurtə ɨmblə'nitə]
down coat	**scurtă** (f) **de puf**	['skurtə de 'puf]
jacket (e.g., leather ~)	**scurtă** (f)	['skurtə]
raincoat (trenchcoat, etc.)	**trenci** (f)	[trentʃi]
waterproof (adj)	**impermeabil** (n)	[imperme'abil]

34. Men's & women's clothing

shirt (button shirt)	**cămaşă** (f)	[kə'maʃə]
pants	**pantaloni** (m pl)	[panta'lonʲ]
jeans	**blugi** (m pl)	[bludʒʲ]
suit jacket	**sacou** (n)	[sa'kou]
suit	**costum** (n)	[kos'tum]
dress (frock)	**rochie** (f)	['rokie]
skirt	**fustă** (f)	['fustə]
blouse	**bluză** (f)	['bluzə]
knitted jacket (cardigan, etc.)	**jachetă** (f) **tricotată**	[ʒa'ketə triko'tatə]
jacket (of woman's suit)	**jachetă** (f)	[ʒa'ketə]
T-shirt	**tricou** (n)	[tri'kou]
shorts (short trousers)	**şorturi** (n pl)	['ʃorturʲ]
tracksuit	**costum** (n) **sportiv**	[kos'tum spor'tiv]
bathrobe	**halat** (n)	[ha'lat]
pajamas	**pijama** (f)	[piʒa'ma]
sweater	**sveter** (n)	['sveter]
pullover	**pulover** (n)	[pu'lover]
vest	**vestă** (f)	['vestə]
tailcoat	**frac** (n)	[frak]
tuxedo	**smoching** (n)	['smoking]

uniform	**uniformă** (f)	[uni'formə]
workwear	**haină** (f) **de lucru**	['hajnə de 'lukru]
overalls	**salopetă** (f)	[salo'petə]
coat (e.g., doctor's smock)	**halat** (n)	[ha'lat]

35. Clothing. Underwear

underwear	**lenjerie** (f) **de corp**	[lenʒe'rie de 'korp]
boxers, briefs	**boxeri, chiloți** (m pl)	[bokserʲ], [ki'lotsʲ]
panties	**chiloți** (m pl)	[ki'lotsʲ]
undershirt (A-shirt)	**maiou** (n)	[ma'jou]
socks	**şosete** (f pl)	[ʃo'sete]
nightdress	**cămaşă** (f) **de noapte**	[kə'maʃə de no'apte]
bra	**sutien** (n)	[su'tjen]
knee highs (knee-high socks)	**ciorapi** (m pl)	[tʃio'rapʲ]
pantyhose	**ciorapi pantalon** (m pl)	[tʃio'rapʲ panta'lon]
stockings (thigh highs)	**ciorapi** (m pl)	[tʃio'rapʲ]
bathing suit	**costum** (n) **de baie**	[kos'tum de 'bae]

36. Headwear

hat	**căciulă** (f)	[kə'tʃiulə]
fedora	**pălărie** (f)	[pələ'rie]
baseball cap	**şapcă** (f)	['ʃapkə]
flatcap	**chipiu** (n)	[ki'pju]
beret	**beretă** (f)	[be'retə]
hood	**glugă** (f)	['glugə]
panama hat	**panama** (f)	[pana'ma]
knit cap (knitted hat)	**căciulă** (f) **împletită**	[kə'tʃiulə imple'titə]
headscarf	**basma** (f)	[bas'ma]
women's hat	**pălărie** (f) **de damă**	[pələ'rie de 'damə]
hard hat	**cască** (f)	['kaskə]
garrison cap	**bonetă** (f)	[bo'netə]
helmet	**coif** (n)	[kojf]
derby	**pălărie** (f)	[pələ'rie]
top hat	**joben** (n)	[ʒo'ben]

37. Footwear

footwear	**încălțăminte** (f)	[inkəltsə'minte]
shoes (men's shoes)	**ghete** (f pl)	['gete]

shoes (women's shoes)	**pantofi** (m pl)	[pan'tofʲ]
boots (e.g., cowboy ~)	**cizme** (f pl)	['ʧizme]
slippers	**şlapi** (m pl)	[ʃlapʲ]
tennis shoes (e.g., Nike ~)	**adidaşi** (m pl)	[a'didaʃ]
sneakers (e.g., Converse ~)	**tenişi** (m pl)	['teniʃ]
sandals	**sandale** (f pl)	[san'dale]
cobbler (shoe repairer)	**cizmar** (m)	[ʧiz'mar]
heel	**toc** (n)	[tok]
pair (of shoes)	**pereche** (f)	[pe'reke]
shoestring	**şiret** (n)	[ʃi'ret]
to lace (vt)	**a şnurui**	[a ʃnuru'i]
shoehorn	**lingură** (f) **pentru pantofi**	['lingurə 'pentru pan'tofʲ]
shoe polish	**cremă** (f) **de ghete**	['kremə de 'gete]

38. Textile. Fabrics

cotton (n)	**bumbac** (m)	[bum'bak]
cotton (as adj)	**de, din bumbac**	[de, din bum'bak]
flax (n)	**in** (n)	[in]
flax (as adj)	**de, din in**	[de, din in]
silk (n)	**mătase** (f)	[mə'tase]
silk (as adj)	**de, din mătase**	[de, din mə'tase]
wool (n)	**lână** (f)	['lɨnə]
wool (as adj)	**de, din lână**	[de, din 'lɨnə]
velvet	**catifea** (f)	[kati'fʲa]
suede	**piele** (f) **întoarsă**	['pjele ɨnto'arsə]
corduroy	**ţesătură de bumbac catifelată** (f)	[tsesə'turə de bum'bak katife'latə]
nylon (n)	**nailon** (n)	[naj'lon]
nylon (as adj)	**de, din nailon**	[de, din naj'lon]
polyester (n)	**poliester** (n)	[polies'ter]
polyester (as adj)	**de, din poliester**	[de, din polies'ter]
leather (n)	**piele** (f)	['pjele]
leather (as adj)	**de, din piele**	[de, din 'pjele]
fur (n)	**blană** (f)	['blanə]
fur (e.g., ~ coat)	**de, din blană**	[de, din 'blanə]

39. Personal accessories

gloves	**mănuşi** (f pl)	[mə'nuʃ]
mittens	**mănuşi** (f pl) **cu un singur deget**	[mə'nuʃ ku un 'singur 'deʤet]

scarf (muffler)	**fular** (m)	[fu'lar]
glasses (eyeglasses)	**ochelari** (m pl)	[oke'lar^{j}]
frame (eyeglass ~)	**ramă** (f)	['ramə]
umbrella	**umbrelă** (f)	[um'brelə]
walking stick	**baston** (n)	[bas'ton]
hairbrush	**perie** (f) **de păr**	[pe'rie de pər]
fan	**evantai** (n)	[evan'taj]
tie (necktie)	**cravată** (f)	[kra'vatə]
bow tie	**papion** (n)	[papi'on]
suspenders	**bretele** (f pl)	[bre'tele]
handkerchief	**batistă** (f)	[ba'tistə]
comb	**pieptene** (m)	['pjeptəne]
barrette	**agrafă** (f)	[a'grafə]
hairpin	**ac** (n) **de păr**	[ak de pər]
buckle	**cataramă** (f)	[kata'ramə]
belt	**cordon** (n)	[kor'don]
shoulder strap	**curea** (f)	[ku'r^{j}a]
bag (handbag)	**geantă** (f)	['dʒantə]
purse	**poşetă** (f)	[po'ʃetə]
backpack	**rucsac** (n)	[ruk'sak]

40. Clothing. Miscellaneous

fashion	**modă** (f)	['modə]
in vogue (adj)	**la modă**	[la 'modə]
fashion designer	**modelier** (n)	[mode'ljer]
collar	**guler** (n)	['guler]
pocket	**buzunar** (n)	[buzu'nar]
pocket (as adj)	**de buzunar**	[de buzu'nar]
sleeve	**mânecă** (f)	['minekə]
hanging loop	**gaică** (f)	['gajkə]
fly (on trousers)	**şliț** (n)	[ʃlits]
zipper (fastener)	**fermoar** (n)	[fermo'ar]
fastener	**capsă** (f)	['kapsə]
button	**nasture** (m)	['nasture]
buttonhole	**butonieră** (f)	[buto'njerə]
to come off (ab. button)	**a se rupe**	[a se 'rupe]
to sew (vi, vt)	**a coase**	[a ko'ase]
to embroider (vi, vt)	**a broda**	[a bro'da]
embroidery	**broderie** (f)	[brode'rie]
sewing needle	**ac** (n)	[ak]
thread	**ață** (f)	['atsə]
seam	**cusătură** (f)	[kusə'turə]

to get dirty (vi)	**a se murdări**	[a se murdə'ri]
stain (mark, spot)	**pată** (f)	['patə]
to crease, crumple (vi)	**a se şifona**	[a se ʃifo'na]
to tear, to rip (vt)	**a rupe**	[a 'rupe]
clothes moth	**molie** (f)	['molie]

41. Personal care. Cosmetics

toothpaste	**pastă** (f) **de dinți**	['pastə de dintsʲ]
toothbrush	**periuță** (f) **de dinți**	[peri'utsə de dintsʲ]
to brush one's teeth	**a se spăla pe dinți**	[a se spə'la pe dintsʲ]
razor	**brici** (n)	['britʃi]
shaving cream	**cremă** (f) **de bărbierit**	['kremə de bərbie'rit]
to shave (vi)	**a se bărbieri**	[a se bərbie'ri]
soap	**săpun** (n)	[sə'pun]
shampoo	**şampon** (n)	[ʃam'pon]
scissors	**foarfece** (n)	[fo'arfetʃe]
nail file	**pilă** (f) **de unghii**	['pilə de 'ungij]
nail clippers	**cleştişor** (n)	[kleʃti'ʃor]
tweezers	**pensetă** (f)	[pen'setə]
cosmetics	**cosmetică** (f)	[kos'metikə]
face mask	**mască** (f)	['maskə]
manicure	**manichiură** (f)	[mani'kjurə]
to have a manicure	**a face manichiura**	[a 'fatʃe mani'kjura]
pedicure	**pedichiură** (f)	[pedi'kjurə]
make-up bag	**trusă** (f) **de cosmetică**	['trusə de kos'metikə]
face powder	**pudră** (f)	['pudrə]
powder compact	**pudrieră** (f)	[pudri'erə]
blusher	**fard de obraz** (n)	[fard de o'braz]
perfume (bottled)	**parfum** (n)	[par'fum]
toilet water (lotion)	**apă de toaletă** (f)	['apə de toa'letə]
lotion	**loțiune** (f)	[lotsi'une]
cologne	**colonie** (f)	[ko'lonie]
eyeshadow	**fard** (n) **de pleoape**	[fard 'pentru pleo'ape]
eyeliner	**creion** (n) **de ochi**	[kre'jon 'pentru okʲ]
mascara	**rimel** (n)	[ri'mel]
lipstick	**ruj** (n)	[ruʒ]
nail polish, enamel	**ojă** (f)	['oʒə]
hair spray	**gel** (n) **de păr**	[dʒel de pər]
deodorant	**deodorant** (n)	[deodo'rant]
cream	**cremă** (f)	['kremə]
face cream	**cremă** (f) **de față**	['kremə de 'fatsə]

hand cream	**cremă** (f) **pentru mâini**	['kremə 'pentru mɨnʲ]
anti-wrinkle cream	**cremă** (f) **anti-rid**	['kremə 'anti rid]
day cream	**cremă** (f) **de zi**	['kremə de zi]
night cream	**cremă** (f) **de noapte**	['kremə de no'apte]
day (as adj)	**de zi**	[de zi]
night (as adj)	**de noapte**	[de no'apte]
tampon	**tampon** (n)	[tam'pon]
toilet paper (toilet roll)	**hârtie** (f) **igienică**	[hɨr'tie idʒi'enikə]
hair dryer	**uscător** (n) **de păr**	[uskə'tor de pər]

42. Jewelry

jewelry, jewels	**giuvaeruri** (n pl)	[dʒiuva'erurʲ]
precious (e.g., ~ stone)	**prețios**	[preʦi'os]
hallmark stamp	**marcă** (f)	['markə]
ring	**inel** (n)	[i'nel]
wedding ring	**verighetă** (f)	[veri'getə]
bracelet	**brățară** (f)	[brə'ʦarə]
earrings	**cercei** (m pl)	[ʧer'ʧej]
necklace (~ of pearls)	**colier** (n)	[ko'ljer]
crown	**coroană** (f)	[koro'anə]
bead necklace	**mărgele** (f pl)	[mər'dʒele]
diamond	**briliant** (n)	[brili'ant]
emerald	**smarald** (n)	[sma'rald]
ruby	**rubin** (n)	[ru'bin]
sapphire	**safir** (n)	[sa'fir]
pearl	**perlă** (f)	['perlə]
amber	**chihlimbar** (n)	[kihlim'bar]

43. Watches. Clocks

watch (wristwatch)	**ceas** (n) **de mână**	[ʧas de 'mɨnə]
dial	**cadran** (n)	[ka'dran]
hand (of clock, watch)	**acul** (n) **ceasornicului**	['akul ʧasor'nikuluj]
metal watch band	**brățară** (f)	[brə'ʦarə]
watch strap	**curea** (f)	[ku'rʲa]
battery	**baterie** (f)	[bate'rie]
to be dead (battery)	**a se termina**	[a se termi'na]
to change a battery	**a schimba bateria**	[a skim'ba bate'rija]
to run fast	**a merge înainte**	[a 'merdʒe ɨna'inte]
to run slow	**a rămâne în urmă**	[a rə'mɨne ɨn 'urmə]
wall clock	**pendulă** (f)	[pen'dulə]
hourglass	**clepsidră** (f)	[klep'sidrə]

sundial	**cadran** (n) **solar**	[ka'dran so'lar]
alarm clock	**ceas** (n) **deşteptător**	[ʧas deʃteptə'tor]
watchmaker	**ceasornicar** (m)	[ʧasorni'kar]
to repair (vt)	**a repara**	[a repa'ra]

Food. Nutricion

44. Food

meat	**carne** (f)	['karne]
chicken	**carne** (f) **de găină**	['karne de gə'inə]
Rock Cornish hen (poussin)	**carne** (f) **de pui**	['karne de puj]
duck	**carne** (f) **de rață**	['karne de 'ratsə]
goose	**carne** (f) **de gâscă**	['karne de 'giskə]
game	**vânat** (n)	[vi'nat]
turkey	**carne** (f) **de curcan**	['karne de 'kurkan]
pork	**carne** (f) **de porc**	['karne de pork]
veal	**carne** (f) **de vițel**	['karne de vi'tsel]
lamb	**carne** (f) **de berbec**	['karne de ber'bek]
beef	**carne** (f) **de vită**	['karne de 'vitə]
rabbit	**carne** (f) **de iepure de casă**	['karne de 'epure de 'kasə]
sausage (bologna, etc.)	**salam** (n)	[sa'lam]
vienna sausage (frankfurter)	**crenvurşt** (n)	[kren'vurʃt]
bacon	**costiță** (f) **afumată**	[kos'titsə afu'matə]
ham	**şuncă** (f)	['ʃunkə]
gammon	**pulpă** (f)	['pulpə]
pâté	**pateu** (n)	[pa'teu]
liver	**ficat** (m)	[fi'kat]
hamburger (ground beef)	**carne** (f) **tocată**	['karne to'katə]
tongue	**limbă** (f)	['limbə]
egg	**ou** (n)	['ow]
eggs	**ouă** (n pl)	['owə]
egg white	**albuş** (n)	[al'buʃ]
egg yolk	**gălbenuş**	[gəlbe'nuʃ]
fish	**peşte** (m)	['peʃte]
seafood	**produse** (n pl) **marine**	[pro'duse ma'rine]
caviar	**icre** (f pl) **de peşte**	['ikre de 'peʃte]
crab	**crab** (m)	[krab]
shrimp	**crevetă** (f)	[kre'vetə]
oyster	**stridie** (f)	['stridie]
spiny lobster	**langustă** (f)	[lan'gustə]
octopus	**caracatiță** (f)	[kara'katitsə]

squid	**calmar** (m)	[kal'mar]
sturgeon	**carne** (f) **de nisetru**	['karne de ni'setru]
salmon	**somon** (m)	[so'mon]
halibut	**calcan** (m)	[kal'kan]
cod	**batog** (m)	[ba'tog]
mackerel	**macrou** (n)	[ma'krou]
tuna	**ton** (m)	[ton]
eel	**țipar** (m)	[ʦi'par]
trout	**păstrăv** (m)	[pəs'trəv]
sardine	**sardea** (f)	[sar'dʲa]
pike	**ştiucă** (f)	['ʃtjukə]
herring	**scrumbie** (f)	[skrum'bie]
bread	**pâine** (f)	['pɨne]
cheese	**caşcaval** (n)	['brɨnzə]
sugar	**zahăr** (n)	['zahər]
salt	**sare** (f)	['sare]
rice	**orez** (n)	[o'rez]
pasta (macaroni)	**paste** (f pl)	['paste]
noodles	**tăiței** (m)	[təi'ʦej]
butter	**unt** (n)	['unt]
vegetable oil	**ulei** (n) **vegetal**	[u'lej veʤe'tal]
sunflower oil	**ulei** (n) **de floarea-soarelui**	[u'lej de flo'arʲa so'areluj]
margarine	**margarină** (f)	[marga'rinə]
olives	**olive** (f pl)	[o'live]
olive oil	**ulei** (n) **de măsline**	[u'lej de məs'line]
milk	**lapte** (n)	['lapte]
condensed milk	**lapte** (n) **condensat**	['lapte konden'sat]
yogurt	**iaurt** (n)	[ja'urt]
sour cream	**smântână** (f)	[smɨn'tɨnə]
cream (of milk)	**frişcă** (f)	['friʃkə]
mayonnaise	**maioneză** (f)	[majo'nezə]
buttercream	**cremă** (f)	['kremə]
groats (barley ~, etc.)	**crupe** (f pl)	['krupe]
flour	**făină** (f)	[fə'inə]
canned food	**conserve** (f pl)	[kon'serve]
cornflakes	**fulgi** (m pl) **de porumb**	['fulʤʲ de po'rumb]
honey	**miere** (f)	['mjere]
jam	**gem** (n)	[ʤem]
chewing gum	**gumă** (f) **de mestecat**	['gumə de meste'kat]

45. Drinks

water	**apă** (f)	['apə]
drinking water	**apă** (f) **potabilă**	['apə po'tabilə]
mineral water	**apă** (f) **minerală**	['apə mine'ralə]
still (adj)	**necarbogazoasă**	[nekarbogazo'asə]
carbonated (adj)	**carbogazoasă**	[karbogazo'asə]
sparkling (adj)	**gazoasă**	[gazo'asə]
ice	**gheață** (f)	['gʲaʦə]
with ice	**cu gheață**	[ku 'gʲaʦə]
non-alcoholic (adj)	**fără alcool**	['fərə alko'ol]
soft drink	**băutură** (f) **fără alcool**	[bəu'turə fərə alko'ol]
refreshing drink	**băutură** (f) **răcoritoare**	[bəu'turə rəkorito'are]
lemonade	**limonadă** (f)	[limo'nadə]
liquors	**băuturi** (f pl) **alcoolice**	[bəu'turʲ alko'oliʧe]
wine	**vin** (n)	[vin]
white wine	**vin** (n) **alb**	[vin alb]
red wine	**vin** (n) **roșu**	[vin 'roʃu]
liqueur	**lichior** (n)	[li'kør]
champagne	**șampanie** (f)	[ʃam'panie]
vermouth	**vermut** (n)	[ver'mut]
whiskey	**whisky** (n)	['wiski]
vodka	**votcă** (f)	['votkə]
gin	**gin** (n)	[ʤin]
cognac	**coniac** (n)	[ko'njak]
rum	**rom** (n)	[rom]
coffee	**cafea** (f)	[ka'fʲa]
black coffee	**cafea** (f) **neagră**	[ka'fʲa 'nʲagrə]
coffee with milk	**cafea** (f) **cu lapte**	[ka'fʲa ku 'lapte]
cappuccino	**cafea** (f) **cu frișcă**	[ka'fʲa ku 'friʃkə]
instant coffee	**cafea** (f) **solubilă**	[ka'fʲa so'lubilə]
milk	**lapte** (n)	['lapte]
cocktail	**cocteil** (n)	[kok'tejl]
milkshake	**cocteil** (n) **din lapte**	[kok'tejl din 'lapte]
juice	**suc** (n)	[suk]
tomato juice	**suc** (n) **de roșii**	[suk de 'roʃij]
orange juice	**suc** (n) **de portocale**	[suk de porto'kale]
freshly squeezed juice	**suc** (n) **natural**	[suk natu'ral]
beer	**bere** (f)	['bere]
light beer	**bere** (f) **blondă**	['bere 'blondə]
dark beer	**bere** (f) **brună**	['bere 'brunə]
tea	**ceai** (n)	[ʧaj]

black tea	**ceai** (n) **negru**	[ʧaj 'negru]
green tea	**ceai** (n) **verde**	[ʧaj 'verde]

46. Vegetables

vegetables	**legume** (f pl)	[le'gume]
greens	**verdeață** (f)	[ver'dʲaʦə]
tomato	**roşie** (f)	['roʃie]
cucumber	**castravete** (m)	[kastra'vete]
carrot	**morcov** (m)	['morkov]
potato	**cartof** (m)	[kar'tof]
onion	**ceapă** (f)	['ʧapə]
garlic	**usturoi** (m)	[ustu'roj]
cabbage	**varză** (f)	['varzə]
cauliflower	**conopidă** (f)	[kono'pidə]
Brussels sprouts	**varză** (f) **de Bruxelles**	['varzə de bruk'sel]
broccoli	**broccoli** (m)	['brokoli]
beet	**sfeclă** (f)	['sfeklə]
eggplant	**pătlăgea** (f) **vânătă**	[pətlə'ʤʲa 'vinətə]
zucchini	**dovlecel** (m)	[dovle'ʧel]
pumpkin	**dovleac** (m)	[dov'lʲak]
turnip	**nap** (m)	[nap]
parsley	**pătrunjel** (m)	[pətrun'ʒel]
dill	**mărar** (m)	[mə'rar]
lettuce	**salată** (f)	[sa'latə]
celery	**țelină** (f)	['ʦelinə]
asparagus	**sparanghel** (m)	[sparan'gel]
spinach	**spanac** (n)	[spa'nak]
pea	**mazăre** (f)	['mazəre]
beans	**boabe** (f pl)	[bo'abe]
corn (maize)	**porumb** (m)	[po'rumb]
kidney bean	**fasole** (f)	[fa'sole]
bell pepper	**piper** (m)	[pi'per]
radish	**ridiche** (f)	[ri'dike]
artichoke	**anghinare** (f)	[angi'nare]

47. Fruits. Nuts

fruit	**fruct** (n)	[frukt]
apple	**măr** (n)	[mər]
pear	**pară** (f)	['parə]
lemon	**lămâie** (f)	[lə'mie]

orange	**portocală** (f)	[porto'kalə]
strawberry (garden ~)	**căpşună** (f)	[kəp'ʃunə]
mandarin	**mandarină** (f)	[manda'rinə]
plum	**prună** (f)	['prunə]
peach	**piersică** (f)	['pjersikə]
apricot	**caisă** (f)	[ka'isə]
raspberry	**zmeură** (f)	['zmeurə]
pineapple	**ananas** (m)	[ana'nas]
banana	**banană** (f)	[ba'nanə]
watermelon	**pepene** (m) **verde**	['pepene 'verde]
grape	**struguri** (m pl)	['strugurʲ]
sour cherry	**vişină** (f)	['viʃinə]
sweet cherry	**cireaşă** (f)	[tʃi'rʲaʃə]
melon	**pepene** (m) **galben**	['pepene 'galben]
grapefruit	**grepfrut** (n)	['grepfrut]
avocado	**avocado** (n)	[avo'kado]
papaya	**papaia** (f)	[pa'paja]
mango	**mango** (n)	['mango]
pomegranate	**rodie** (f)	['rodie]
redcurrant	**coacăză** (f) **roşie**	[ko'akəzə 'roʃie]
blackcurrant	**coacăză** (f) **neagră**	[ko'akəzə 'nʲagrə]
gooseberry	**agrişă** (f)	[a'griʃə]
bilberry	**afină** (f)	[a'finə]
blackberry	**mură** (f)	['murə]
raisin	**stafidă** (f)	[sta'fidə]
fig	**smochină** (f)	[smo'kinə]
date	**curmală** (f)	[kur'malə]
peanut	**arahidă** (f)	[ara'hidə]
almond	**migdală** (f)	[mig'dalə]
walnut	**nucă** (f)	['nukə]
hazelnut	**alună** (f) **de pădure**	[a'lunə de pə'dure]
coconut	**nucă** (f) **de cocos**	['nukə de 'kokos]
pistachios	**fistic** (m)	['fistik]

48. Bread. Candy

bakers' confectionery (pastry)	**produse** (n pl) **de cofetărie**	[pro'duse də kofetə'rie]
bread	**pâine** (f)	['pine]
cookies	**biscuit** (m)	[bisku'it]
chocolate (n)	**ciocolată** (f)	[tʃioko'latə]
chocolate (as adj)	**de, din ciocolată**	[de, din tʃioko'latə]
candy (wrapped)	**bomboană** (f)	[bombo'anə]

cake (e.g., cupcake)	**prăjitură** (f)	[prəʒi'turə]
cake (e.g., birthday ~)	**tort** (n)	[tort]
pie (e.g., apple ~)	**plăcintă** (f)	[plə'ʧintə]
filling (for cake, pie)	**umplutură** (f)	[umplu'turə]
jam (whole fruit jam)	**dulceață** (f)	[dul'ʧaʦə]
marmalade	**marmeladă** (f)	[marme'ladə]
wafers	**napolitane** (f pl)	[napoli'tane]
ice-cream	**înghețată** (f)	[ɨnge'ʦatə]

49. Cooked dishes

course, dish	**fel** (n) **de mâncare**	[fel de mɨ'nkare]
cuisine	**bucătărie** (f)	[bukətə'rie]
recipe	**rețetă** (f)	[re'ʦetə]
portion	**porție** (f)	['porʦie]
salad	**salată** (f)	[sa'latə]
soup	**supă** (f)	['supə]
clear soup (broth)	**supă** (f) **de carne**	['supə de 'karne]
sandwich (bread)	**tartină** (f)	[tar'tinə]
fried eggs	**omletă** (f)	[om'letə]
hamburger (beefburger)	**hamburger** (m)	['hamburger]
beefsteak	**biftec** (n)	[bif'tek]
side dish	**garnitură** (f)	[garni'turə]
spaghetti	**spaghete** (f pl)	[spa'gete]
mashed potatoes	**piure** (n) **de cartofi**	[pju're de kar'tofʲ]
pizza	**pizza** (f)	['piʦa]
porridge (oatmeal, etc.)	**cașă** (f)	['kaʃə]
omelet	**omletă** (f)	[om'letə]
boiled (e.g., ~ beef)	**fiert**	[fiert]
smoked (adj)	**afumat**	[afu'mat]
fried (adj)	**prăjit**	[prə'ʒit]
dried (adj)	**uscat**	[us'kat]
frozen (adj)	**congelat**	[konʤe'lat]
pickled (adj)	**marinat**	[mari'nat]
sweet (sugary)	**dulce**	['dulʧe]
salty (adj)	**sărat**	[sə'rat]
cold (adj)	**rece**	['reʧe]
hot (adj)	**fierbinte**	[fier'binte]
bitter (adj)	**amar**	[a'mar]
tasty (adj)	**gustos**	[gus'tos]
to cook in boiling water	**a fierbe**	[a 'fjerbe]
to cook (dinner)	**a găti**	[a gə'ti]

to fry (vt)	**a prăji**	[a prə'ʒi]
to heat up (food)	**a încălzi**	[a ɨnkəl'zi]
to salt (vt)	**a săra**	[a sə'ra]
to pepper (vt)	**a pipera**	[a pipe'ra]
to grate (vt)	**a da prin răzătoare**	[a da prin rəzəto'are]
peel (n)	**coajă** (f)	[ko'aʒə]
to peel (vt)	**a curăța**	[a kurə'tsa]

50. Spices

salt	**sare** (f)	['sare]
salty (adj)	**sărat**	[sə'rat]
to salt (vt)	**a săra**	[a sə'ra]
black pepper	**piper** (m) **negru**	[pi'per 'negru]
red pepper (milled ~)	**piper** (m) **roşu**	[pi'per 'roʃu]
mustard	**muştar** (m)	[muʃ'tar]
horseradish	**hrean** (n)	[hrʲan]
condiment	**condiment** (n)	[kondi'ment]
spice	**condiment** (n)	[kondi'ment]
sauce	**sos** (n)	[sos]
vinegar	**oțet** (n)	[o'tset]
anise	**anason** (m)	[ana'son]
basil	**busuioc** (n)	[busu'jok]
cloves	**cuişoare** (f pl)	[kuiʃo'are]
ginger	**ghimber** (m)	[gim'ber]
coriander	**coriandru** (m)	[kori'andru]
cinnamon	**scorțişoară** (f)	[skortsiʃo'arə]
sesame	**susan** (m)	[su'san]
bay leaf	**foi** (f) **de dafin**	[foj de 'dafin]
paprika	**paprică** (f)	['paprikə]
caraway	**chimen** (m)	[ki'men]
saffron	**şofran** (m)	[ʃo'fran]

51. Meals

food	**mâncare** (f)	[mɨn'kare]
to eat (vi, vt)	**a mânca**	[a mɨn'ka]
breakfast	**micul dejun** (n)	['mikul de'ʒun]
to have breakfast	**a lua micul dejun**	[a lu'a 'mikul de'ʒun]
lunch	**prânz** (n)	[prɨnz]
to have lunch	**a lua prânzul**	[a lu'a 'prɨnzul]
dinner	**cină** (f)	['tʃinə]

to have dinner	**a cina**	[a ʧi'na]
appetite	**poftă** (f) **de mâncare**	['poftə de mɨ'nkare]
Enjoy your meal!	**Poftă bună!**	['poftə 'bunə]
to open (~ a bottle)	**a deschide**	[a des'kide]
to spill (liquid)	**a vărsa**	[a vər'sa]
to spill out (vi)	**a se vărsa**	[a se vər'sa]
to boil (vi)	**a fierbe**	[a 'fjerbe]
to boil (vt)	**a fierbe**	[a 'fjerbe]
boiled (~ water)	**fiert**	[fiert]
to chill, cool down (vt)	**a răci**	[a rə'ʧi]
to chill (vi)	**a se răci**	[a se rə'ʧi]
taste, flavor	**gust** (n)	[gust]
aftertaste	**aromă** (f)	[a'romə]
to slim down (lose weight)	**a slăbi**	[a slə'bi]
diet	**dietă** (f)	[di'etə]
vitamin	**vitamină** (f)	[vita'minə]
calorie	**calorie** (f)	[kalo'rie]
vegetarian (n)	**vegetarian** (m)	[veʤetari'an]
vegetarian (adj)	**vegetarian**	[veʤetari'an]
fats (nutrient)	**grăsimi** (f pl)	[grə'simʲ]
proteins	**proteine** (f pl)	[prote'ine]
carbohydrates	**hidrați** (m pl) **de carbon**	[hi'dratsʲ de kar'bon]
slice (of lemon, ham)	**felie** (f)	[fe'lie]
piece (of cake, pie)	**bucată** (f)	[bu'katə]
crumb (of bread, cake, etc.)	**firimitură** (f)	[firimi'turə]

52. Table setting

spoon	**lingură** (f)	['lingurə]
knife	**cuțit** (n)	[ku'tsit]
fork	**furculiță** (f)	[furku'litsə]
cup (e.g., coffee ~)	**ceaşcă** (f)	['ʧaʃkə]
plate (dinner ~)	**farfurie** (f)	[farfu'rie]
saucer	**farfurioară** (f)	[farfurio'arə]
napkin (on table)	**şervețel** (n)	[ʃərve'tsel]
toothpick	**scobitoare** (f)	[skobito'are]

53. Restaurant

restaurant	**restaurant** (n)	[restau'rant]
coffee house	**cafenea** (f)	[kafe'nʲa]

pub, bar	**bar** (n)	[bar]
tearoom	**salon** (n) **de ceai**	[sa'lon de tʃaj]
waiter	**chelner** (m)	['kelner]
waitress	**chelneriță** (f)	[kelne'ritsə]
bartender	**barman** (m)	['barman]
menu	**meniu** (n)	[me'nju]
wine list	**meniu** (n) **de vinuri**	[menju de 'vinurʲ]
to book a table	**a rezerva o masă**	[a rezer'va o 'masə]
course, dish	**mâncare** (f)	[mɨn'kare]
to order (meal)	**a comanda**	[a koman'da]
to make an order	**a face comandă**	[a 'fatʃe ko'mandə]
aperitif	**aperitiv** (n)	[aperi'tiv]
appetizer	**gustare** (f)	[gus'tare]
dessert	**desert** (n)	[de'sert]
check	**notă** (f) **de plată**	['notə de 'platə]
to pay the check	**a achita nota de plată**	[a aki'ta 'nota de 'platə]
to give change	**a da rest**	[a da 'rest]
tip	**bacşiş** (n)	[bak'ʃiʃ]

Family, relatives and friends

54. Personal information. Forms

name (first name)	**prenume** (n)	[pre'nume]
surname (last name)	**nume** (n)	['nume]
date of birth	**data** (f) **naşterii**	['data 'naʃterij]
place of birth	**locul** (n) **naşterii**	['lokul 'naʃterij]
nationality	**naţionalitate** (f)	[natsionali'tate]
place of residence	**locul** (n) **de reşedinţă**	['lokul de reʃə'dintsə]
country	**ţară** (f)	['tsarə]
profession (occupation)	**profesie** (f)	[pro'fesie]
gender, sex	**sex** (n)	[seks]
height	**înălţime** (f)	[ɨnəl'tsime]
weight	**greutate** (f)	[greu'tate]

55. Family members. Relatives

mother	**mamă** (f)	['mamə]
father	**tată** (m)	['tatə]
son	**fiu** (m)	['fju]
daughter	**fiică** (f)	['fiikə]
younger daughter	**fiica** (f) **mai mică**	['fiika maj 'mikə]
younger son	**fiul** (m) **mai mic**	['fjul maj mik]
eldest daughter	**fiica** (f) **mai mare**	['fiika maj 'mare]
eldest son	**fiul** (m) **mai mare**	['fjul maj 'mare]
brother	**frate** (m)	['frate]
elder brother	**frate** (m) **mai mare**	['frate maj 'mare]
younger brother	**frate** (m) **mai mic**	['frate maj mik]
sister	**soră** (f)	['sorə]
elder sister	**soră** (f) **mai mare**	['sorə maj 'mare]
younger sister	**soră** (f) **mai mică**	['sorə maj 'mikə]
cousin (masc.)	**văr** (m)	[vər]
cousin (fem.)	**vară** (f)	['varə]
mom, mommy	**mamă** (f)	['mamə]
dad, daddy	**tată** (m)	['tatə]
parents	**părinţi** (m pl)	[pə'rintsʲ]
child	**copil** (m)	[ko'pil]
children	**copii** (m pl)	[ko'pij]

grandmother	**bunică** (f)	[bu'nikə]
grandfather	**bunic** (m)	[bu'nik]
grandson	**nepot** (m)	[ne'pot]
granddaughter	**nepoată** (f)	[nepo'atə]
grandchildren	**nepoți** (m pl)	[ne'poʦʲ]
uncle	**unchi** (m)	[unkʲ]
aunt	**mătuşă** (f)	[mə'tuʃə]
nephew	**nepot** (m)	[ne'pot]
niece	**nepoată** (f)	[nepo'atə]
mother-in-law (wife's mother)	**soacră** (f)	[so'akrə]
father-in-law (husband's father)	**socru** (m)	['sokru]
son-in-law (daughter's husband)	**cumnat** (m)	[kum'nat]
stepmother	**mamă vitregă** (f)	['mamə 'vitregə]
stepfather	**tată vitreg** (m)	['tatə 'vitreg]
infant	**sugaci** (m)	[su'gaʧi]
baby (infant)	**prunc** (m)	[prunk]
little boy, kid	**pici** (m)	[piʧi]
wife	**soție** (f)	[so'ʦie]
husband	**soț** (m)	[soʦ]
spouse (husband)	**soț** (m)	[soʦ]
spouse (wife)	**soție** (f)	[so'ʦie]
married (masc.)	**căsătorit**	[kəsəto'rit]
married (fem.)	**căsătorită**	[kəsəto'ritə]
single (unmarried)	**celibatar** (m)	[ʧeliba'tar]
bachelor	**burlac** (m)	[bur'lak]
divorced (masc.)	**divorțat**	[divor'ʦat]
widow	**văduvă** (f)	[vəduvə]
widower	**văduv** (m)	[vəduv]
relative	**rudă** (f)	['rudə]
close relative	**rudă** (f) **apropiată**	['rudə apropi'jatə]
distant relative	**rudă** (f) **îndepărtată**	['rudə indeper'tatə]
relatives	**rude** (f pl) **de sânge**	['rude de 'sinʤe]
orphan (boy or girl)	**orfan** (m)	[or'fan]
guardian (of a minor)	**tutore** (m)	[tu'tore]
to adopt (a boy)	**a adopta**	[a adop'ta]
to adopt (a girl)	**a adopta**	[a adop'ta]

56. Friends. Coworkers

friend (masc.)	**prieten** (m)	[pri'eten]
friend (fem.)	**prietenă** (f)	[pri'etenə]

friendship	**prietenie** (f)	[priete'nie]
to be friends	**a prieteni**	[a priete'ni]
buddy (masc.)	**amic** (m)	[a'mik]
buddy (fem.)	**amică** (f)	[a'mikə]
partner	**partener** (m)	[parte'ner]
chief (boss)	**şef** (m)	[ʃef]
superior (n)	**director** (m)	[di'rektor]
owner, proprietor	**proprietar** (m)	[proprie'tar]
subordinate (n)	**subordonat** (m)	[subordo'nat]
colleague	**coleg** (m)	[ko'leg]
acquaintance (person)	**cunoscut** (m)	[kunos'kut]
fellow traveler	**tovarăş** (m) **de drum**	[to'varəʃ de drum]
classmate	**coleg** (m) **de clasă**	[ko'leg de 'klasə]
neighbor (masc.)	**vecin** (m)	[ve'ʧin]
neighbor (fem.)	**vecină** (f)	[ve'ʧinə]
neighbors	**vecini** (m pl)	[ve'ʧinʲ]

57. Man. Woman

woman	**femeie** (f)	[fe'meje]
girl (young woman)	**domnişoară** (f)	[domniʃo'arə]
bride	**mireasă** (f)	[mi'rʲasə]
beautiful (adj)	**frumoasă**	[frumo'asə]
tall (adj)	**înaltă**	[ɨ'naltə]
slender (adj)	**zveltă**	['zveltə]
short (adj)	**scundă**	['skundə]
blonde (n)	**blondă** (f)	['blondə]
brunette (n)	**brunetă** (f)	[bru'netə]
ladies' (adj)	**de damă**	[de 'damə]
virgin (girl)	**virgină** (f)	[vir'ʤinə]
pregnant (adj)	**gravidă** (f)	[gra'vidə]
man (adult male)	**bărbat** (m)	[bər'bat]
blond (n)	**blond** (m)	[blond]
brunet (n)	**brunet** (m)	[bru'net]
tall (adj)	**înalt**	[ɨ'nalt]
short (adj)	**scund**	[skund]
rude (rough)	**grosolan**	[groso'lan]
stocky (adj)	**robust**	[ro'bust]
robust (adj)	**tare**	['tare]
strong (adj)	**puternic**	[pu'ternik]
strength	**forţă** (f)	['fortsə]

stout, fat (adj)	**gras**	[gras]
swarthy (adj)	**negricios**	[negri'tʃios]
slender (well-built)	**zvelt**	[zvelt]
elegant (adj)	**elegant**	[ele'gant]

58. Age

age	**vârstă** (f)	['vɨrstə]
youth (young age)	**tinerețe** (f)	[tine'retse]
young (adj)	**tânăr**	['tɨnər]
younger (adj)	**mai mic**	[maj mik]
older (adj)	**mai mare**	[maj 'mare]
young man	**tânăr** (m)	['tɨnər]
teenager	**adolescent** (m)	[adoles'tʃent]
guy, fellow	**flăcău** (m)	[fləkəu]
old man	**bătrân** (m)	[bə'trɨn]
old woman	**bătrână** (f)	[bə'trɨnə]
adult (adj)	**adult** (m)	[a'dult]
middle-aged (adj)	**de vârstă medie**	[de 'vɨrstə 'medie]
elderly (adj)	**în vârstă**	[ɨn 'vɨrstə]
old (adj)	**bătrân**	[bə'trɨn]
retirement	**pensie** (f)	['pensie]
to retire (from job)	**a se pensiona**	[a se pensio'na]
retiree	**pensionar** (m)	[pensio'nar]

59. Children

child	**copil** (m)	[ko'pil]
children	**copii** (m pl)	[ko'pij]
twins	**gemeni** (m pl)	['dʒemenʲ]
cradle	**leagăn** (n)	['lʲagən]
rattle	**sunătoare** (f)	[sunəto'are]
diaper	**scutec** (n)	['skutek]
pacifier	**biberon** (n)	[bibe'ron]
baby carriage	**cărucior** (n) **pentru copii**	[kəru'tʃior 'pentru ko'pij]
kindergarten	**grădiniță** (f) **de copii**	[grədi'nitsə de ko'pij]
babysitter	**dădacă** (f)	[də'dakə]
childhood	**copilărie** (f)	[kopilə'rie]
doll	**păpușă** (f)	[pə'puʃə]
toy	**jucărie** (f)	[ʒukə'rie]

construction set (toy)	**constructor** (m)	[kon'struktor]
well-bred (adj)	**bine crescut**	['bine kres'kut]
ill-bred (adj)	**needucat**	[needu'kat]
spoiled (adj)	**răsfăţat**	[rəsfə'tsat]
to be naughty	**a face pozne**	[a 'fatʃe 'pozne]
mischievous (adj)	**năzbâtios**	[nəzbɨti'os]
mischievousness	**năzbâtie** (f)	[nəz'bɨtie]
mischievous child	**ştrengar** (m)	[ʃtren'gar]
obedient (adj)	**ascultător**	[askultə'tor]
disobedient (adj)	**neascultător**	[neaskultə'tor]
docile (adj)	**inteligent**	[inteli'dʒent]
clever (smart)	**deştept**	[deʃ'tept]
child prodigy	**copil** (m) **minune**	[ko'pil mi'nune]

60. Married couples. Family life

to kiss (vt)	**a săruta**	[a səru'ta]
to kiss (vi)	**a se săruta**	[a se səru'ta]
family (n)	**familie** (f)	[fa'milie]
family (as adj)	**de familie**	[de fa'milie]
couple	**pereche** (f)	[pe'reke]
marriage (state)	**căsătorie** (f)	[kəsəto'rie]
hearth (home)	**cămin** (n)	[kə'min]
dynasty	**dinastie** (f)	[dinas'tie]
date	**întâlnire** (f)	[ɨntɨl'nire]
kiss	**sărut** (n)	[sə'rut]
love (for sb)	**iubire** (f)	[ju'bire]
to love (sb)	**a iubi**	[a ju'bi]
beloved	**iubit**	[ju'bit]
tenderness	**gingăşie** (f)	[dʒingə'ʃie]
tender (affectionate)	**tandru**	['tandru]
faithfulness	**fidelitate** (f)	[fideli'tate]
faithful (adj)	**fidel**	[fi'del]
care (attention)	**grijă** (f)	['griʒə]
caring (~ father)	**grijuliu**	[griʒu'lju]
newlyweds	**tineri** (m pl) **căsătoriţi**	['tiner[j] kəsəto'rits]
honeymoon	**lună** (f) **de miere**	['lunə de 'mjere]
to get married (ab. woman)	**a se mărita**	[a se məri'ta]
to get married (ab. man)	**a se căsători**	[a se kəsəto'ri]
wedding	**nuntă** (f)	['nuntə]
golden wedding	**nuntă** (f) **de aur**	['nuntə de 'aur]

anniversary	**aniversare** (f)	[aniver'sare]
lover (masc.)	**amant** (m)	[a'mant]
mistress (lover)	**amantă** (f)	[a'mantə]
adultery	**adulter** (n)	[adul'ter]
to cheat on ... (commit adultery)	**a înşela**	[a inʃə'la]
jealous (adj)	**gelos**	[ʤe'los]
to be jealous	**a fi gelos**	[a fi ʤe'los]
divorce	**divorț** (n)	[di'vorʦ]
to divorce (vi)	**a divorța**	[a divor'ʦa]
to quarrel (vi)	**a se certa**	[a se ʧer'ta]
to be reconciled (after an argument)	**a se împăca**	[a se impə'ka]
together (adv)	**împreună**	[impre'unə]
sex	**sex** (n)	[seks]
happiness	**fericire** (f)	[feri'ʧire]
happy (adj)	**fericit**	[feri'ʧit]
misfortune (accident)	**nenorocire** (f)	[nenoro'ʧire]
unhappy (adj)	**nefericit**	[neferi'ʧit]

Character. Feelings. Emotions

61. Feelings. Emotions

feeling (emotion)	**sentiment** (n)	[senti'ment]
feelings	**sentimente** (n pl)	[senti'mente]
to feel (vt)	**a simți**	[a sim'ʦʲ]
hunger	**foame** (f)	[fo'ame]
to be hungry	**a fi foame**	[a fi fo'ame]
thirst	**sete** (f)	['sete]
to be thirsty	**a fi sete**	[a fi 'sete]
sleepiness	**somnolență** (f)	[somno'lenʦə]
to feel sleepy	**a fi somn**	[a fi somn]
tiredness	**oboseală** (f)	[obo'sʲalə]
tired (adj)	**obosit**	[obo'sit]
to get tired	**a obosi**	[a obo'si]
mood (humor)	**dispoziție** (f)	[dispo'ziʦie]
boredom	**plictiseală** (f)	[plikti'sʲalə]
to be bored	**a se plictisi**	[a se plikti'si]
seclusion	**singurătate** (f)	[singurə'tate]
to seclude oneself	**a se izola**	[a se izo'la]
to worry (make anxious)	**a nelinişti**	[a nelinij'ti]
to be worried	**a se nelinişti**	[a se nelinij'ti]
worrying (n)	**nelinişte** (f)	[ne'linijte]
anxiety	**nelinişte** (f)	[ne'linijte]
preoccupied (adj)	**preocupat**	[preoku'pat]
to be nervous	**a se enerva**	[a se ener'va]
to panic (vi)	**a panica**	[a pani'ka]
hope	**speranță** (f)	[spe'ranʦə]
to hope (vi, vt)	**a spera**	[a spe'ra]
certainty	**siguranță** (f)	[sigu'ranʦə]
certain, sure (adj)	**sigur**	['sigur]
uncertainty	**nesiguranță** (f)	[nesigu'ranʦə]
uncertain (adj)	**nesigur**	[ne'sigur]
drunk (adj)	**beat**	[bʲat]
sober (adj)	**treaz**	[trʲaz]
weak (adj)	**slab**	[slab]
happy (adj)	**norocos**	[noro'kos]
to scare (vt)	**a speria**	[a speri'ja]

fury (madness)	**turbare** (f)	[tur'bare]
rage (fury)	**furie** (f)	[fu'rie]
depression	**depresie** (f)	[de'presie]
discomfort (unease)	**disconfort** (n)	[diskon'fort]
comfort	**confort** (n)	[kon'fort]
to regret (be sorry)	**a regreta**	[a regre'ta]
regret	**regret** (n)	[re'gret]
bad luck	**ghinion** (n)	[gini'on]
sadness	**întristare** (f)	[ɨntri'stare]
shame (remorse)	**ruşine** (f)	[ru'ʃine]
gladness	**veselie** (f)	[vese'lie]
enthusiasm, zeal	**entuziasm** (n)	[entuzi'asm]
enthusiast	**entuziast** (m)	[entuzi'ast]
to show enthusiasm	**a arăta entuziasm**	[a arə'ta entuzi'asm]

62. Character. Personality

character	**caracter** (n)	[karak'ter]
character flaw	**viciu** (n)	['vitʃiu]
mind	**minte** (f)	['minte]
reason	**raţiune** (f)	[ratsi'une]
conscience	**conştiinţă** (f)	[konʃti'intsə]
habit (custom)	**obişnuinţă** (f)	[obiʃnu'intsə]
ability (talent)	**talent** (n)	[ta'lent]
can (e.g., ~ swim)	**a putea**	[a pu'tʲa]
patient (adj)	**răbdător**	[rəbdə'tor]
impatient (adj)	**nerăbdător**	[nerəbdə'tor]
curious (inquisitive)	**curios**	[kuri'os]
curiosity	**curiozitate** (f)	[kuriozi'tate]
modesty	**modestie** (f)	[modes'tie]
modest (adj)	**modest**	[mo'dest]
immodest (adj)	**lipsit de modestie**	[lip'sit de modes'tie]
laziness	**lene** (f)	['lene]
lazy (adj)	**leneş**	['leneʃ]
lazy person (masc.)	**leneş** (m)	['leneʃ]
cunning (n)	**viclenie** (f)	[vikle'nie]
cunning (as adj)	**viclean**	[vik'lʲan]
distrust	**neîncredere** (f)	[neɨn'kredere]
distrustful (adj)	**neîncrezător**	[neɨnkrezə'tor]
generosity	**generozitate** (f)	[dʒenerozi'tate]
generous (adj)	**generos**	[dʒene'ros]
talented (adj)	**talentat**	[talen'tat]

talent	**talent** (n)	[ta'lent]
courageous (adj)	**îndrăzneț**	[ɨndrəz'nets]
courage	**îndrăzneală** (f)	[ɨndrəz'nʲalə]
honest (adj)	**onest**	[o'nest]
honesty	**onestitate** (f)	[onesti'tate]
careful (cautious)	**prudent**	[pru'dent]
brave (courageous)	**curajos**	[kura'ʒos]
serious (adj)	**serios**	[se'rjos]
strict (severe, stern)	**sever**	[se'ver]
decisive (adj)	**hotărât**	[hotə'rɨt]
indecisive (adj)	**nehotărât**	[nehotə'rɨt]
shy, timid (adj)	**sfios**	[sfi'os]
shyness, timidity	**sfială** (f)	[sfi'jalə]
confidence (trust)	**încredere** (f)	[ɨn'kredere]
to believe (trust)	**a avea încredere**	[a a'vʲa ɨn'kredere]
trusting (credulous)	**credul**	[kre'dul]
sincerely (adv)	**sincer**	['sintʃer]
sincere (adj)	**sincer**	['sintʃer]
sincerity	**sinceritate** (f)	[sintʃeri'tate]
open (person)	**deschis**	[des'kis]
calm (adj)	**liniştit**	[liniʃ'tit]
frank (sincere)	**sincer**	['sintʃer]
naïve (adj)	**naiv**	[na'iv]
absent-minded (adj)	**distrat**	[dis'trat]
funny (odd)	**hazliu**	[haz'lju]
greed, stinginess	**lăcomie** (f)	[ləko'mie]
greedy, stingy (adj)	**lacom**	['lakom]
stingy (adj)	**zgârcit**	[zgɨr'tʃit]
evil (adj)	**rău**	['rəu]
stubborn (adj)	**încăpățânat**	[ɨnkəpətsɨ'nat]
unpleasant (adj)	**neplăcut**	[neplə'kut]
selfish person (masc.)	**egoist** (m)	[ego'ist]
selfish (adj)	**egoist**	[ego'ist]
coward	**laş** (m)	[laʃ]
cowardly (adj)	**fricos**	[fri'kos]

63. Sleep. Dreams

to sleep (vi)	**a dormi**	[a dor'mi]
sleep, sleeping	**somn** (n)	[somn]
dream	**vis** (n)	[vis]
to dream (in sleep)	**a visa**	[a vi'sa]
sleepy (adj)	**somnoros**	[somno'ros]

bed	**pat** (n)	[pat]
mattress	**saltea** (f)	[sal'tʲa]
blanket (comforter)	**plapumă** (f)	['plapumə]
pillow	**pernă** (f)	['pernə]
sheet	**cearşaf** (n)	[ʧar'ʃaf]
insomnia	**insomnie** (f)	[insom'nie]
sleepless (adj)	**fără somn**	['fərə somn]
sleeping pill	**somnifer** (n)	[somni'fer]
to take a sleeping pill	**a lua somnifere**	[a lu'a somni'fere]
to feel sleepy	**a fi somn**	[a fi somn]
to yawn (vi)	**a căsca**	[a kəs'ka]
to go to bed	**a merge la culcare**	[a 'merʤe la kul'kare]
to make up the bed	**a face patul**	[a 'faʧe 'patul]
to fall asleep	**a adormi**	[a ador'mi]
nightmare	**coşmar** (n)	[koʃ'mar]
snore, snoring	**sforăit** (n)	[sforə'it]
to snore (vi)	**a sforăi**	[a sforə'i]
alarm clock	**ceas** (n) **deşteptător**	[ʧas deʃteptə'tor]
to wake (vt)	**a trezi**	[a tre'zi]
to wake up	**a se trezi**	[a se tre'zi]
to get up (vi)	**a se ridica**	[a se ridi'ka]
to wash up (wash face)	**a se spăla**	[a se spə'la]

64. Humour. Laughter. Gladness

humor (wit, fun)	**umor** (n)	[u'mor]
sense of humor	**simţ** (n)	[simʦ]
to enjoy oneself	**a se veseli**	[a se vese'li]
cheerful (merry)	**vesel**	['vesel]
merriment (gaiety)	**veselie** (f)	[vese'lie]
smile	**zâmbet** (n)	['zɨmbet]
to smile (vi)	**a zâmbi**	[a zɨm'bi]
to start laughing	**a izbucni în râs**	[a izbuk'ni ɨn rɨs]
to laugh (vi)	**a râde**	[a 'rɨde]
laugh, laughter	**râs** (n)	[rɨs]
anecdote	**anecdotă** (f)	[anek'dotə]
funny (anecdote, etc.)	**hazliu**	[haz'lju]
funny (odd)	**hazliu**	[haz'lju]
to joke (vi)	**a glumi**	[a glu'mi]
joke (verbal)	**glumă** (f)	['glumə]
joy (emotion)	**bucurie** (f)	[buku'rie]
to rejoice (vi)	**a se bucura**	[a se buku'ra]
joyful (adj)	**bucuros**	[buku'ros]

65. Discussion, conversation. Part 1

communication	**comunicare** (f)	[komuni'kare]
to communicate	**a comunica**	[a komuni'ka]
conversation	**convorbire** (f)	[konvor'bire]
dialog	**dialog** (n)	[dia'log]
discussion (discourse)	**dezbatere** (f)	[dez'batere]
dispute (debate)	**polemică** (f)	[po'lemikə]
to dispute	**a revendica**	[a revendi'ka]
interlocutor	**interlocutor** (m)	[interloku'tor]
topic (theme)	**temă** (f)	['temə]
point of view	**punct** (n) **de vedere**	[punkt de ve'dere]
opinion (point of view)	**părere** (f)	[pə'rere]
speech (talk)	**discurs** (n)	[dis'kurs]
discussion (of report, etc.)	**discuție** (f)	[dis'kutsie]
to discuss (vt)	**a discuta**	[a disku'ta]
talk (conversation)	**conversație** (f)	[konver'satsie]
to talk (to chat)	**a conversa**	[a konver'sa]
meeting (encounter)	**întâlnire** (f)	[ɨntɨl'nire]
to meet (vi, vt)	**a se întâlni**	[a se ɨntɨl'ni]
proverb	**proverb** (n)	[pro'verb]
saying	**zicătoare** (f)	[zikəto'are]
riddle (poser)	**ghicitoare** (f)	[gitʃito'are]
to pose a riddle	**a ghici o ghicitoare**	[a gi'tʃi o gitʃito'are]
password	**parolă** (f)	[pa'rolə]
secret	**secret** (n)	[se'kret]
oath (vow)	**jurământ** (n)	[ʒurə'mɨnt]
to swear (an oath)	**a jura**	[a ʒu'ra]
promise	**promisiune** (f)	[promisi'une]
to promise (vt)	**a promite**	[a pro'mite]
advice (counsel)	**sfat** (n)	[sfat]
to advise (vt)	**a sfătui**	[a sfətu'i]
to listen to ... (obey)	**a asculta**	[a askul'ta]
news	**noutate** (f)	[nou'tate]
sensation (news)	**senzație** (f)	[sen'zatsie]
information (report)	**informații** (f pl)	[infor'matsij]
conclusion (decision)	**concluzie** (f)	[kon'kluzie]
voice	**voce** (f)	['votʃe]
compliment	**compliment** (n)	[kompli'ment]
kind (nice)	**amabil**	[a'mabil]
word	**cuvânt** (n)	[ku'vɨnt]
phrase	**frază** (f)	['frazə]
answer	**răspuns** (n)	[rəs'puns]

truth	**adevăr** (n)	[ade'vər]
lie	**minciună** (f)	[min'tʃiunə]
thought	**gând** (f)	[gɨnd]
idea (inspiration)	**gând** (n)	[gɨnd]
fantasy	**imaginație** (f)	[imadʒi'natsie]

66. Discussion, conversation. Part 2

respected (adj)	**stimat**	[sti'mat]
to respect (vt)	**a respecta**	[a respek'ta]
respect	**respect** (n)	[res'pekt]
Dear ... (letter)	**Stimate ...**	[sti'mate]
to introduce (sb to sb)	**a prezenta**	[a prezen'ta]
to make acquaintance	**a face cunoştinţă**	[a 'fatʃe kunoʃ'tintsə]
intention	**intenție** (f)	[in'tentsie]
to intend (have in mind)	**a intenționa**	[a intentsio'na]
wish	**urare** (f)	[u'rare]
to wish (~ good luck)	**a ura**	[a u'ra]
surprise (astonishment)	**mirare** (f)	[mi'rare]
to surprise (amaze)	**a mira**	[a mi'ra]
to be surprised	**a se mira**	[a se mi'ra]
to give (vt)	**a da**	[a da]
to take (get hold of)	**a lua**	[a lu'a]
to give back	**a restitui**	[a restitu'i]
to return (give back)	**a înapoia**	[a ɨnapo'ja]
to apologize (vi)	**a cere scuze**	[a 'tʃere 'skuze]
apology	**scuză** (f)	['skuzə]
to forgive (vt)	**a ierta**	[a er'ta]
to talk (speak)	**a vorbi**	[a vor'bi]
to listen (vi)	**a asculta**	[a askul'ta]
to hear out	**a asculta**	[a askul'ta]
to understand (vt)	**a înțelege**	[a ɨntse'ledʒe]
to show (to display)	**a arăta**	[a arə'ta]
to look at ...	**a se uita**	[a se uj'ta]
to call (yell for sb)	**a chema**	[a ke'ma]
to distract (disturb)	**a distrage**	[a dis'tradʒe]
to disturb (vt)	**a deranja**	[a deran'ʒa]
to pass (to hand sth)	**a transmite**	[a trans'mite]
demand (request)	**rugăminte** (f)	[rugə'minte]
to request (ask)	**a ruga**	[a ru'ga]
demand (firm request)	**cerere** (f)	['tʃerere]
to demand (request firmly)	**a cere**	[a 'tʃere]

to tease (call names)	**a tachina**	[a taki'na]
to mock (make fun of)	**a-şi bate joc**	[aʃ 'bate ʒok]
mockery, derision	**derâdere** (f)	[de'ridere]
nickname	**poreclă** (f)	[po'reklə]
insinuation	**aluzie** (f)	[a'luzie]
to insinuate (imply)	**a face aluzie**	[a 'fatʃe a'luzie]
to mean (vt)	**a se subînțelege**	[a se subɨntse'ledʒe]
description	**descriere** (f)	[de'skriere]
to describe (vt)	**a descrie**	[a de'skrie]
praise (compliments)	**laudă** (f)	['laudə]
to praise (vt)	**a lăuda**	[a ləu'da]
disappointment	**dezamăgire** (f)	[dezamə'dʒire]
to disappoint (vt)	**a dezamăgi**	[a dezamə'dʒi]
to be disappointed	**a se dezamăgi**	[a se dezamə'dʒi]
supposition	**presupunere** (f)	[presu'punere]
to suppose (assume)	**a presupune**	[a presu'pune]
warning (caution)	**avertisment** (n)	[avertis'ment]
to warn (vt)	**a preveni**	[a preve'ni]

67. Discussion, conversation. Part 3

to talk into (convince)	**a convinge**	[a kon'vindʒe]
to calm down (vt)	**a linişti**	[a liniʃ'ti]
silence (~ is golden)	**tăcere** (f)	[tə'tʃere]
to be silent (not speaking)	**a tăcea**	[a tə'tʃa]
to whisper (vi, vt)	**a şopti**	[a ʃop'ti]
whisper	**şoaptă** (f)	[ʃo'aptə]
frankly, sincerely (adv)	**sincer**	['sintʃer]
in my opinion ...	**după părerea mea ...**	['dupə pə'rerʲa mʲa]
detail (of the story)	**amănunt** (n)	[amə'nunt]
detailed (adj)	**amănunțit**	[amənun'tsit]
in detail (adv)	**amănunțit**	[amənun'tsit]
hint, clue	**indiciu** (n)	[in'ditʃiu]
to give a hint	**a şopti**	[a ʃop'ti]
look (glance)	**privire** (f)	[pri'vire]
to have a look	**a privi**	[a pri'vi]
fixed (look)	**fix**	[fiks]
to blink (vi)	**a clipi**	[a kli'pi]
to wink (vi)	**a clipi**	[a kli'pi]
to nod (in assent)	**a da din cap**	[a da din 'kap]
sigh	**oftat** (n)	[of'tat]

to sigh (vi)	**a ofta**	[a of'ta]
to shudder (vi)	**a tresări**	[a tresə'ri]
gesture	**gest** (n)	[dʒest]
to touch (one's arm, etc.)	**a se atinge**	[a se a'tindʒe]
to seize (e.g., ~ by the arm)	**a apuca**	[a apu'ka]
to tap (on the shoulder)	**a bate**	[a 'bate]
Look out!	**Atenție!**	[a'tentsie]
Really?	**Oare?**	[o'are]
Are you sure?	**Eşti sigur?**	[eʃtʲ 'sigur]
Good luck!	**Succes!**	[suk'tʃes]
I see!	**Clar!**	[klar]
What a pity!	**Ce păcat!**	[tʃe pə'kat]

68. Agreement. Refusal

consent	**consimțământ** (n)	[konsimtsə'mɨnt]
to consent (vi)	**a fi de acord cu ...**	[a fi de a'kord ku]
approval	**aprobare** (f)	[apro'bare]
to approve (vt)	**a aproba**	[a apro'ba]
refusal	**refuz** (n)	[re'fuz]
to refuse (vi, vt)	**a refuza**	[a refu'za]
Great!	**Perfect!**	[per'fekt]
All right!	**Bine!**	['bine]
Okay! (I agree)	**De acord!**	[de a'kord]
forbidden (adj)	**interzis**	[inter'zis]
it's forbidden	**nu se poate**	[nu se po'ate]
it's impossible	**imposibil**	[impo'sibil]
incorrect (adj)	**incorect**	[inko'rekt]
to reject (~ a demand)	**a respinge**	[a res'pindʒe]
to support (cause, idea)	**a susține**	[a sus'tsine]
to accept (~ an apology)	**a accepta**	[a aktʃep'ta]
to confirm (vt)	**a confirma**	[a konfir'ma]
confirmation	**confirmare** (f)	[konfir'mare]
permission	**permisiune** (f)	[permisi'une]
to permit (vt)	**a permite**	[a per'mite]
decision	**hotărâre** (f)	[hotə'rɨre]
to say nothing (hold one's tongue)	**a tăcea**	[a tə'tʃa]
condition (term)	**condiție** (f)	[kon'ditsie]
excuse (pretext)	**pretext** (n)	[pre'tekst]
praise (compliments)	**laudă** (f)	['laudə]
to praise (vt)	**a lăuda**	[a ləu'da]

69. Success. Good luck. Failure

success	**reuşită** (f)	[reu'ʃitə]
successfully (adv)	**reuşit**	[reu'ʃit]
successful (adj)	**reuşit**	[reu'ʃit]
luck (good luck)	**succes** (n)	[suk'ʧes]
Good luck!	**Succes!**	[suk'ʧes]
lucky (e.g., ~ day)	**norocos**	[noro'kos]
lucky (fortunate)	**norocos**	[noro'kos]
failure	**eşec** (n)	[e'ʃək]
misfortune	**ghinion** (n)	[gini'on]
bad luck	**ghinion** (n)	[gini'on]
unsuccessful (adj)	**nereuşit**	[nereu'ʃit]
catastrophe	**catastrofă** (f)	[katas'trofə]
pride	**mândrie** (f)	[mɨn'drie]
proud (adj)	**mândru**	['mɨndru]
to be proud	**a se mândri**	[a se mɨn'dri]
winner	**învingător** (m)	[ɨnvingə'tor]
to win (vi)	**a învinge**	[a ɨn'vinʤe]
to lose (not win)	**a pierde**	[a 'pjerde]
try	**încercare** (f)	[ɨnʧer'kare]
to try (vi)	**a se strădui**	[a se strədu'i]
chance (opportunity)	**şansă** (f)	['ʃansə]

70. Quarrels. Negative emotions

shout (scream)	**strigăt** (n)	['strigət]
to shout (vi)	**a striga**	[a stri'ga]
to start to cry out	**a striga**	[a stri'ga]
quarrel	**ceartă** (f)	['ʧartə]
to quarrel (vi)	**a se certa**	[a se ʧer'ta]
fight (squabble)	**scandal** (n)	[skan'dal]
to make a scene	**a face scandal**	[a 'faʧe skan'dal]
conflict	**conflict** (n)	[kon'flikt]
misunderstanding	**neînţelegere** (f)	[neinʦe'leʤere]
insult	**insultă** (f)	[in'sultə]
to insult (vt)	**a insulta**	[a insul'ta]
insulted (adj)	**ofensat**	[ofen'sat]
resentment	**jignire** (f)	[ʒig'nire]
to offend (vt)	**a jigni**	[a ʒig'ni]
to take offense	**a se supăra**	[a se supə'ra]
indignation	**indignare** (f)	[indig'nare]
to be indignant	**a se indigna**	[a se indig'na]

complaint	**plângere** (f)	['plɨndʒere]
to complain (vi, vt)	**a se plânge**	[a se 'plɨndʒe]
apology	**scuză** (f)	['skuzə]
to apologize (vi)	**a cere scuze**	[a 'tʃere 'skuze]
to beg pardon	**a cere iertare**	[a 'tʃere er'tare]
criticism	**critică** (f)	['kritikə]
to criticize (vt)	**a critica**	[a kriti'ka]
accusation (charge)	**învinuire** (f)	[ɨnvinu'ire]
to accuse (vt)	**a învinui**	[a ɨnvinu'i]
revenge	**răzbunare** (f)	[rəzbu'nare]
to avenge (get revenge)	**a răzbuna**	[a rəzbu'na]
to pay back	**a se revanşa**	[a se revan'ʃa]
disdain	**dispreț** (n)	[dis'prets]
to despise (vt)	**a disprețui**	[a dispretsu'i]
hatred, hate	**ură** (f)	['urə]
to hate (vt)	**a urî**	[a u'rɨ]
nervous (adj)	**nervos**	[ner'vos]
to be nervous	**a se enerva**	[a se ener'va]
angry (mad)	**supărat**	[supə'rat]
to make angry	**a supăra**	[a supə'ra]
humiliation	**umilire** (f)	[umi'lire]
to humiliate (vt)	**a umili**	[a umi'li]
to humiliate oneself	**a se umili**	[a se umi'li]
shock	**şoc** (n)	[ʃok]
to shock (vt)	**a şoca**	[a ʃo'ka]
trouble (e.g., serious ~)	**neplăcere** (f)	[neplə'tʃere]
unpleasant (adj)	**neplăcut**	[neplə'kut]
fear (dread)	**frică** (f)	['frikə]
terrible (storm, heat)	**năprasnic**	[nə'prasnik]
scary (e.g., ~ story)	**de groază**	[de gro'azə]
horror	**groază** (f)	[gro'azə]
awful (crime, news)	**înspăimântător**	[ɨnspəjmɨntə'tor]
to cry (weep)	**a plânge**	[a 'plɨndʒe]
to start crying	**a plânge**	[a 'plɨndʒe]
tear	**lacrimă** (f)	['lakrimə]
fault	**greşeală** (f)	[gre'ʃalə]
guilt (feeling)	**vină** (f)	['vinə]
dishonor (disgrace)	**ruşine** (f)	[ru'ʃine]
protest	**protest** (n)	[pro'test]
stress	**stres** (n)	[stres]
to disturb (vt)	**a deranja**	[a deran'ʒa]

to be furious	**a se supăra**	[a se supə'ra]
mad, angry (adj)	**supărat**	[supə'rat]
to end (~ a relationship)	**a pune capăt**	[a 'pune 'kapət]
to swear (at sb)	**a se sfădi**	[a se sfə'di]
to scare (become afraid)	**a se speria**	[a se speri'ja]
to hit (strike with hand)	**a lovi**	[a lo'vi]
to fight (street fight, etc.)	**a se bate**	[a se 'bate]
to settle (a conflict)	**a aplana**	[a apla'na]
discontented (adj)	**nemulțumit**	[nemultsu'mit]
furious (adj)	**furios**	[furi'os]
It's not good!	**Nu e bine!**	[nu e 'bine]
It's bad!	**E rău!**	[e rəu]

Medicine

71. Diseases

sickness	**boală** (f)	[bo'alə]
to be sick	**a fi bolnav**	[a fi bol'nav]
health	**sănătate** (f)	[sənə'tate]
runny nose (coryza)	**guturai** (n)	[gutu'raj]
tonsillitis	**anghină** (f)	[a'nginə]
cold (illness)	**răceală** (f)	[rə'ʧalə]
to catch a cold	**a răci**	[a rə'ʧi]
bronchitis	**bronşită** (f)	[bron'ʃitə]
pneumonia	**pneumonie** (f)	[pneumo'nie]
flu, influenza	**gripă** (f)	['gripə]
nearsighted (adj)	**miop**	[mi'op]
farsighted (adj)	**prezbit**	[prez'bit]
strabismus (crossed eyes)	**strabism** (n)	[stra'bism]
cross-eyed (adj)	**saşiu**	[sa'ʃiu]
cataract	**cataractă** (f)	[kata'raktə]
glaucoma	**glaucom** (n)	[glau'kom]
stroke	**congestie** (f)	[kon'ʤestie]
heart attack	**infarct** (n)	[in'farkt]
myocardial infarction	**infarct** (n) **miocardic**	[in'farkt mio'kardik]
paralysis	**paralizie** (f)	[parali'zie]
to paralyze (vt)	**a paraliza**	[a parali'za]
allergy	**alergie** (f)	[aler'ʤie]
asthma	**astmă** (f)	['astmə]
diabetes	**diabet** (n)	[dia'bet]
toothache	**durere** (f) **de dinți**	[du'rere de dints]
caries	**carie** (f)	['karie]
diarrhea	**diaree** (f)	[dia'ree]
constipation	**constipație** (f)	[konsti'patsie]
stomach upset	**deranjament** (n) **la stomac**	[deranʒa'ment la sto'mak]
food poisoning	**intoxicare** (f)	[intoksi'kare]
to get food poisoning	**a se intoxica**	[a se intoksi'ka]
arthritis	**artrită** (f)	[ar'tritə]
rickets	**rahitism** (n)	[rahi'tism]

rheumatism	**reumatism** (n)	[reuma'tism]
atherosclerosis	**ateroscleroză** (f)	[arterioskle'rozə]
gastritis	**gastrită** (f)	[gas'tritə]
appendicitis	**apendicită** (f)	[apendi'tʃitə]
cholecystitis	**colecistită** (f)	[koletʃis'titə]
ulcer	**ulcer** (n)	[ul'tʃer]
measles	**pojar**	[po'ʒar]
rubella (German measles)	**rubeolă** (f)	[ruʒe'olə]
jaundice	**icter** (n)	['ikter]
hepatitis	**hepatită** (f)	[hepa'titə]
schizophrenia	**schizofrenie** (f)	[skizofre'nie]
rabies (hydrophobia)	**turbare** (f)	[tur'bare]
neurosis	**nevroză** (f)	[ne'vrozə]
concussion	**comoție** (f) **cerebrală**	[ko'motsie tʃerə'bralə]
cancer	**cancer** (n)	['kantʃer]
sclerosis	**scleroză** (f)	[skle'rozə]
multiple sclerosis	**scleroză multiplă** (f)	[skle'rozə mul'tiplə]
alcoholism	**alcoolism** (n)	[alkoo'lizm]
alcoholic (n)	**alcoolic** (m)	[alko'olik]
syphilis	**sifilis** (n)	['sifilis]
AIDS	**SIDA** (f)	['sida]
tumor	**tumoare** (f)	[tumo'are]
malignant (adj)	**malignă**	[ma'lignə]
benign (adj)	**benignă**	[be'nignə]
fever	**friguri** (n pl)	['friguri]
malaria	**malarie** (f)	[mala'rie]
gangrene	**cangrenă** (f)	[kan'grenə]
seasickness	**rău** (n) **de mare**	[rəu de 'mare]
epilepsy	**epilepsie** (f)	[epilep'sie]
epidemic	**epidemie** (f)	[epide'mie]
typhus	**tifos** (n)	['tifos]
tuberculosis	**tuberculoză** (f)	[tuberku'lozə]
cholera	**holeră** (f)	['holerə]
plague (bubonic ~)	**ciumă** (f)	['tʃiumə]

72. Symptoms. Treatments. Part 1

symptom	**simptom** (n)	[simp'tom]
temperature	**temperatură** (f)	[tempera'turə]
high temperature (fever)	**febră** (f)	['febrə]
pulse (heartbeat)	**puls** (n)	[puls]
dizziness (vertigo)	**amețeală** (f)	[ame'tsʲalə]

hot (adj)	**fierbinte**	[fier'binte]
shivering	**frisoane** (n pl)	[friso'ane]
pale (e.g., ~ face)	**palid**	['palid]
cough	**tuse** (f)	['tuse]
to cough (vi)	**a tuşi**	[a tu'ʃi]
to sneeze (vi)	**a strănuta**	[a strənu'ta]
faint	**leşin** (n)	[le'ʃin]
to faint (vi)	**a leşina**	[a leʃi'na]
bruise (hématome)	**vânătaie** (f)	[vɨnə'tae]
bump (lump)	**cucui** (n)	[ku'kuj]
to bang (bump)	**a se lovi**	[a se lo'vi]
contusion (bruise)	**contuzie** (f)	[kon'tuzie]
to get a bruise	**a se lovi**	[a se lo'vi]
to limp (vi)	**a şchiopăta**	[a ʃkiopə'ta]
dislocation	**luxație** (f)	[luk'satsie]
to dislocate (vt)	**a luxa**	[a luk'sa]
fracture	**fractură** (f)	[frak'turə]
to have a fracture	**a fractura**	[a fraktu'ra]
cut (e.g., paper ~)	**tăietură** (f)	[təe'turə]
to cut oneself	**a se tăia**	[a se tə'ja]
bleeding	**sângerare** (f)	[sɨndʒe'rare]
burn (injury)	**arsură** (f)	[ar'surə]
to get burned	**a se frige**	[a se 'fridʒe]
to prick (vt)	**a înțepa**	[a ɨntse'pa]
to prick oneself	**a se înțepa**	[a s ɨntse'pa]
to injure (vt)	**a se răni**	[a se rə'ni]
injury	**vătămare** (f)	[vətə'mare]
wound	**rană** (f)	['ranə]
trauma	**traumă** (f)	['traumə]
to be delirious	**a delira**	[a deli'ra]
to stutter (vi)	**a se bâlbâi**	[a se bɨlbɨ'i]
sunstroke	**insolație** (f)	[inso'latsie]

73. Symptoms. Treatments. Part 2

pain, ache	**durere** (f)	[du'rere]
splinter (in foot, etc.)	**ghimpe** (m)	['gimpe]
sweat (perspiration)	**transpirație** (f)	[transpi'ratsie]
to sweat (perspire)	**a transpira**	[a transpi'ra]
vomiting	**vomă** (f)	['vomə]
convulsions	**convulsii** (f pl)	[kon'vulsij]
pregnant (adj)	**gravidă** (f)	[gra'vidə]

to be born	**a se naşte**	[a se 'naʃte]
delivery, labor	**naştere** (f)	['naʃtere]
to deliver (~ a baby)	**a naşte**	[a 'naʃte]
abortion	**avort** (n)	[a'vort]
breathing, respiration	**respirație** (f)	[respi'ratsie]
in-breath (inhalation)	**inspirație** (f)	[inspi'ratsie]
out-breath (exhalation)	**expirație** (f)	[ekspi'ratsie]
to exhale (breathe out)	**a expira**	[a ekspi'ra]
to inhale (vi)	**a inspira**	[a inspi'ra]
disabled person	**invalid** (m)	[inva'lid]
cripple	**infirm** (m)	[in'firm]
drug addict	**narcoman** (m)	[narko'man]
deaf (adj)	**surd**	[surd]
mute (adj)	**mut**	[mut]
deaf mute (adj)	**surdo-mut**	[surdo'mut]
mad, insane (adj)	**nebun**	[ne'bun]
madman (demented person)	**nebun** (m)	[ne'bun]
madwoman	**nebună** (f)	[ne'bunə]
to go insane	**a înnebuni**	[a ɨnnebu'ni]
gene	**genă** (f)	['dʒenə]
immunity	**imunitate** (f)	[imuni'tate]
hereditary (adj)	**ereditar**	[eredi'tar]
congenital (adj)	**congenital**	[kondʒeni'tal]
virus	**virus** (m)	['virus]
microbe	**microb** (m)	[mi'krob]
bacterium	**bacterie** (f)	[bak'terie]
infection	**infecție** (f)	[in'fektsie]

74. Symptoms. Treatments. Part 3

hospital	**spital** (n)	[spi'tal]
patient	**pacient** (m)	[patʃi'ent]
diagnosis	**diagnostic** (n)	[diag'nostik]
cure	**tratament** (n)	[trata'ment]
to get treatment	**a urma tratament**	[a ur'ma trata'ment]
to treat (~ a patient)	**a trata**	[a tra'ta]
to nurse (look after)	**a îngriji**	[a ɨngri'ʒi]
care (nursing ~)	**îngrijire** (f)	[ɨngri'ʒire]
operation, surgery	**operație** (f)	[ope'ratsie]
to bandage (head, limb)	**a pansa**	[a pan'sa]
bandaging	**pansare** (f)	[pan'sare]

vaccination	**vaccin** (n)	[vak'ʧin]
to vaccinate (vt)	**a vaccina**	[a vakʧi'na]
injection, shot	**injecție** (f)	[in'ʒektsie]
to give an injection	**a face injecție**	[a 'faʧe in'ʒektsie]
amputation	**amputare** (f)	[ampu'tare]
to amputate (vt)	**a amputa**	[a ampu'ta]
coma	**comă** (f)	['komə]
to be in a coma	**a fi în comă**	[a fi ɨn 'komə]
intensive care	**reanimare** (f)	[reani'mare]
to recover (~ from flu)	**a se vindeca**	[a se vinde'ka]
condition (patient's ~)	**stare** (f)	['stare]
consciousness	**conştiinţă** (f)	[konʃti'intsə]
memory (faculty)	**memorie** (f)	[me'morie]
to pull out (tooth)	**a extrage**	[a eks'traʤe]
filling	**plombă** (f)	['plombə]
to fill (a tooth)	**a plomba**	[a plom'ba]
hypnosis	**hipnoză** (f)	[hip'nozə]
to hypnotize (vt)	**a hipnotiza**	[a hipnoti'za]

75. Doctors

doctor	**medic** (m)	['medik]
nurse	**asistentă** (f) **medicală**	[asis'tentə medi'kalə]
personal doctor	**medic** (m) **personal**	['medik perso'nal]
dentist	**stomatolog** (m)	[stomato'log]
eye doctor	**oculist** (m)	[oku'list]
internist	**terapeut** (m)	[terape'ut]
surgeon	**chirurg** (m)	[ki'rurg]
psychiatrist	**psihiatru** (m)	[psihi'atru]
pediatrician	**pediatru** (m)	[pedi'atru]
psychologist	**psiholog** (m)	[psiho'log]
gynecologist	**ginecolog** (m)	[ʤineko'log]
cardiologist	**cardiolog** (m)	[kardio'log]

76. Medicine. Drugs. Accessories

medicine, drug	**medicament** (n)	[medika'ment]
remedy	**remediu** (n)	[re'medju]
to prescribe (vt)	**a prescrie**	[a pre'skrie]
prescription	**rețetă** (f)	[re'tsetə]
tablet, pill	**pastilă** (f)	[pas'tilə]
ointment	**unguent** (n)	[ungu'ent]

ampule	**fiolă** (f)	[fi'olə]
mixture, solution	**mixtură** (f)	[miks'turə]
syrup	**sirop** (n)	[si'rop]
capsule	**pilulă** (f)	[pi'lulə]
powder	**praf** (n)	[praf]
gauze bandage	**bandaj** (n)	[ban'daʒ]
cotton wool	**vată** (f)	['vatə]
iodine	**iod** (n)	[jod]
Band-Aid	**leucoplast** (n)	[leuko'plast]
eyedropper	**pipetă** (f)	[pi'petə]
thermometer	**termometru** (n)	[termo'metru]
syringe	**seringă** (f)	[se'ringə]
wheelchair	**cărucior** (n) **pentru invalizi**	[kəru'ʧior 'pentru inva'lizʲ]
crutches	**cârje** (f pl)	['kɨrʒe]
painkiller	**anestezic** (n)	[anes'tezik]
laxative	**laxativ** (n)	[laksa'tiv]
spirits (ethanol)	**spirt** (n)	[spirt]
medicinal herbs	**plante** (f pl) **medicinale**	['plante mediʧi'nale]
herbal (~ tea)	**din plante medicinale**	[din 'plante mediʧi'nale]

77. Smoking. Tobacco products

tobacco	**tutun** (n)	[tu'tun]
cigarette	**țigară** (f)	[ʦi'garə]
cigar	**țigară** (f) **de foi**	[ʦi'garə de foj]
pipe	**pipă** (f)	['pipə]
pack (of cigarettes)	**pachet** (n)	[pa'ket]
matches	**chibrituri** (n pl)	[ki'briturʲ]
matchbox	**cutie** (f) **de chibrituri**	[ku'tie de ki'briturʲ]
lighter	**brichetă** (f)	[bri'ketə]
ashtray	**scrumieră** (f)	[skru'mjerə]
cigarette case	**tabacheră** (n)	[taba'kerə]
cigarette holder	**muştiuc** (n)	[muʃ'tjuk]
filter (cigarette tip)	**filtru** (n)	['filtru]
to smoke (vi, vt)	**a fuma**	[a fu'ma]
to light a cigarette	**a începe să fumeze**	[a ɨn'ʧepe sə fu'meze]
smoking	**fumat** (n)	[fu'mat]
smoker	**fumător** (m)	[fumə'tor]
stub, butt (of cigarette)	**muc** (n) **de țigară**	[muk de ʦi'garə]
smoke, fumes	**fum** (n)	[fum]
ash	**scrum** (n)	[skrum]

HUMAN HABITAT

City

78. City. Life in the city

city, town	**oraş** (n)	[o'raʃ]
capital city	**capitală** (f)	[kapi'talə]
village	**sat** (n)	[sat]
city map	**planul** (n) **oraşului**	['planul o'raʃuluj]
downtown	**centrul** (n) **oraşului**	['ʧentrul o'raʃuluj]
suburb	**suburbie** (f)	[subur'bie]
suburban (adj)	**din suburbie**	[din subur'bie]
outskirts	**margine** (f)	['marʤine]
environs (suburbs)	**împrejurimi** (f pl)	[ɨmpreʒu'rimʲ]
city block	**cartier** (n)	[kar'tjer]
residential block (area)	**cartier** (n) **locativ**	[ka'rtjer loka'tiv]
traffic	**circulaţie** (f)	[ʧirku'laʦie]
traffic lights	**semafor** (n)	[sema'for]
public transportation	**transport** (n) **urban**	[trans'port ur'ban]
intersection	**intersecţie** (f)	[inter'sekʦie]
crosswalk	**trecere** (f)	['treʧere]
pedestrian underpass	**trecere** (f) **subterană**	['treʧere subte'ranə]
to cross (~ the street)	**a traversa**	[a traver'sa]
pedestrian	**pieton** (m)	[pie'ton]
sidewalk	**trotuar** (n)	[trotu'ar]
bridge	**pod** (n)	[pod]
embankment (river walk)	**faleză** (f)	[fa'lezə]
fountain	**havuz** (n)	[ha'vuz]
allée (garden walkway)	**alee** (f)	[a'lee]
park	**parc** (n)	[park]
boulevard	**bulevard** (n)	[bule'vard]
square	**piaţă** (f)	['pjaʦə]
avenue (wide street)	**prospect** (n)	[pros'pekt]
street	**stradă** (f)	['stradə]
side street	**stradelă** (f)	[stra'delə]
dead end	**fundătură** (f)	[fundə'turə]
house	**casă** (f)	['kasə]
building	**clădire** (f)	[klə'dire]

skyscraper	**zgârie-nori** (m)	['zgɨrie norʲ]
facade	**fațadă** (f)	[fa'tsadə]
roof	**acoperiş** (n)	[akope'riʃ]
window	**fereastră** (f)	[fe'rʲastrə]
arch	**arc** (n)	[ark]
column	**coloană** (f)	[kolo'anə]
corner	**colț** (n)	[kolts]
store window	**vitrină** (f)	[vi'trinə]
signboard (store sign, etc.)	**firmă** (f)	['firmə]
poster (e.g., playbill)	**afiş** (n)	[a'fiʃ]
advertising poster	**afişaj** (n)	[afi'ʃaʒ]
billboard	**panou** (n) **publicitar**	[pa'nu publitʃi'tar]
garbage, trash	**gunoi** (n)	[gu'noj]
trash can (public ~)	**coş** (n) **de gunoi**	[koʃ de gu'noj]
to litter (vi)	**a face murdărie**	[a 'fatʃe murdə'rie]
garbage dump	**groapă** (f) **de gunoi**	[gro'apə de gu'noj]
phone booth	**cabină** (f) **telefonică**	[ka'binə tele'fonikə]
lamppost	**stâlp** (m) **de felinar**	[stɨlp de feli'nar]
bench (park ~)	**bancă** (f)	['bankə]
police officer	**polițist** (m)	[poli'tsist]
police	**poliție** (f)	[po'litsie]
beggar	**cerşetor** (m)	[tʃerʃə'tor]
homeless (n)	**vagabond** (m)	[vaga'bond]

79. Urban institutions

store	**magazin** (n)	[maga'zin]
drugstore, pharmacy	**farmacie** (f)	[farma'tʃie]
eyeglass store	**optică** (f)	['optikə]
shopping mall	**centru** (n) **comercial**	['tʃentru komertʃi'al]
supermarket	**supermarket** (n)	[super'market]
bakery	**brutărie** (f)	[brutə'rie]
baker	**brutar** (m)	[bru'tar]
pastry shop	**cofetărie** (f)	[kofetə'rie]
grocery store	**băcănie** (f)	[bəkə'nie]
butcher shop	**hală** (f) **de carne**	['halə de 'karne]
produce store	**magazin** (m) **de legume**	[maga'zin de le'gume]
market	**piață** (f)	['pjatsə]
coffee house	**cafenea** (f)	[kafe'nʲa]
restaurant	**restaurant** (n)	[restau'rant]
pub, bar	**berărie** (f)	[berə'rie]
pizzeria	**pizzerie** (f)	[pitse'rie]
hair salon	**frizerie** (f)	[frize'rie]

post office	**poştă** (f)	['poʃtə]
dry cleaners	**curățătorie** (f) **chimică**	[kurətsəto'rie 'kimikə]
photo studio	**atelier** (n) **foto**	[ate'ljer 'foto]
shoe store	**magazin** (n) **de încălțăminte**	[maga'zin de ɨnkəltsə'minte]
bookstore	**librărie** (f)	[librə'rie]
sporting goods store	**magazin** (n) **sportiv**	[maga'zin spor'tiv]
clothes repair shop	**croitorie** (f)	[kroito'rie]
formal wear rental	**închiriere** (f) **de haine**	[ɨnki'rjere de 'hajne]
video rental store	**închiriere** (f) **de filme**	[ɨnki'rjere de 'filme]
circus	**circ** (n)	[tʃirk]
zoo	**grădină** (f) **zoologică**	[grə'dinə zoo'lodʒikə]
movie theater	**cinematograf** (n)	[tʃinemato'graf]
museum	**muzeu** (n)	[mu'zeu]
library	**bibliotecă** (f)	[biblio'tekə]
theater	**teatru** (n)	[te'atru]
opera (opera house)	**operă** (f)	['operə]
nightclub	**club** (n) **de noapte**	['klub de no'apte]
casino	**cazinou** (n)	[kazi'nou]
mosque	**moschee** (f)	[mos'kee]
synagogue	**sinagogă** (f)	[sina'gogə]
cathedral	**catedrală** (f)	[kate'dralə]
temple	**templu** (n)	['templu]
church	**biserică** (f)	[bi'serikə]
college	**institut** (n)	[insti'tut]
university	**universitate** (f)	[universi'tate]
school	**şcoală** (f)	[ʃko'alə]
prefecture	**prefectură** (f)	[prefek'turə]
city hall	**primărie** (f)	[primə'rie]
hotel	**hotel** (n)	[ho'tel]
bank	**bancă** (f)	['bankə]
embassy	**ambasadă** (f)	[amba'sadə]
travel agency	**agenție** (f) **de turism**	[adʒen'tsie de tu'rism]
information office	**birou** (n) **de informații**	[bi'rou de infor'matsij]
currency exchange	**schimb** (n) **valutar**	[skimb valu'tar]
subway	**metrou** (n)	[me'trou]
hospital	**spital** (n)	[spi'tal]
gas station	**benzinărie** (f)	[benzinə'rie]
parking lot	**parcare** (f)	[par'kare]

80. Signs

signboard (store sign, etc.)	**firmă** (f)	['firmə]
notice (door sign, etc.)	**inscripție** (f)	[in'skriptsie]
poster	**afiş** (n)	[a'fiʃ]
direction sign	**semn** (n)	[semn]
arrow (sign)	**indicator** (n)	[indika'tor]
caution	**avertisment** (n)	[avertis'ment]
warning sign	**avertisment** (n)	[avertis'ment]
to warn (vt)	**a avertiza**	[a averti'za]
rest day (weekly ~)	**zi** (f) **de odihnă**	[zi de o'dihnə]
timetable (schedule)	**orar** (n)	[o'rar]
opening hours	**ore** (f pl) **de lucru**	['ore de 'lukru]
WELCOME!	**BINE AȚI VENIT!**	['bine 'atsʲ ve'nit]
ENTRANCE	**INTRARE**	[in'trare]
EXIT	**IEŞIRE**	[je'ʃire]
PUSH	**ÎMPINGE**	[ɨm'pindʒe]
PULL	**TRAGE**	['tradʒe]
OPEN	**DESCHIS**	[des'kis]
CLOSED	**ÎNCHIS**	[ɨn'kis]
WOMEN	**PENTRU FEMEI**	['pentru fe'mej]
MEN	**PENTRU BĂRBAȚI**	['pentru bər'batsʲ]
DISCOUNTS	**REDUCERI**	[re'dutʃerʲ]
SALE	**LICHIDARE DE STOC**	[liki'dare de stok]
NEW!	**NOU**	['nou]
FREE	**GRATUIT**	[gratu'it]
ATTENTION!	**ATENȚIE!**	[a'tentsie]
NO VACANCIES	**NU SUNT LOCURI**	[nu 'sunt 'lokurʲ]
RESERVED	**REZERVAT**	[rezer'vat]
ADMINISTRATION	**ADMINISTRAȚIE**	[adminis'tratsie]
STAFF ONLY	**NUMAI PENTRU ANGAJAȚI**	['numaj 'pentru anga'ʒats]
BEWARE OF THE DOG!	**CÂINE RĂU**	['kɨne 'rəu]
NO SMOKING	**NU FUMAȚI!**	[nu fu'mats]
DO NOT TOUCH!	**NU ATINGEȚI!**	[nu a'tindʒets]
DANGEROUS	**PERICULOS**	[periku'los]
DANGER	**PERICOL**	[pe'rikol]
HIGH VOLTAGE	**TENSIUNE ÎNALTĂ**	[tensi'une ɨ'naltə]
NO SWIMMING!	**SCĂLDATUL INTERZIS!**	[skəl'datul inter'zis]
OUT OF ORDER	**NU FUNCȚIONEAZĂ**	[nu funktsio'nʲazə]
FLAMMABLE	**INFLAMABIL**	[infla'mabil]

FORBIDDEN	**INTERZIS**	[inter'zis]
NO TRESPASSING!	**TRECEREA INTERZISĂ**	['tretʃerʲa inter'zisə]
WET PAINT	**PROASPĂT VOPSIT**	[pro'aspət vop'sit]

81. Urban transportation

bus	**autobuz** (n)	[auto'buz]
streetcar	**tramvai** (n)	[tram'vaj]
trolley bus	**troleibuz** (n)	[trolej'buz]
route (of bus, etc.)	**rută** (f)	['rutə]
number (e.g., bus ~)	**număr** (n)	['numər]
to go by ...	**a merge cu ...**	[a 'merdʒe ku]
to get on (~ the bus)	**a se urca**	[a se ur'ka]
to get off ...	**a coborî**	[a kobo'rɨ]
stop (e.g., bus ~)	**stație** (f)	['statsie]
next stop	**stația** (f) **următoare**	['statsija urməto'are]
terminus	**ultima stație** (f)	['ultima 'statsie]
schedule	**orar** (n)	[o'rar]
to wait (vt)	**a aştepta**	[a aʃtep'ta]
ticket	**bilet** (n)	[bi'let]
fare	**costul** (n) **biletului**	['kostul bi'letuluj]
cashier (ticket seller)	**casier** (m)	[ka'sjer]
ticket inspection	**control** (n)	[kon'trol]
ticket inspector	**controlor** (m)	[kontro'lor]
to be late (for ...)	**a întârzia**	[a ɨntɨr'zija]
to miss (~ the train, etc.)	**a pierde ...**	[a 'pjerdə]
to be in a hurry	**a se grăbi**	[a se grə'bi]
taxi, cab	**taxi** (n)	[ta'ksi]
taxi driver	**taximetrist** (m)	[taksime'trist]
by taxi	**cu taxiul**	[ku ta'ksjul]
taxi stand	**stație** (f) **de taxiuri**	['statsie de ta'ksjurʲ]
to call a taxi	**a chema un taxi**	[a ke'ma un ta'ksi]
to take a taxi	**a lua un taxi**	[a lu'a un ta'ksi]
traffic	**circulație** (f) **pe stradă**	[tʃirku'latsie pe 'stradə]
traffic jam	**ambuteiaj** (n)	[ambute'jaʒ]
rush hour	**oră** (f) **de vârf**	[orə de vɨrf]
to park (vi)	**a se parca**	[a se par'ka]
to park (vt)	**a parca**	[a par'ka]
parking lot	**parcare** (f)	[par'kare]
subway	**metrou** (n)	[me'trou]
station	**stație** (f)	['statsie]
to take the subway	**a merge cu metroul**	[a 'merdʒe ku me'troul]

train	**tren** (n)	[tren]
train station	**gară** (f)	['garə]

82. Sightseeing

monument	**monument** (n)	[monu'ment]
fortress	**cetate** (f)	[tʃe'tate]
palace	**palat** (n)	[pa'lat]
castle	**castel** (n)	[kas'tel]
tower	**turn** (n)	[turn]
mausoleum	**mausoleu** (n)	[mawzo'leu]
architecture	**arhitectură** (f)	[arhitek'turə]
medieval (adj)	**medieval**	[medie'val]
ancient (adj)	**vechi**	[vekʲ]
national (adj)	**național**	[natsio'nal]
famous (monument, etc.)	**cunoscut**	[kunos'kut]
tourist	**turist** (m)	[tu'rist]
guide (person)	**ghid** (m)	[gid]
excursion, sightseeing tour	**excursie** (f)	[eks'kursie]
to show (vt)	**a arăta**	[a arə'ta]
to tell (vt)	**a povesti**	[a poves'ti]
to find (vt)	**a găsi**	[a gə'si]
to get lost (lose one's way)	**a se pierde**	[a se 'pjerde]
map (e.g., subway ~)	**schemă** (f)	['skemə]
map (e.g., city ~)	**plan** (m)	[plan]
souvenir, gift	**suvenir** (n)	[suve'nir]
gift shop	**magazin** (n) **de suveniruri**	[maga'zin de suve'nirurʲ]
to take pictures	**a fotografia**	[a fotografi'ja]
to have one's picture taken	**a se fotografia**	[a se fotografi'ja]

83. Shopping

to buy (purchase)	**a cumpăra**	[a kumpə'ra]
purchase	**cumpărătură** (f)	[kumpərə'turə]
to go shopping	**a face cumpărături**	[a 'fatʃe kumpərə'turʲ]
shopping	**shopping** (n)	['ʃoping]
to be open (ab. store)	**a fi deschis**	[a fi des'kis]
to be closed	**a se închide**	[a se ɨn'kide]
footwear, shoes	**încălțăminte** (f)	[ɨnkəltsə'minte]
clothes, clothing	**haine** (f pl)	['hajne]
cosmetics	**cosmetică** (f)	[kos'metikə]

food products	**produse** (n pl)	[pro'duse]
gift, present	**cadou** (n)	[ka'dou]
salesman	**vânzător** (m)	[vɨnzə'tor]
saleswoman	**vânzătoare** (f)	[vɨnzəto'are]
check out, cash desk	**casă** (f)	['kasə]
mirror	**oglindă** (f)	[og'lində]
counter (store ~)	**tejghea** (f)	[teʒ'gʲa]
fitting room	**cabină** (f) **de probă**	[ka'binə de 'probə]
to try on	**a proba**	[a pro'ba]
to fit (ab. dress, etc.)	**a veni**	[a ve'ni]
to like (I like ...)	**a plăcea**	[a plə'ʧa]
price	**preț** (n)	[preʦ]
price tag	**indicator** (n) **de prețuri**	[indika'tor de 'preʦurʲ]
to cost (vt)	**a costa**	[a kos'ta]
How much?	**Cât?**	[kɨt]
discount	**reducere** (f)	[re'duʧere]
inexpensive (adj)	**ieftin**	['jeftin]
cheap (adj)	**ieftin**	['jeftin]
expensive (adj)	**scump**	[skump]
It's expensive	**E scump**	[e skump]
rental (n)	**închiriere** (f)	[ɨnkiri'ere]
to rent (~ a tuxedo)	**a lua în chirie**	[a lu'a ɨn ki'rie]
credit (trade credit)	**credit** (n)	['kredit]
on credit (adv)	**în credit**	[ɨn 'kredit]

84. Money

money	**bani** (m pl)	[banʲ]
currency exchange	**schimb** (n)	[skimb]
exchange rate	**curs** (n)	[kurs]
ATM	**bancomat** (n)	[banko'mat]
coin	**monedă** (f)	[mo'nedə]
dollar	**dolar** (m)	[do'lar]
euro	**euro** (m)	['euro]
lira	**liră** (f)	['lirə]
Deutschmark	**marcă** (f)	['markə]
franc	**franc** (m)	[frank]
pound sterling	**liră** (f) **sterlină**	['lirə ster'linə]
yen	**yen** (f)	['jen]
debt	**datorie** (f)	[dato'rie]
debtor	**datornic** (m)	[da'tornik]

to lend (money)	**a da cu împrumut**	[a da ku ɨmpru'mut]
to borrow (vi, vt)	**a lua cu împrumut**	[a lu'a ku ɨmpru'mut]
bank	**bancă** (f)	['bankə]
account	**cont** (n)	[kont]
to deposit (vt)	**a pune**	[a 'pune]
to deposit into the account	**a pune în cont**	[a 'pune ɨn 'kont]
to withdraw (vt)	**a scoate din cont**	[a sko'ate din kont]
credit card	**carte** (f) **de credit**	['karte de 'kredit]
cash	**numerar** (n)	[nume'rar]
check	**cec** (n)	[ʧek]
to write a check	**a scrie un cec**	[a 'skrie un ʧek]
checkbook	**carte** (f) **de cecuri**	['karte de 'ʧekurʲ]
wallet	**portvizit** (n)	[portvi'zit]
change purse	**portofel** (n)	[porto'fel]
safe	**seif** (n)	['sejf]
heir	**moştenitor** (m)	[moʃteni'tor]
inheritance	**moştenire** (f)	[moʃte'nire]
fortune (wealth)	**avere** (f)	[a'vere]
lease	**arendă** (f)	[a'rendə]
rent (money)	**chirie** (f)	[ki'rie]
to rent (sth from sb)	**a închiria**	[a ɨnkiri'ja]
price	**preț** (n)	[prets]
cost	**valoare** (f)	[valo'are]
sum	**sumă** (f)	['sumə]
to spend (vt)	**a cheltui**	[a keltu'i]
expenses	**cheltuieli** (f pl)	[keltu'elʲ]
to economize (vi, vt)	**a economisi**	[a ekonomi'si]
economical	**econom**	[eko'nom]
to pay (vi, vt)	**a plăti**	[a plə'ti]
payment	**plată** (f)	['platə]
change (give the ~)	**rest** (n)	[rest]
tax	**impozit** (n)	[im'pozit]
fine	**amendă** (f)	[a'mendə]
to fine (vt)	**a amenda**	[a amen'da]

85. Post. Postal service

post office	**poştă** (f)	['poʃtə]
mail (letters, etc.)	**corespondență** (f)	[korespon'dentsə]
mailman	**poştaş** (m)	[poʃ'taʃ]
opening hours	**ore** (f pl) **de lucru**	['ore de 'lukru]

letter	**scrisoare** (f)	[skriso'are]
registered letter	**scrisoare** (f) **recomandată**	[skriso'are rekoman'datə]
postcard	**carte** (f) **poştală**	['karte poʃ'talə]
telegram	**telegramă** (f)	[tele'gramə]
package (parcel)	**colet** (n)	[ko'let]
money transfer	**mandat** (n) **poştal**	[man'dat poʃ'tal]
to receive (vt)	**a primi**	[a pri'mi]
to send (vt)	**a expedia**	[a ekspedi'ja]
sending	**expediere** (f)	[ekspe'djere]
address	**adresă** (f)	[a'dresə]
ZIP code	**cod** (n) **poştal**	[kod poʃ'tal]
sender	**expeditor** (m)	[ekspedi'tor]
receiver	**destinatar** (m)	[destina'tar]
name (first name)	**prenume** (n)	[pre'nume]
surname (last name)	**nume** (n)	['nume]
postage rate	**tarif** (n)	[ta'rif]
standard (adj)	**normal**	[nor'mal]
economical (adj)	**econom**	[eko'nom]
weight	**greutate** (f)	[greu'tate]
to weigh (~ letters)	**a cântări**	[a kintə'ri]
envelope	**plic** (n)	[plik]
postage stamp	**timbru** (n)	['timbru]
to stamp an envelope	**a lipi timbrul**	[a li'pi 'timbrul]

Dwelling. House. Home

86. House. Dwelling

house	**casă** (f)	['kasə]
at home (adv)	**acasă**	[a'kasə]
yard	**curte** (f)	['kurte]
fence (iron ~)	**gard** (n)	[gard]
brick (n)	**cărămidă** (f)	[kərə'midə]
brick (as adj)	**de, din cărămidă**	[de, din kərə'midə]
stone (n)	**piatră** (f)	['pjatrə]
stone (as adj)	**de, din piatră**	[de, din 'pjatrə]
concrete (n)	**beton** (n)	[be'ton]
concrete (as adj)	**de, din beton**	[de, din be'ton]
new (new-built)	**nou**	['nou]
old (adj)	**vechi**	[vekʲ]
decrepit (house)	**vechi**	[vekʲ]
modern (adj)	**contemporan**	[kontempo'ran]
multistory (adj)	**cu multe etaje**	[ku 'multe e'taʒe]
tall (~ building)	**înalt**	[ɨ'nalt]
floor, story	**etaj** (n)	[e'taʒ]
single-story (adj)	**cu un singur etaj**	[ku un 'singur e'taʒ]
1st floor	**etajul** (n) **de jos**	[e'taʒul de ʒos]
top floor	**etajul** (n) **de sus**	[e'taʒul de sus]
roof	**acoperiş** (n)	[akope'riʃ]
chimney	**tub** (n)	[tub]
roof tiles	**ţiglă** (f)	['ʦiglə]
tiled (adj)	**de, din ţiglă**	[de, din 'ʦiglə]
attic (storage place)	**mansardă** (f)	[man'sardə]
window	**fereastră** (f)	[fe'rʲastrə]
glass	**sticlă** (f)	['stiklə]
window ledge	**pervaz** (n)	[per'vaz]
shutters	**oblon** (n) **la fereastră**	[o'blon la fe'rʲastrə]
wall	**perete** (m)	[pe'rete]
balcony	**balcon** (n)	[bal'kon]
downspout	**burlan** (n)	[bur'lan]
upstairs (to be ~)	**deasupra**	[dʲa'supra]
to go upstairs	**a urca**	[a ur'ka]

to come down (the stairs)	**a coborî**	[a kobo'ri]
to move (to new premises)	**a se muta**	[a se mu'ta]

87. House. Entrance. Lift

entrance	**intrare** (f)	[in'trare]
stairs (stairway)	**scară** (f)	['skarə]
steps	**trepte** (f pl)	['trepte]
banister	**balustradă** (f)	[balu'stradə]
lobby (hotel ~)	**hol** (n)	[hol]
mailbox	**cutie** (f) **poştală**	[ku'tie poʃ'talə]
garbage can	**ladă** (f) **de gunoi**	['ladə de gu'noj]
trash chute	**conductă** (f) **de gunoi**	[kon'duktə de gu'noj]
elevator	**lift** (n)	[lift]
freight elevator	**ascensor** (n) **de marfă**	[astʃen'sor de 'marfə]
elevator cage	**cabină** (f)	[ka'binə]
to take the elevator	**a merge cu liftul**	[a 'merdʒe ku 'liftul]
apartment	**apartament** (n)	[aparta'ment]
residents (~ of a building)	**locatari** (m pl)	[loka'tarʲ]
neighbor (masc.)	**vecin** (m)	[ve'tʃin]
neighbor (fem.)	**vecină** (f)	[ve'tʃinə]
neighbors	**vecini** (m pl)	[ve'tʃinʲ]

88. House. Electricity

electricity	**electricitate** (f)	[elektritʃi'tate]
light bulb	**bec** (n)	[bek]
switch	**întrerupător** (n)	[intrerupə'tor]
fuse (plug fuse)	**siguranță** (f)	[sigu'rantsə]
cable, wire (electric ~)	**cablu** (n)	['kablu]
wiring	**instalație** (f) **electrică**	[insta'latsie e'lektrikə]
electricity meter	**contor** (n)	[kon'tor]
readings	**indicație** (f)	[indi'katsie]

89. House. Doors. Locks

door	**uşă** (f)	['uʃə]
gate (vehicle ~)	**poartă** (f)	[po'artə]
handle, doorknob	**clanță** (f)	['klantsə]
to unlock (unbolt)	**a descuia**	[a desku'ja]
to open (vt)	**a deschide**	[a des'kide]
to close (vt)	**a închide**	[a ɨ'nkide]

key	**cheie** (f)	['kee]
bunch (of keys)	**legătură** (f) **de chei**	[ləgə'turə de 'kej]
to creak (door, etc.)	**a scârțâi**	[a skɨrtsɨ'i]
creak	**scârțâit** (n)	[skɨrtsɨ'it]
hinge (door ~)	**balama** (f)	[bala'ma]
doormat	**covoraş** (n)	[kovo'raʃ]
door lock	**încuietoare** (f)	[ɨnkueto'are]
keyhole	**gaura** (f) **cheii**	['gaura 'keij]
crossbar (sliding bar)	**zăvor** (n)	[zə'vor]
door latch	**zăvor** (n)	[zə'vor]
padlock	**lacăt** (n)	['lakət]
to ring (~ the door bell)	**a suna**	[a su'na]
ringing (sound)	**sunet** (n)	['sunet]
doorbell	**sonerie** (f)	[sone'rie]
doorbell button	**buton** (n)	[bu'ton]
knock (at the door)	**bătaie** (f)	[bə'tae]
to knock (vi)	**a bate**	[a 'bate]
code	**cod** (n)	[kod]
combination lock	**lacăt** (n) **cu cod**	['lakət ku kod]
intercom	**interfon** (n)	[inter'fon]
number (on the door)	**număr** (n)	['numər]
doorplate	**placă** (f)	['plakə]
peephole	**vizor** (f)	[vi'zor]

90. Country house

village	**sat** (n)	[sat]
vegetable garden	**grădină** (f) **de zarzavat**	[grə'dinə de zarza'vat]
fence	**gard** (n)	[gard]
picket fence	**îngrăditură** (f)	[ɨngrədi'turə]
wicket gate	**portiță** (f)	[por'titsə]
granary	**hambar** (n)	[ham'bar]
root cellar	**beci** (n)	[betʃi]
shed (garden ~)	**magazie** (f)	[maga'zie]
water well	**fântână** (f)	[fɨn'tɨnə]
stove (wood-fired ~)	**sobă** (f)	['sobə]
to stoke the stove	**a face focul**	[a 'fatʃe 'fokul]
firewood	**lemne** (n pl)	['lemne]
log (firewood)	**bucată** (f) **de lemn**	[bu'katə de lemn]
veranda	**verandă** (f)	[ve'randə]
deck (terrace)	**terasă** (f)	[te'rasə]
stoop (front steps)	**verandă** (f)	[ve'randə]
swing (hanging seat)	**scrânciob** (n)	['skrɨntʃiob]

91. Villa. Mansion

country house	**casă** (f) **în afara localității**	['kasə ɨn a'fara lokali'tətsij]
villa (seaside ~)	**vilă** (f)	['vilə]
wing (~ of a building)	**aripă** (f)	[a'ripə]
garden	**grădină** (f)	[grə'dinə]
park	**parc** (n)	[park]
conservatory (greenhouse)	**seră** (f)	['serə]
to look after (garden, etc.)	**a îngriji**	[a ɨngri'ʒi]
swimming pool	**bazin** (n)	[ba'zin]
gym (home gym)	**sală** (f) **de sport**	['salə de sport]
tennis court	**teren** (n) **de tenis**	[te'ren de 'tenis]
home theater (room)	**cinematograf** (n)	[tʃinemato'graf]
garage	**garaj** (n)	[ga'raʒ]
private property	**proprietate** (f) **privată**	[proprie'tate pri'vatə]
private land	**proprietate** (f) **privată**	[proprie'tate pri'vatə]
warning (caution)	**avertizare** (f)	[averti'zare]
warning sign	**avertisment** (n)	[avertis'ment]
security	**pază** (f)	['pazə]
security guard	**paznic** (m)	['paznik]
burglar alarm	**alarmă** (f)	[a'larmə]

92. Castle. Palace

castle	**castel** (n)	[kas'tel]
palace	**palat** (n)	[pa'lat]
fortress	**cetate** (f)	[tʃe'tate]
wall (round castle)	**zid** (n)	[zid]
tower	**turn** (n)	[turn]
keep, donjon	**turnul** (n) **principal**	['turnul printʃi'pal]
portcullis	**porți** (f pl) **rulante**	['portsʲ ru'lante]
underground passage	**subsol** (n)	[sub'sol]
moat	**șanț** (n)	[ʃants]
chain	**lanț** (n)	[lants]
arrow loop	**meterez** (n)	[mete'rez]
magnificent (adj)	**măreț**	[mə'rets]
majestic (adj)	**maiestuos**	[maestu'os]
impregnable (adj)	**de necucerit**	[de nekutʃe'rit]
medieval (adj)	**medieval**	[medie'val]

93. Apartment

apartment	**apartament** (n)	[aparta'ment]
room	**cameră** (f)	['kamerə]
bedroom	**dormitor** (n)	[dormi'tor]
dining room	**sufragerie** (f)	[sufradʒe'rie]
living room	**salon** (n)	[sa'lon]
study (home office)	**cabinet** (n)	[kabi'net]
entry room	**antreu** (n)	[an'treu]
bathroom (room with a bath or shower)	**baie** (f)	['bae]
half bath	**toaletă** (f)	[toa'letə]
ceiling	**pod** (n)	[pod]
floor	**podea** (f)	[po'dʲa]
corner	**colț** (n)	[kolts]

94. Apartment. Cleaning

to clean (vi, vt)	**a face ordine**	[a 'fatʃe 'ordine]
to put away (to stow)	**a strânge**	[a 'strindʒe]
dust	**praf** (n)	[praf]
dusty (adj)	**prăfuit**	[prəfu'it]
to dust (vt)	**a şterge praful**	[a 'ʃterdʒe 'praful]
vacuum cleaner	**aspirator** (n)	[aspira'tor]
to vacuum (vt)	**a da cu aspiratorul**	[a da ku aspira'torul]
to sweep (vi, vt)	**a mătura**	[a mətu'ra]
sweepings	**gunoi** (n)	[gu'noj]
order	**ordine** (f)	['ordine]
disorder, mess	**dezordine** (f)	[de'zordine]
mop	**teu** (n)	['teu]
dust cloth	**cârpă** (f)	['kirpə]
short broom	**mătură** (f)	['məturə]
dustpan	**făraş** (n)	[fə'raʃ]

95. Furniture. Interior

furniture	**mobilă** (f)	['mobilə]
table	**masă** (f)	['masə]
chair	**scaun** (n)	['skaun]
bed	**pat** (n)	[pat]
couch, sofa	**divan** (n)	[di'van]
armchair	**fotoliu** (n)	[fo'tolju]
bookcase	**dulap** (n) **de cărți**	[du'lap de kərts]

shelf	**raft** (n)	[raft]
wardrobe	**dulap** (n) **de haine**	[du'lap de 'hajne]
coat rack (wall-mounted ~)	**cuier** (n) **perete**	[ku'jer pe'rete]
coat stand	**cuier** (n) **pom**	[ku'jer pom]
bureau, dresser	**comodă** (f)	[ko'modə]
coffee table	**măsuță** (f)	[mə'sutsə]
mirror	**oglindă** (f)	[og'lində]
carpet	**covor** (n)	[ko'vor]
rug, small carpet	**carpetă** (f)	[kar'petə]
fireplace	**şemineu** (n)	[ʃəmi'neu]
candle	**lumânare** (f)	[lumɨ'nare]
candlestick	**sfeşnic** (n)	['sfeʃnik]
drapes	**draperii** (f pl)	[drape'rij]
wallpaper	**tapet** (n)	[ta'pet]
blinds (jalousie)	**jaluzele** (f pl)	[ʒalu'zele]
table lamp	**lampă** (f) **de birou**	['lampə de bi'rou]
wall lamp (sconce)	**lampă** (f)	['lampə]
floor lamp	**lampă** (f) **cu picior**	['lampə ku pi'ʧior]
chandelier	**lustră** (f)	['lustrə]
leg (of chair, table)	**picior** (n)	[pi'ʧior]
armrest	**braț** (n) **la fotoliu**	['brats la fo'tolju]
back (backrest)	**spătar** (n)	[spə'tar]
drawer	**sertar** (n)	[ser'tar]

96. Bedding

bedclothes	**lenjerie** (f)	[lenʒe'rie]
pillow	**pernă** (f)	['pernə]
pillowcase	**față** (f) **de pernă**	['fatsə de 'pernə]
duvet, comforter	**plapumă** (f)	['plapumə]
sheet	**cearşaf** (n)	[ʧar'ʃaf]
bedspread	**pătură** (f)	[pəturə]

97. Kitchen

kitchen	**bucătărie** (f)	[bukətə'rie]
gas	**gaz** (n)	[gaz]
gas stove (range)	**aragaz** (n)	[ara'gaz]
electric stove	**plită** (f) **electrică**	['plitə e'lektrikə]
oven	**cuptor** (n)	[kup'tor]
microwave oven	**cuptor** (n) **cu microunde**	[kup'tor ku mikro'unde]
refrigerator	**frigider** (n)	[fridʒi'der]

freezer	**congelator** (n)	[kondʒela'tor]
dishwasher	**maşină** (f) **de spălat vase**	[ma'ʃinə de spə'lat 'vase]
meat grinder	**maşină** (f) **de tocat carne**	[ma'ʃinə de to'kat 'karne]
juicer	**storcător** (n)	[storkə'tor]
toaster	**prăjitor** (n) **de pâine**	[prəʒi'tor de 'pɨne]
mixer	**mixer** (n)	['mikser]
coffee machine	**fierbător** (n) **de cafea**	[fierbə'tor de ka'fʲa]
coffee pot	**ibric** (n)	[i'brik]
coffee grinder	**râşniță** (f) **de cafea**	['rɨʃnitsə de ka'fʲa]
kettle	**ceainic** (n)	['ʧajnik]
teapot	**ceainic** (n)	['ʧajnik]
lid	**capac** (n)	[ka'pak]
tea strainer	**strecurătoare** (f)	[strekurəto'are]
spoon	**lingură** (f)	['lingurə]
teaspoon	**lingurită** (f) **de ceai**	[lingu'ritsə de ʧaj]
soup spoon	**lingură** (f)	['lingurə]
fork	**furculiță** (f)	[furku'litsə]
knife	**cuțit** (n)	[ku'tsit]
tableware (dishes)	**vase** (n pl)	['vase]
plate (dinner ~)	**farfurie** (f)	[farfu'rie]
saucer	**farfurioară** (f)	[farfurio'arə]
shot glass	**păhărel** (n)	[pəhə'rel]
glass (tumbler)	**pahar** (n)	[pa'har]
cup	**ceaşcă** (f)	['ʧaʃkə]
sugar bowl	**zaharniță** (f)	[za'harnitsə]
salt shaker	**solniță** (f)	['solnitsə]
pepper shaker	**piperniță** (f)	[pi'pernitsə]
butter dish	**untieră** (f)	[un'tjerə]
stock pot (soup pot)	**cratiță** (f)	['kratitsə]
frying pan (skillet)	**tigaie** (f)	[ti'gae]
ladle	**polonic** (n)	[polo'nik]
colander	**strecurătoare** (f)	[strekurəto'are]
tray (serving ~)	**tavă** (f)	['tavə]
bottle	**sticlă** (f)	['stiklə]
jar (glass)	**borcan** (n)	[bor'kan]
can	**cutie** (f)	[ku'tie]
bottle opener	**deschizător** (n) **de sticle**	[deskizə'tor de 'stikle]
can opener	**deschizător** (n) **de conserve**	[deskizə'tor de kon'serve]
corkscrew	**tirbuşon** (n)	[tirbu'ʃon]
filter	**filtru** (n)	['filtru]
to filter (vt)	**a filtra**	[a fil'tra]

trash, garbage (food waste, etc.)	**gunoi** (n)	[gu'noj]
trash can (kitchen ~)	**coş** (n) **de gunoi**	[koʃ de gu'noj]

98. Bathroom

bathroom	**baie** (f)	['bae]
water	**apă** (f)	['apə]
faucet	**robinet** (n)	[robi'net]
hot water	**apă** (f) **fierbinte**	['apə fjer'binte]
cold water	**apă** (f) **rece**	['apə 'retʃe]
toothpaste	**pastă** (f) **de dinți**	['pastə de dintsʲ]
to brush one's teeth	**a se spăla pe dinți**	[a se spə'la pe dintsʲ]
toothbrush	**periuță** (f) **de dinți**	[peri'utsə de dintsʲ]
to shave (vi)	**a se bărbieri**	[a se bərbie'ri]
shaving foam	**spumă** (f) **de ras**	['spumə de 'ras]
razor	**brici** (n)	['britʃi]
to wash (one's hands, etc.)	**a spăla**	[a spə'la]
to take a bath	**a se spăla**	[a se spə'la]
shower	**duş** (n)	[duʃ]
to take a shower	**a face duş**	[a 'fatʃe duʃ]
bathtub	**cadă** (f)	['kadə]
toilet (toilet bowl)	**closet** (n)	[klo'set]
sink (washbasin)	**chiuvetă** (f)	[kju'vetə]
soap	**săpun** (n)	[sə'pun]
soap dish	**săpunieră** (f)	[səpu'njerə]
sponge	**burete** (n)	[bu'rete]
shampoo	**şampon** (n)	[ʃam'pon]
towel	**prosop** (n)	[pro'sop]
bathrobe	**halat** (n)	[ha'lat]
laundry (laundering)	**spălat** (n)	[spə'lat]
washing machine	**maşină** (f) **de spălat**	[ma'ʃinə de spə'lat]
to do the laundry	**a spăla haine**	[a spə'la 'hajne]
laundry detergent	**detergent** (n)	[deter'dʒent]

99. Household appliances

TV set	**televizor** (n)	[televi'zor]
tape recorder	**casetofon** (n)	[kaseto'fon]
VCR (video recorder)	**videomagnetofon** (n)	[videomagneto'fon]
radio	**aparat** (n) **de radio**	[apa'rat de 'radio]

player (CD, MP3, etc.)	**CD player** (n)	[si'di 'pleer]
video projector	**proiector** (n) **video**	[proek'tor 'video]
home movie theater	**sistem** (n) **home cinema**	[sis'tem 'houm 'sinema]
DVD player	**DVD-player** (n)	[divi'di 'pleer]
amplifier	**amplificator** (n)	[amplifi'kator]
video game console	**consolă** (f) **de jocuri**	[kon'solə de 'ʒokurʲ]
video camera	**cameră** (f) **video**	['kamerə 'video]
camera (photo)	**aparat** (n) **foto**	[apa'rat 'foto]
digital camera	**aparat** (n) **foto digital**	[apa'rat 'foto didʒi'tal]
vacuum cleaner	**aspirator** (n)	[aspira'tor]
iron (e.g., steam ~)	**fier** (n) **de călcat**	[fier de kəl'kat]
ironing board	**masă** (f) **de călcat**	['masə de kəl'kat]
telephone	**telefon** (n)	[tele'fon]
cell phone	**telefon** (n) **mobil**	[tele'fon mo'bil]
typewriter	**maşină** (f) **de scris**	[ma'ʃinə de skris]
sewing machine	**maşină** (f) **de cusut**	[ma'ʃine de ku'sut]
microphone	**microfon** (n)	[mikro'fon]
headphones	**căşti** (f pl)	[kəʃtʲ]
remote control (TV)	**telecomandă** (f)	[teleko'mandə]
CD, compact disc	**CD** (n)	[si'di]
cassette, tape	**casetă** (f)	[ka'setə]
vinyl record	**placă** (f)	['plakə]

100. Repairs. Renovation

renovations	**reparaţie** (f)	[repa'ratsie]
to renovate (vt)	**a face reparaţie**	[a 'fatʃe repa'ratsie]
to repair, to fix (vt)	**a repara**	[a repa'ra]
to put in order	**a pune în ordine**	[a 'pune ɨn 'ordine]
to redo (do again)	**a reface**	[a re'fatʃe]
paint	**vopsea** (f)	[vop'sʲa]
to paint (~ a wall)	**a vopsi**	[a vop'si]
house painter	**zugrav** (m)	[zu'grav]
paintbrush	**pensulă** (f)	['pensulə]
whitewash	**var** (n)	[var]
to whitewash (vt)	**a vărui**	[a vəru'i]
wallpaper	**tapet** (n)	[ta'pet]
to wallpaper (vt)	**a tapeta**	[a tape'ta]
varnish	**lac** (n)	[lak]
to varnish (vt)	**a lăcui**	[a ləku'i]

101. Plumbing

water	**apă** (f)	['apə]
hot water	**apă** (f) **fierbinte**	['apə fjer'binte]
cold water	**apă** (f) **rece**	['apə 'retʃe]
faucet	**robinet** (n)	[robi'net]
drop (of water)	**picătură** (f)	[pikə'turə]
to drip (vi)	**a picura**	[a piku'ra]
to leak (ab. pipe)	**a curge**	[a 'kurdʒe]
leak (pipe ~)	**scurgere** (f)	['skurdʒere]
puddle	**baltă** (f)	['baltə]
pipe	**țeavă** (f)	['tsʲavə]
valve (e.g., ball ~)	**ventil** (n)	[ven'til]
to be clogged up	**a se înfunda**	[a se ɨnfun'da]
tools	**instrumente** (n pl)	[instru'mente]
adjustable wrench	**cheie** (f) **reglabilă**	['kee re'glabilə]
to unscrew (lid, filter, etc.)	**a deşuruba**	[a deʃuru'ba]
to screw (tighten)	**a înşuruba**	[a ɨnʃuru'ba]
to unclog (vt)	**a curăța**	[a kurə'tsa]
plumber	**instalator** (m)	[instala'tor]
basement	**subsol** (n)	[sub'sol]
sewerage (system)	**canalizare** (f)	[kanali'zare]

102. Fire. Conflagration

fire (accident)	**foc** (n)	[fok]
flame	**flacără** (f)	['flakərə]
spark	**scânteie** (f)	[skɨn'tee]
smoke (from fire)	**fum** (n)	[fum]
torch (flaming stick)	**făclie** (f)	[fək'lie]
campfire	**foc** (n)	[fok]
gas, gasoline	**benzină** (f)	[ben'zinə]
kerosene (type of fuel)	**petrol** (n)	[pe'trol]
flammable (adj)	**inflamabil**	[infla'mabil]
explosive (adj)	**explozibil**	[eksplo'zibil]
NO SMOKING	**NU FUMAȚI!**	[nu fu'mats]
safety	**siguranță** (f)	[sigu'rantsə]
danger	**pericol** (n)	[pe'rikol]
dangerous (adj)	**periculos**	[periku'los]
to catch fire	**a lua foc**	[a lu'a 'fok]
explosion	**explozie** (f)	[eks'plozie]
to set fire	**a incendia**	[a intʃendi'a]

arsonist	**incendiator** (m)	[intʃendia'tor]
arson	**incendiere** (f)	[intʃen'djere]
to blaze (vi)	**a arde cu flăcări mari**	[a 'arde ku fləkə'ri 'mari]
to burn (be on fire)	**a arde**	[a 'arde]
to burn down	**a arde din temelie**	[a 'arde din teme'lie]
firefighter, fireman	**pompier** (m)	[pom'pjer]
fire truck	**maşină** (f) **de pompieri**	[ma'ʃinə de pom'pjeri]
fire department	**echipă** (f) **de pompieri**	[ekipə de pom'pjeri]
fire truck ladder	**scară** (f) **de incendiu**	['skarə de in'tʃendju]
fire hose	**furtun** (n)	[fur'tun]
fire extinguisher	**stingător** (n)	[stingə'tor]
helmet	**cască** (f)	['kaskə]
siren	**sirenă** (f)	[si'renə]
to cry (for help)	**a striga**	[a stri'ga]
to call for help	**a chema în ajutor**	[a ke'ma ɨn aʒu'tor]
rescuer	**salvator** (m)	[salva'tor]
to rescue (vt)	**a salva**	[a sal'va]
to arrive (vi)	**a veni**	[a ve'ni]
to extinguish (vt)	**a stinge**	[a 'stindʒe]
water	**apă** (f)	['apə]
sand	**nisip** (n)	[ni'sip]
ruins (destruction)	**ruine** (f pl)	[ru'ine]
to collapse (building, etc.)	**a se prăbuşi**	[a se prəbu'ʃi]
to fall down (vi)	**a se dărâma**	[a se dərɨ'ma]
to cave in (ceiling, floor)	**a se surpa**	[a se sur'pa]
piece of debris	**dărâmătură** (f)	[dərəmə'turə]
ash	**scrum** (n)	[skrum]
to suffocate (die)	**a se sufoca**	[a se sufo'ka]
to be killed (perish)	**a deceda**	[a detʃe'da]

HUMAN ACTIVITIES

Job. Business. Part 1

103. Office. Working in the office

office (company ~)	**oficiu** (n)	[o'fitʃiu]
office (of director, etc.)	**cabinet** (n)	[kabi'net]
reception desk	**recepție** (f)	[re'tʃeptsie]
secretary	**secretar** (m)	[sekre'tar]
director	**director** (m)	[di'rektor]
manager	**manager** (m)	['menedʒə]
accountant	**contabil** (f)	[kon'tabil]
employee	**colaborator** (m)	[kolabora'tor]
furniture	**mobilă** (f)	['mobilə]
desk	**masă** (f)	['masə]
desk chair	**fotoliu** (n)	[fo'tolju]
drawer unit	**noptieră** (f)	[nop'tjerə]
coat stand	**cuier** (n) **pom**	[ku'jer pom]
computer	**calculator** (n)	[kalkula'tor]
printer	**imprimantă** (f)	[impri'mantə]
fax machine	**fax** (n)	[faks]
photocopier	**copiator** (n)	[kopia'tor]
paper	**hârtie** (f)	[hɨr'tie]
office supplies	**rechizite** (n pl) **de birou**	[reki'zite de bi'rou]
mouse pad	**pad** (n)	[pad], [pəd]
sheet (of paper)	**foaie** (f)	[fo'ae]
binder	**mapă** (f)	['mapə]
catalog	**catalog** (n)	[kata'log]
phone directory	**îndrumar** (n)	[ɨndru'mar]
documentation	**documentație** (f)	[dokumen'tatsie]
brochure (e.g., 12 pages ~)	**broşură** (f)	[bro'ʃurə]
leaflet (promotional ~)	**foaie** (f)	[fo'ae]
sample	**model** (n)	[mo'del]
training meeting	**trening** (n)	['trening]
meeting (of managers)	**şedință** (f)	[ʃe'dintsə]
lunch time	**pauză** (f) **de prânz**	['pauzə de 'prɨnz]
to make a copy	**a face copie**	[a 'fatʃe 'kopie]

to make multiple copies	**a multiplica**	[a multipli'ka]
to receive a fax	**a primi fax**	[a pri'mi 'faks]
to send a fax	**a trimite fax**	[a tri'mite 'faks]
to call (by phone)	**a suna**	[a su'na]
to answer (vt)	**a răspunde**	[a rəs'punde]
to put through	**a face legătura**	[a 'fatʃe legə'tura]
to arrange, to set up	**a stabili**	[a stabi'li]
to demonstrate (vt)	**a demonstra**	[a demonst'ra]
to be absent	**a lipsi**	[a lip'si]
absence	**lipsă** (f)	['lipsə]

104. Business processes. Part 1

business	**business** (n)	['biznis]
occupation	**ocupație** (f)	[oku'patsie]
firm	**firmă** (f)	['firmə]
company	**companie** (f)	[kompa'nie]
corporation	**corporație** (f)	[korpo'ratsie]
enterprise	**întreprindere** (f)	[ɨntre'prindere]
agency	**agenție** (f)	[adʒen'tsie]
agreement (contract)	**acord** (n)	[a'kord]
contract	**contract** (n)	[kon'trakt]
deal	**afacere** (f)	[a'fatʃere]
order (to place an ~)	**comandă** (f)	[ko'mandə]
terms (of the contract)	**condiție** (f)	[kon'ditsie]
wholesale (adv)	**en-gros**	[an'gro]
wholesale (adj)	**en-gros**	[an'gro]
wholesale (n)	**vânzare** (f) **en-gros**	[vɨn'zare an'gro]
retail (adj)	**cu bucata**	[ku bu'kata]
retail (n)	**vânzare** (f) **cu bucata**	[vɨn'zare ku bu'kata]
competitor	**concurent** (m)	[konku'rent]
competition	**concurență** (f)	[konku'rentsə]
to compete (vi)	**a concura**	[a konku'ra]
partner (associate)	**partener** (m)	[parte'ner]
partnership	**parteneriat** (n)	[parteneri'at]
crisis	**criză** (f)	['krizə]
bankruptcy	**faliment** (n)	[fali'ment]
to go bankrupt	**a da faliment**	[a da fali'ment]
difficulty	**dificultate** (f)	[difikul'tate]
problem	**problemă** (f)	[pro'blemə]
catastrophe	**catastrofă** (f)	[katas'trofə]
economy	**economie** (f)	[ekono'mie]
economic (~ growth)	**economic**	[eko'nomik]

economic recession	**scădere** (f) **economică**	[skə'dere eko'nomikə]
goal (aim)	**scop** (n)	[skop]
task	**obiectiv** (n)	[objek'tiv]
to trade (vi)	**a face comerț**	[a 'fatʃe ko'merts]
network (distribution ~)	**rețea** (f)	[re'tsʲa]
inventory (stock)	**depozit** (n)	[de'pozit]
range (assortment)	**sortiment** (n)	[sorti'ment]
leader (leading company)	**lider** (m)	['lider]
large (~ company)	**mare**	['mare]
monopoly	**monopol** (n)	[mono'pol]
theory	**teorie** (f)	[teo'rie]
practice	**practică** (f)	['praktikə]
experience (in my ~)	**experiență** (f)	[ekspe'rjentsə]
trend (tendency)	**tendință** (f)	[ten'dintsə]
development	**dezvoltare** (f)	[dezvol'tare]

105. Business processes. Part 2

profit (foregone ~)	**profit** (n)	[pro'fit]
profitable (~ deal)	**profitabil**	[profi'tabil]
delegation (group)	**delegație** (f)	[dele'gatsie]
salary	**salariu** (n)	[sa'larju]
to correct (an error)	**a corecta**	[a korek'ta]
business trip	**deplasare** (f)	[depla'sare]
commission	**comisie** (f)	[ko'misie]
to control (vt)	**a controla**	[a kontro'la]
conference	**conferință** (f)	[konfe'rintsə]
license	**licență** (f)	[li'tʃentsə]
reliable (~ partner)	**de încredere**	[de ɨn'kredere]
initiative (undertaking)	**început** (n)	[ɨntʃe'put]
norm (standard)	**normă** (f)	['normə]
circumstance	**circumstanță** (f)	[tʃirkum'stantsə]
duty (of employee)	**obligație** (f)	[obli'gatsie]
organization (company)	**organizație** (f)	[organi'zatsie]
organization (process)	**organizare** (f)	[organi'zare]
organized (adj)	**organizat**	[organi'zat]
cancellation	**contramandare** (f)	[kontraman'dare]
to cancel (call off)	**a anula**	[a anu'la]
report (official ~)	**raport** (n)	[ra'port]
patent	**brevet** (f)	[bre'vet]
to patent (obtain patent)	**a breveta**	[a breve'ta]
to plan (vt)	**a planifica**	[a planifi'ka]

bonus (money)	**primă** (f)	['primə]
professional (adj)	**profesional**	[profesio'nal]
procedure	**procedură** (f)	[protʃe'durə]
to examine (contract, etc.)	**a examina**	[a ekzami'na]
calculation	**calcul** (n)	['kalkul]
reputation	**reputație** (f)	[repu'tatsie]
risk	**risc** (n)	[risk]
to manage, to run	**a conduce**	[a kon'dutʃe]
information (report)	**informații** (f pl)	[infor'matsij]
property	**proprietate** (f)	[proprie'tate]
union	**alianță** (f)	[ali'antsə]
life insurance	**asigurare** (f) **de viață**	[asigu'rare de 'vjatsə]
to insure (vt)	**a asigura**	[a asigu'ra]
insurance	**asigurare** (f)	[asigu'rare]
auction (~ sale)	**licitație** (f)	[litʃi'tatsie]
to notify (inform)	**a înştiința**	[a inʃtiin'tsa]
management (process)	**conducere** (f)	[kon'dutʃere]
service (~ industry)	**serviciu** (n)	[ser'vitʃiu]
forum	**for** (n)	[for]
to function (vi)	**a funcționa**	[a funktsio'na]
stage (phase)	**etapă** (f)	[e'tapə]
legal (~ services)	**juridic**	[ʒu'ridik]
lawyer (legal advisor)	**jurist** (m)	[ʒu'rist]

106. Production. Works

plant	**uzină** (f)	[u'zinə]
factory	**fabrică** (f)	['fabrikə]
workshop	**atelier** (n)	[ate'ljer]
works, production site	**fabricație** (f)	[fabri'katsie]
industry (manufacturing)	**industrie** (f)	[in'dustrie]
industrial (adj)	**industrial**	[industri'al]
heavy industry	**industrie** (f) **grea**	[in'dustrie grʲa]
light industry	**industrie** (f) **uşoară**	[in'dustrie uʃo'arə]
products	**producție** (f)	[pro'duktsie]
to produce (vt)	**a produce**	[a pro'dutʃe]
raw materials	**materie** (f) **primă**	[ma'terie 'primə]
foreman (construction ~)	**şef** (m) **de brigadă**	[ʃef de bri'gadə]
workers team (crew)	**brigadă** (f)	[bri'gadə]
worker	**muncitor** (m)	[muntʃi'tor]
working day	**zi** (f) **lucrătoare**	['zi lukrəto'are]
pause (rest break)	**pauză** (f)	['pauzə]

meeting	**adunare** (f)	[adu'nare]
to discuss (vt)	**a discuta**	[a disku'ta]
plan	**plan** (n)	[plan]
to fulfill the plan	**a îndeplini planul**	[a ɨndepli'ni 'planul]
rate of output	**normă** (f)	['normə]
quality	**calitate** (f)	[kali'tate]
control (checking)	**control** (n)	[kon'trol]
quality control	**controlul** (n) **calității**	[kon'trolul kali'təʦij]
workplace safety	**protecția** (f) **muncii**	[pro'tekʦija 'munʧij]
discipline	**disciplină** (f)	[disʧi'plinə]
violation (of safety rules, etc.)	**încălcare** (f)	[ɨnkəl'kare]
to violate (rules)	**a încălca**	[a ɨnkəl'ka]
strike	**grevă** (f)	['grevə]
striker	**grevist** (m)	[gre'vist]
to be on strike	**a face grevă**	[a 'faʧe 'grevə]
labor union	**sindicat** (n)	[sindi'kat]
to invent (machine, etc.)	**a inventa**	[a inven'ta]
invention	**invenție** (f)	[in'venʦie]
research	**cercetare** (f)	[ʧerʧe'tare]
to improve (make better)	**a îmbunătăți**	[a ɨmbunətə'ʦi]
technology	**tehnologie** (f)	[tehnolo'ʤie]
technical drawing	**plan** (n)	[plan]
load, cargo	**încărcătură** (f)	[ɨnkərkə'turə]
loader (person)	**hamal** (m)	[ha'mal]
to load (vehicle, etc.)	**a încărca**	[a ɨnkər'ka]
loading (process)	**încărcătură** (f)	[ɨnkərkə'turə]
to unload (vi, vt)	**a descărca**	[a deskər'ka]
unloading	**descărcare** (f)	[deskər'kare]
transportation	**transport** (n)	[trans'port]
transportation company	**companie** (f) **de transport**	[kompa'nie de trans'port]
to transport (vt)	**a transporta**	[a transpor'ta]
freight car	**vagon** (n) **marfar**	[va'gon mar'far]
tank (e.g., oil ~)	**cisternă** (f)	[ʧis'ternə]
truck	**autocamion** (n)	[autoka'mjon]
machine tool	**maşină-unealtă** (f)	[ma'ʃinə u'nʲaltə]
mechanism	**mecanism** (n)	[meka'nizm]
industrial waste	**deşeuri** (n pl)	[de'ʃəurʲ]
packing (process)	**ambalare** (f)	[amba'lare]
to pack (vt)	**a ambala**	[a amba'la]

107. Contract. Agreement

contract	**contract** (n)	[kon'trakt]
agreement	**contract** (f)	[kon'trakt]
addendum	**anexă** (f)	[a'neksə]
to sign a contract	**a încheia un contract**	[a ɨnke'ja un kon'trakt]
signature	**semnătură** (f)	[semnə'turə]
to sign (vt)	**a semna**	[a sem'na]
seal (stamp)	**ştampilă** (f)	[ʃtam'pilə]
subject of the contract	**obiectul** (n) **contractului**	[o'bjektul kon'traktuluj]
clause	**paragraf** (n)	[para'graf]
parties (in contract)	**părţi** (f pl)	[pərts']
legal address	**adresă** (f) **juridică**	[a'dresə ʒu'ridikə]
to violate the contract	**a încălca contractul**	[a ɨnkəl'ka kon'traktul]
commitment (obligation)	**obligaţie** (f)	[obli'gatsie]
responsibility	**răspundere** (f)	[rəs'pundere]
force majeure	**forţe** (f pl) **majore**	['fortse ma'ʒore]
dispute	**dispută** (f)	[dis'putə]
penalties	**sancţiuni** (f pl)	[sanktsi'un']

108. Import & Export

import	**import** (n)	[im'port]
importer	**importator** (m)	[importa'tor]
to import (vt)	**a importa**	[a impor'ta]
import (as adj.)	**din import**	[din im'port]
export (exportation)	**export** (n)	[eks'port]
exporter	**exportator** (m)	[eksporta'tor]
to export (vi, vt)	**a exporta**	[a ekspor'ta]
export (as adj.)	**din export**	[din eks'port]
goods (merchandise)	**marfă** (f)	['marfə]
consignment, lot	**lot** (n)	[lot]
weight	**greutate** (f)	[greu'tate]
volume	**volum** (n)	[vo'lum]
cubic meter	**metru** (m) **cub**	['metru 'kub]
manufacturer	**producător** (m)	[produkə'tor]
transportation company	**companie** (f) **de transport**	[kompa'nie de trans'port]
container	**container** (m)	[kon'tajner]
border	**graniţă** (f)	['granitsə]
customs	**vamă** (f)	['vamə]
customs duty	**taxă** (f) **vamală**	['taksə va'malə]

customs officer	**vameş** (m)	['vameʃ]
smuggling	**contrabandă** (f)	[kontra'bandə]
contraband (smuggled goods)	**contrabandă** (f)	[kontra'bandə]

109. Finances

stock (share)	**acțiune** (f)	[aktsi'une]
bond (certificate)	**obligație** (f)	[obli'gatsie]
promissory note	**poliță** (f)	['politsə]
stock exchange	**bursă** (f)	['bursə]
stock price	**cursul** (n) **acțiunii**	['kursul aktsi'unij]
to go down (become cheaper)	**a se ieftini**	[a se efti'ni]
to go up (become more expensive)	**a se scumpi**	[a se skum'pi]
share	**parte** (f)	['parte]
controlling interest	**pachet** (n) **de control**	[pa'ket de kon'trol]
investment	**investiții** (f pl)	[inves'titsij]
to invest (vt)	**a investi**	[a inves'ti]
percent	**procent** (n)	[pro'tʃent]
interest (on investment)	**dobândă** (f)	[do'bɨndə]
profit	**profit** (n)	[pro'fit]
profitable (adj)	**profitabil**	[profi'tabil]
tax	**impozit** (n)	[im'pozit]
currency (foreign ~)	**valută** (f)	[va'lutə]
national (adj)	**național**	[natsio'nal]
exchange (currency ~)	**schimb** (n)	[skimb]
accountant	**contabil** (m)	[kon'tabil]
accounting	**contabilitate** (f)	[kontabili'tate]
bankruptcy	**faliment** (n)	[fali'ment]
collapse, crash	**faliment** (n)	[fali'ment]
ruin	**faliment** (n)	[fali'ment]
to be ruined (financially)	**a falimenta**	[a falimen'ta]
inflation	**inflație** (f)	[in'flatsie]
devaluation	**devalorizare** (f)	[devalori'zare]
capital	**capital** (n)	[kapi'tal]
income	**venit** (n)	[ve'nit]
turnover	**rotație** (f)	[ro'tatsie]
resources	**resurse** (f pl)	[re'surse]
monetary resources	**mijloace** (n pl) **băneşti**	[miʒlo'atʃe bə'neʃtʲ]
overhead	**cheltuieli** (f pl) **de operare**	[keltu'elʲ de ope'rare]
to reduce (expenses)	**a reduce**	[a re'dutʃe]

110. Marketing

marketing	**marketing** (n)	['marketing]
market	**piață** (f)	['pjatsə]
market segment	**segment** (n) **de piață**	[seg'ment de 'pjatsə]
product	**produs** (n)	[pro'dus]
goods (merchandise)	**marfă** (f)	['marfə]
brand	**marcă** (f)	['markə]
trademark	**marcă** (f) **comercială**	['markə komertʃi'alə]
logotype	**logotip** (n)	[logo'tip]
logo	**logo** (m)	['logo]
demand	**cerere** (f)	['tʃerere]
supply	**ofertă** (f)	[o'fertə]
need	**necesitate** (f)	[netʃesi'tate]
consumer	**consumator** (m)	[konsu'mator]
analysis	**analiză** (f)	[ana'lizə]
to analyze (vt)	**a analiza**	[a anali'za]
positioning	**poziționare** (f)	[pozitsio'nare]
to position (vt)	**a poziționa**	[a pozitsio'na]
price	**preț** (n)	[prets]
pricing policy	**politica** (f) **prețurilor**	[po'litika 'pretsurilor]
price formation	**stabilirea** (f) **prețurilor**	[stabi'lirʲa 'pretsurilor]

111. Advertising

advertising	**reclamă** (f)	[re'klamə]
to advertise (vt)	**a face reclamă**	[a 'fatʃe re'klamə]
budget	**buget** (n)	[bu'dʒet]
ad, advertisement	**reclamă** (f)	[re'klamə]
TV advertising	**publicitate** (f) **TV**	[publitʃi'tate te've]
radio advertising	**publicitate** (f) **radio**	[publitʃi'tate 'radio]
outdoor advertising	**reclamă** (f) **exterioară**	[re'klamə eksterio'arə]
mass media	**mass-media** (f)	['mas 'media]
periodical (n)	**ediție** (f) **periodică**	[e'ditsie peri'odikə]
image (public appearance)	**imagine** (f)	[i'madʒine]
slogan	**lozincă** (f)	[lo'zinkə]
motto (maxim)	**deviză** (f)	[de'vizə]
campaign	**campanie** (f)	[kam'panie]
advertising campaign	**campanie** (f) **publicitară**	[kam'panie publitʃi'tarə]
target group	**grup** (n) **țintă**	[grup 'tsintə]
business card	**carte** (f) **de vizită**	['karte de 'vizitə]

leaflet (promotional ~)	**foaie** (f)	[fo'ae]
brochure (e.g., 12 pages ~)	**broşură** (f)	[bro'ʃurə]
pamphlet	**pliant** (n)	[pli'ant]
newsletter	**buletin** (n)	[bule'tin]
signboard (store sign, etc.)	**firmă** (f)	['firmə]
poster	**afiş** (n)	[a'fiʃ]
billboard	**panou** (n)	[pa'nou]

112. Banking

bank	**bancă** (f)	['bankə]
branch (of bank, etc.)	**sucursală** (f)	[sukur'salə]
bank clerk, consultant	**consultant** (m)	[konsul'tant]
manager (director)	**director** (m)	[di'rektor]
bank account	**cont** (n)	[kont]
account number	**numărul** (n) **contului**	['numərul 'kontuluj]
checking account	**cont** (n) **curent**	[kont ku'rent]
savings account	**cont** (n) **de acumulare**	[kont de akumu'lare]
to open an account	**a deschide un cont**	[a des'kide un kont]
to close the account	**a închide contul**	[a ɨ'nkide 'kontul]
to deposit into the account	**a pune în cont**	[a 'pune ɨn 'kont]
to withdraw (vt)	**a extrage din cont**	[a eks'tradʒe din kont]
deposit	**depozit** (n)	[de'pozit]
to make a deposit	**a depune**	[a de'pune]
wire transfer	**transfer** (n)	[trans'fer]
to wire, to transfer	**a transfera**	[a transfe'ra]
sum	**sumă** (f)	['sumə]
How much?	**Cât?**	[kɨt]
signature	**semnătură** (f)	[semnə'turə]
to sign (vt)	**a semna**	[a sem'na]
credit card	**carte** (f) **de credit**	['karte de 'kredit]
code (PIN code)	**cod** (n)	[kod]
credit card number	**numărul** (n) **cărţii de credit**	['numərul kərʦij de 'kredit]
ATM	**bancomat** (n)	[banko'mat]
check	**cec** (n)	[ʧek]
to write a check	**a scrie un cec**	[a 'skrie un ʧek]
checkbook	**carte** (f) **de cecuri**	['karte de 'ʧekur^j]
loan (bank ~)	**credit** (n)	['kredit]
to apply for a loan	**a solicita un credit**	[a soliʧi'ta pe 'kredit]

to get a loan	**a lua pe credit**	[a lu'a pe 'kredit]
to give a loan	**a acorda credit**	[a akor'da 'kredit]
guarantee	**garanție** (f)	[garan'tsie]

113. Telephone. Phone conversation

telephone	**telefon** (n)	[tele'fon]
cell phone	**telefon** (n) **mobil**	[tele'fon mo'bil]
answering machine	**răspuns** (n) **automat**	[rəs'puns auto'mat]
to call (by phone)	**a suna, a telefona**	[a su'na], [a tele'fona]
phone call	**apel** (n), **convorbire** (f)	[a'pel], [konvor'bire]
to dial a number	**a forma un număr**	[a for'ma un 'numər]
Hello!	**Alo!**	[a'lo]
to ask (vt)	**a întreba**	[a ɨntre'ba]
to answer (vi, vt)	**a răspunde**	[a rəs'punde]
to hear (vt)	**a auzi**	[a au'zi]
well (adv)	**bine**	['bine]
not well (adv)	**rău**	['rəu]
noises (interference)	**bruiaj** (n)	[bru'jaʒ]
receiver	**receptor** (n)	[retʃep'tor]
to pick up (~ the phone)	**a lua receptorul**	[a lu'a retʃep'torul]
to hang up (~ the phone)	**a pune receptorul**	[a 'pune retʃep'torul]
busy (engaged)	**ocupat**	[oku'pat]
to ring (ab. phone)	**a suna**	[a su'na]
telephone book	**carte** (f) **de telefon**	['karte de tele'fon]
local (adj)	**local**	[lo'kal]
local call	**apel** (n) **local**	[a'pel lo'kal]
long distance (~ call)	**interurban**	[interur'ban]
long-distance call	**apel** (n) **interurban**	[a'pel interur'ban]
international (adj)	**internațional**	[internatsio'nal]
international call	**apel** (n) **interna ional**	[a'pel internatsio'nal]

114. Cell phone

cell phone	**telefon** (n) **mobil**	[tele'fon mo'bil]
display	**ecran** (n)	[e'kran]
button	**buton** (n)	[bu'ton]
SIM card	**cartelă** (f) **SIM**	[kar'telə 'sim]
battery	**baterie** (f)	[bate'rie]
to be dead (battery)	**a se descărca**	[a se deskər'ka]
charger	**încărcător** (m)	[ɨnkərkə'tor]

menu	**meniu** (n)	[me'nju]
settings	**setări** (f)	[se'tərʲ]
tune (melody)	**melodie** (f)	[melo'die]
to select (vt)	**a selecta**	[a selek'ta]
calculator	**calculator** (n)	[kalkula'tor]
voice mail	**răspuns** (n) **automat**	[rəs'puns auto'mat]
alarm clock	**ceas** (n) **deşteptător**	[tʃas deʃteptə'tor]
contacts	**carte** (f) **de telefoane**	['karte de telefo'ane]
SMS (text message)	**SMS** (n)	[ese'mes]
subscriber	**abonat** (m)	[abo'nat]

115. Stationery

ballpoint pen	**stilou** (n)	[sti'lou]
fountain pen	**condei** (n)	[kon'dej]
pencil	**creion** (n)	[kre'jon]
highlighter	**marcher** (n)	['marker]
felt-tip pen	**cariocă** (f)	[kari'okə]
notepad	**carneţel** (n)	[karnə'tsəl]
agenda (diary)	**agendă** (f)	[a'dʒendə]
ruler	**riglă** (f)	['riglə]
calculator	**calculator** (f)	[kalkula'tor]
eraser	**radieră** (f)	[radi'erə]
thumbtack	**piuneză** (f)	[pju'nezə]
paper clip	**clamă** (f)	['klamə]
glue	**lipici** (n)	[li'pitʃi]
stapler	**capsator** (n)	[kapsa'tor]
hole punch	**perforator** (n)	[perfo'rator]
pencil sharpener	**ascuţitoare** (f)	[askutsito'are]

116. Various kinds of documents

account (report)	**raport** (n)	[ra'port]
agreement	**contract** (f)	[kon'trakt]
application form	**cerere** (f)	['tʃerere]
authentic (adj)	**autentic**	[au'tentik]
badge (identity tag)	**ecuson** (n)	[eku'son]
business card	**carte** (f) **de vizită**	['karte de 'vizitə]
certificate (~ of quality)	**certificat** (n)	[tʃertifi'kat]
check (e.g., draw a ~)	**cec** (n)	[tʃek]
check (in restaurant)	**notă** (f) **de plată**	['notə de 'platə]

constitution	**constituție** (f)	[konsti'tutsie]
contract (agreement)	**acord** (n)	[a'kord]
copy	**copie** (f)	['kopie]
copy (of contract, etc.)	**exemplar** (n)	[egzem'plar]
customs declaration	**declarație** (f)	[dekla'ratsie]
document	**act** (n)	[akt]
driver's license	**permis** (n) **de conducere**	[per'mis de kon'dutʃere]
addendum	**anexă** (f)	[a'neksə]
form	**anchetă** (f)	[an'ketə]
ID card (e.g., FBI ~)	**legalizare** (f)	[legali'zare]
inquiry (request)	**solicitare** (f)	[solitʃi'tare]
invitation card	**invitație** (f)	[invi'tatsie]
invoice	**factură** (f)	[fak'turə]
law	**lege** (f)	['ledʒe]
letter (mail)	**scrisoare** (f)	[skriso'are]
letterhead	**formular** (n)	[formu'lar]
list (of names, etc.)	**listă** (f)	['listə]
manuscript	**manuscris** (n)	[manu'skris]
newsletter	**buletin** (n)	[bule'tin]
note (short letter)	**notă** (f)	['notə]
pass (for worker, visitor)	**autorizație** (f)	[autori'zatsie]
passport	**paşaport** (n)	[paʃa'port]
permit	**permis** (n)	[per'mis]
résumé	**CV** (n)	[si'vi]
debt note, IOU	**recipisă** (f)	[retʃi'pisə]
receipt (for purchase)	**chitanță** (f)	[ki'tantsə]
sales slip, receipt	**cec** (n)	[tʃek]
report (mil.)	**raport** (n)	[ra'port]
to show (ID, etc.)	**a prezenta**	[a prezen'ta]
to sign (vt)	**a semna**	[a sem'na]
signature	**semnătură** (f)	[semnə'turə]
seal (stamp)	**ştampilă** (f)	[ʃtam'pilə]
text	**text** (n)	[tekst]
ticket (for entry)	**bilet** (n)	[bi'let]
to cross out	**a tăia**	[a tə'ja]
to fill out (~ a form)	**a completa**	[a komple'ta]
waybill (shipping invoice)	**foaie** (f) **de însoțire**	[fo'ae de inso'tsire]
will (testament)	**testament** (n)	[testa'ment]

117. Kinds of business

accounting services	**servicii** (n pl) **de contabilitate**	[ser'vitʃij de kontabili'tate]
advertising	**reclamă** (f)	[re'klamə]

advertising agency	**agenție** (f) **de reclamă**	[adʒen'tsie de re'klamə]
air-conditioners	**ventilator** (n)	[ventila'tor]
airline	**companie** (f) **aeriană**	[kompa'nie aeri'anə]
alcoholic beverages	**băuturi** (f pl) **alcoolice**	[bəu'turʲ alko'olitʃe]
antiques (antique dealers)	**anticariat** (n)	[antikari'at]
art gallery (contemporary ~)	**galerie** (f)	[gale'rie]
audit services	**servicii** (n pl) **de audit**	[ser'vitʃij de au'dit]
banking industry	**afacere** (f) **bancară**	[a'fatʃere ba'nkarə]
bar	**bar** (n)	[bar]
beauty parlor	**salon** (n) **de frumusețe**	[sa'lon de frumu'setse]
bookstore	**librărie** (f)	[librə'rie]
brewery	**fabricarea** (f) **berii**	[fabri'karʲa 'berij]
business center	**centru** (n) **de afaceri**	['tʃentru de a'fatʃerʲ]
business school	**şcoală** (f) **de afaceri**	[ʃko'alə de a'fatʃerʲ]
casino	**cazinou** (n)	[kazi'nou]
construction	**construcție** (f)	[kon'struktsie]
consulting	**consulting** (n)	[kon'salting]
dental clinic	**stomatologie** (f)	[stomatolo'dʒie]
design	**design** (n)	[di'zajn]
drugstore, pharmacy	**farmacie** (f)	[farma'tʃie]
dry cleaners	**curățătorie** (f) **chimică**	[kurətsəto'rie 'kimikə]
employment agency	**agenție** (f) **de cadre**	[adʒen'tsie de 'kadre]
financial services	**servicii** (n pl) **financiare**	[ser'vitʃij finantʃi'are]
food products	**produse** (n pl) **alimentare**	[pro'duse alimen'tare]
funeral home	**pompe** (f pl) **funebre**	['pompe fu'nebre]
furniture (e.g., house ~)	**mobilă** (f)	['mobilə]
clothing, garment	**haine** (f pl)	['hajne]
hotel	**hotel** (n)	[ho'tel]
ice-cream	**îngheţată** (f)	[ɨnge'tsatə]
industry (manufacturing)	**industrie** (f)	[in'dustrie]
insurance	**asigurare** (f) **medicală**	[asigu'rare medi'kalə]
Internet	**internet** (n)	[inter'net]
investments (finance)	**investiții** (f pl)	[inves'titsij]
jeweler	**bijutier** (m)	[biʒu'tjer]
jewelry	**bijuterii** (f pl)	[biʒute'rij]
laundry (shop)	**spălătorie** (f)	[spələto'rie]
legal advisor	**servicii** (n pl) **juridice**	[ser'vitʃij ʒu'riditʃe]
light industry	**industrie** (f) **uşoară**	[in'dustrie uʃo'arə]
magazine	**revistă** (f)	[re'vistə]
mail order selling	**vânzare** (f) **după catalog**	[vɨn'zare 'dupə kata'log]
medicine	**medicină** (f)	[medi'tʃinə]
movie theater	**cinematograf** (n)	[tʃinemato'graf]

museum	**muzeu** (n)	[mu'zeu]
news agency	**birou** (n) **de informații**	[bi'rou de infor'matsij]
newspaper	**ziar** (n)	[zjar]
nightclub	**club** (n) **de noapte**	['klub de no'apte]
oil (petroleum)	**petrol** (n)	[pe'trol]
courier services	**curierat** (n)	[kurie'rat]
pharmaceutics	**farmaceutică** (f)	[farmatʃe'utikə]
printing (industry)	**poligrafie** (f)	[poligra'fie]
publishing house	**editură** (f)	[edi'turə]
radio (~ station)	**radio** (n)	['radio]
real estate	**bunuri** (n pl) **imobiliare**	['bunurʲ imobili'are]
restaurant	**restaurant** (n)	[restau'rant]
security company	**agenție** (f) **de pază**	[adʒen'tsie de 'pazə]
sports	**sport** (n)	[sport]
stock exchange	**bursă** (f)	['bursə]
store	**magazin** (n)	[maga'zin]
supermarket	**supermarket** (n)	[super'market]
swimming pool (public ~)	**bazin** (n)	[ba'zin]
tailor shop	**atelier** (n)	[ate'ljer]
television	**televiziune** (f)	[televizi'une]
theater	**teatru** (n)	[te'atru]
trade (commerce)	**comerț** (n)	[ko'merts]
transportation	**transporturi** (n)	[trans'porturʲ]
travel	**turism** (n)	[tu'rism]
veterinarian	**veterinar** (m)	[veteri'nar]
warehouse	**depozit** (n)	[de'pozit]
waste collection	**transportarea** (f) **deşeurilor**	[transpor'tarʲa de'ʃəurilor]

Job. Business. Part 2

118. Show. Exhibition

exhibition, show	**expoziție** (f)	[ekspo'zitsie]
trade show	**expoziție** (f) **de comerț**	[ekspo'zitsie de ko'merts]
participation	**participare** (f)	[partitʃi'pare]
to participate (vi)	**a participa**	[a partitʃi'pa]
participant (exhibitor)	**participant** (m)	[partitʃi'pant]
director	**director** (m)	[di'rektor]
organizers' office	**direcție** (f)	[di'rektsie]
organizer	**organizator** (m)	[organiza'tor]
to organize (vt)	**a organiza**	[a organi'za]
participation form	**cerere** (f) **de participare**	['tʃerere de partitʃi'pare]
to fill out (vt)	**a completa**	[a komple'ta]
details	**detalii** (n pl)	[de'talij]
information	**informație** (f)	[infor'matsie]
price (cost, rate)	**preț** (n)	[prets]
including	**inclusiv**	[inklu'siv]
to include (vt)	**a include**	[a in'klude]
to pay (vi, vt)	**a plăti**	[a plə'ti]
registration fee	**tarif** (n) **de înregistrare**	[tarif de ɨnredʒis'trare]
entrance	**intrare** (f)	[in'trare]
pavilion, hall	**pavilion** (n)	[pavili'on]
to register (vt)	**a înscrie**	[a ɨn'skrie]
badge (identity tag)	**ecuson** (n)	[eku'son]
booth, stand	**stand** (n)	[stand]
to reserve, to book	**a rezerva**	[a rezer'va]
display case	**vitrină** (f)	[vi'trinə]
spotlight	**corp** (n) **de iluminat**	['korp de ilumi'nat]
design	**design** (n)	[di'zajn]
to place (put, set)	**a instala**	[a insta'la]
distributor	**distribuitor** (m)	[distribui'tor]
supplier	**furnizor** (m)	[furni'zor]
to supply (vt)	**a furniza**	[a furni'za]
country	**țară** (f)	['tsarə]
foreign (adj)	**străin**	[strə'in]

product	**produs** (n)	[pro'dus]
association	**asociație** (f)	[asotʃi'atsie]
conference hall	**sală** (f) **de conferințe**	['salə de konfe'rintse]
congress	**congres** (n)	[kon'gres]
contest (competition)	**concurs** (n)	[ko'nkurs]
visitor (attendee)	**vizitator** (m)	[vizita'tor]
to visit (attend)	**a vizita**	[a vizi'ta]
customer	**client** (m)	[kli'ent]

119. Mass Media

newspaper	**ziar** (n)	[zjar]
magazine	**revistă** (f)	[re'vistə]
press (printed media)	**presă** (f)	['presə]
radio	**radio** (n)	['radio]
radio station	**post** (n) **de radio**	[post de 'radio]
television	**televiziune** (f)	[televizi'une]
presenter, host	**prezentator** (m)	[prezenta'tor]
newscaster	**prezentator** (m)	[prezenta'tor]
commentator	**comentator** (m)	[komenta'tor]
journalist	**jurnalist** (m)	[ʒurna'list]
correspondent (reporter)	**corespondent** (m)	[korespon'dent]
press photographer	**foto-reporter** (m)	['foto re'porter]
reporter	**reporter** (m)	[re'porter]
editor	**redactor** (m)	[re'daktor]
editor-in-chief	**redactor-şef** (m)	[re'daktor 'ʃef]
to subscribe (to ...)	**a se abona**	[a se abo'na]
subscription	**abonare** (f)	[abo'nare]
subscriber	**abonat** (m)	[abo'nat]
to read (vi, vt)	**a citi**	[a tʃi'ti]
reader	**cititor** (m)	[tʃiti'tor]
circulation (of newspaper)	**tiraj** (n)	[ti'raʒ]
monthly (adj)	**lunar**	[lu'nar]
weekly (adj)	**săptămânal**	[səptəmɨ'nal]
issue (edition)	**număr** (n)	['numər]
new (~ issue)	**nou**	['nou]
headline	**titlu** (n)	['titlu]
short article	**notă** (f)	['notə]
column (regular article)	**rubrică** (f)	['rubrikə]
article	**articol** (n)	[ar'tikol]
page	**pagină** (f)	['padʒinə]
reportage, report	**reportaj** (n)	[repor'taʒ]
event (happening)	**eveniment** (n)	[eveni'ment]

sensation (news)	**senzație** (f)	[sen'zatsie]
scandal	**scandal** (n)	[skan'dal]
scandalous (adj)	**scandalos**	[skanda'los]
great (~ scandal)	**zgomotos**	[zgomo'tos]
show (e.g., cooking ~)	**emisiune** (f)	[emisi'une]
interview	**interviu** (n)	[inter'vju]
live broadcast	**în direct** (m)	[ɨn di'rekt]
channel	**post** (n)	[post]

120. Agriculture

agriculture	**agricultură** (f)	[agrikul'turə]
peasant (masc.)	**țăran** (m)	[tsə'ran]
peasant (fem.)	**țărancă** (f)	[tsə'rankə]
farmer	**fermier** (m)	[fer'mjer]
tractor (farm ~)	**tractor** (n)	[trak'tor]
combine, harvester	**combină** (f)	[kom'binə]
plow	**plug** (n)	[plug]
to plow (vi, vt)	**a ara**	[a a'ra]
plowland	**ogor** (n)	[o'gor]
furrow (in field)	**brazdă** (f)	['brazdə]
to sow (vi, vt)	**a semăna**	[a semə'na]
seeder	**semănătoare** (f)	[semənəto'are]
sowing (process)	**semănare** (f)	[semə'nare]
scythe	**coasă** (f)	[ko'asə]
to mow, to scythe	**a cosi**	[a ko'si]
spade (tool)	**hârleț** (n)	[hɨr'lets]
to till (vt)	**a săpa**	[a sə'pa]
hoe	**sapă** (f)	['sapə]
to hoe, to weed	**a plivi**	[a pli'vi]
weed (plant)	**buruiană** (f)	[buru'janə]
watering can	**stropitoare** (f)	[stropito'are]
to water (plants)	**a uda**	[a u'da]
watering (act)	**irigare** (f)	[iri'gare]
pitchfork	**furcă** (f)	['furkə]
rake	**greblă** (f)	['greblə]
fertilizer	**îngrășământ** (n)	[ɨngrəʃə'mɨnt]
to fertilize (vt)	**a îngrășa**	[a ɨngrə'ʃa]
manure (fertilizer)	**gunoi** (n) **de grajd**	[gu'noj de graʒd]
field	**câmp** (n)	[kɨmp]

meadow	**luncă** (f)	['lunkə]
vegetable garden	**grădină** (f) **de zarzavat**	[grə'dinə de zarza'vat]
orchard (e.g., apple ~)	**grădină** (f)	[grə'dinə]
to graze (vt)	**a paşte**	[a 'paʃte]
herder (herdsman)	**păstor** (m)	[pəs'tor]
pasture	**păşune** (f)	[pə'ʃune]
cattle breeding	**zootehnie** (f)	[zooteh'nie]
sheep farming	**ovicultură** (f)	[ovikul'turə]
plantation	**plantaţie** (f)	[plan'tatsie]
row (garden bed ~s)	**strat** (n)	[strat]
hothouse	**răsadniţă** (f)	[rə'sadnitsə]
drought (lack of rain)	**secetă** (f)	['setʃetə]
dry (~ summer)	**secetos**	[setʃe'tos]
cereal crops	**cereale** (f pl)	[tʃere'ale]
to harvest, to gather	**a strânge**	[a 'strindʒe]
miller (person)	**morar** (m)	[mo'rar]
mill (e.g., gristmill)	**moară** (f)	[mo'arə]
to grind (grain)	**a măcina grăunţe**	[a mətʃi'na grə'untse]
flour	**făină** (f)	[fə'inə]
straw	**paie** (n pl)	['pae]

121. Building. Building process

construction site	**şantier** (n)	[ʃan'tjer]
to build (vt)	**a construi**	[a konstru'i]
construction worker	**constructor** (m)	[kon'struktor]
project	**proiect** (n)	[pro'ekt]
architect	**arhitect** (m)	[arhi'tekt]
worker	**muncitor** (m)	[muntʃi'tor]
foundation (of a building)	**fundament** (n)	[funda'ment]
roof	**acoperiş** (n)	[akope'riʃ]
foundation pile	**pilon** (m)	[pi'lon]
wall	**perete** (m)	[pe'rete]
reinforcing bars	**armătură** (f)	[armə'turə]
scaffolding	**schele** (f)	['skele]
concrete	**beton** (n)	[be'ton]
granite	**granit** (n)	[gra'nit]
stone	**piatră** (f)	['pjatrə]
brick	**cărămidă** (f)	[kərə'midə]
sand	**nisip** (n)	[ni'sip]

cement	**ciment** (n)	[tʃi'ment]
plaster (for walls)	**tencuială** (f)	[tenku'jalə]
to plaster (vt)	**a tencui**	[a tenku'i]
paint	**vopsea** (f)	[vop'sʲa]
to paint (~ a wall)	**a vopsi**	[a vop'si]
barrel	**butoi** (n)	[bu'toj]
crane	**macara** (f)	[maka'ra]
to lift, to hoist (vt)	**a ridica**	[a ridi'ka]
to lower (vt)	**a coborî**	[a kobo'rɨ]
bulldozer	**buldozer** (n)	[bul'dozer]
excavator	**excavator** (n)	[ekskava'tor]
scoop, bucket	**căuş** (n)	[kə'uʃ]
to dig (excavate)	**a săpa**	[a sə'pa]
hard hat	**cască** (f)	['kaskə]

122. Science. Research. Scientists

science	**ştiinţă** (f)	[ʃti'intsə]
scientific (adj)	**ştiinţific**	[ʃtiin'tsifik]
scientist	**savant** (m)	[sa'vant]
theory	**teorie** (f)	[teo'rie]
axiom	**axiomă** (f)	[aksi'omə]
analysis	**analiză** (f)	[ana'lizə]
to analyze (vt)	**a analiza**	[a anali'za]
argument (strong ~)	**argument** (n)	[argu'ment]
substance (matter)	**substanţă** (f)	[sub'stantsə]
hypothesis	**ipoteză** (f)	[ipo'tezə]
dilemma	**dilemă** (f)	[di'lemə]
dissertation	**disertaţie** (f)	[diser'tatsie]
dogma	**dogmă** (f)	['dogmə]
doctrine	**doctrină** (f)	[dok'trinə]
research	**cercetare** (f)	[tʃertʃe'tare]
to research (vt)	**a cerceta**	[a tʃertʃe'ta]
tests (laboratory ~)	**verificare** (f)	[verifi'kare]
laboratory	**laborator** (n)	[labora'tor]
method	**metodă** (f)	[me'todə]
molecule	**moleculă** (f)	[mole'kulə]
monitoring	**monitorizare** (n)	[monitori'zare]
discovery (act, event)	**descoperire** (f)	[deskope'rire]
postulate	**postulat** (n)	[postu'lat]
principle	**principiu** (n)	[prin'tʃipju]
forecast	**prognoză** (f)	[prog'nozə]

to forecast (vt)	**a prognoza**	[a progno'za]
synthesis	**sinteză** (f)	[sin'tezə]
trend (tendency)	**tendință** (f)	[ten'dinʦə]
theorem	**teoremă** (f)	[teo'remə]
teachings	**învățătură** (f)	[ɨnvəʦə'turə]
fact	**fapt** (n)	[fapt]
expedition	**expediție** (f)	[ekspe'diʦie]
experiment	**experiment** (n)	[eksperi'ment]
academician	**academician** (m)	[akdemi'ʧian]
bachelor (e.g., ~ of Arts)	**bacalaureat** (n)	[bakalaure'at]
doctor (PhD)	**doctor** (m)	['doktor]
Associate Professor	**docent** (m)	[do'ʧent]
Master (e.g., ~ of Arts)	**magistru** (m)	[ma'ʤistru]
professor	**profesor** (m)	[pro'fesor]

Professions and occupations

123. Job search. Dismissal

job	**serviciu** (n)	[ser'vitʃiu]
staff (work force)	**cadre** (n pl)	['kadre]
personnel	**personal** (n)	[perso'nal]
career	**carieră** (f)	[ka'rjerə]
prospects (chances)	**perspectivă** (f)	[perspek'tivə]
skills (mastery)	**îndemânare** (f)	[ɨndemɨ'nare]
selection (screening)	**alegere** (f)	[a'ledʒere]
employment agency	**agenție** (f) **de cadre**	[adʒen'tsie de 'kadre]
résumé	**CV** (n)	[si'vi]
job interview	**interviu** (n)	[inter'vju]
vacancy, opening	**post** (n) **vacant**	['post va'kant]
salary, pay	**salariu** (n)	[sa'larju]
fixed salary	**salariu** (n)	[sa'larju]
pay, compensation	**plată** (f)	['platə]
position (job)	**funcție** (f)	['funktsie]
duty (of employee)	**obligație** (f)	[obli'gatsie]
range of duties	**domeniu** (n)	[do'menju]
busy (I'm ~)	**ocupat**	[oku'pat]
to fire (dismiss)	**a concedia**	[a kontʃedi'a]
dismissal	**concediere** (f)	[kontʃe'djere]
unemployment	**şomaj** (n)	[ʃo'maʒ]
unemployed (n)	**şomer** (m)	[ʃo'mer]
retirement	**pensie** (f)	['pensie]
to retire (from job)	**a se pensiona**	[a se pensio'na]

124. Business people

director	**director** (m)	[di'rektor]
manager (director)	**administrator** (m)	[adminis'trator]
boss	**conducător** (m)	[kondukə'tor]
superior	**şef** (m)	[ʃef]
superiors	**conducere** (f)	[kon'dutʃere]
president	**preşedinte** (m)	[preʃə'dinte]

chairman	**preşedinte** (m)	[preʃə'dinte]
deputy (substitute)	**adjunct** (m)	[a'dʒunkt]
assistant	**asistent** (m)	[asis'tent]
secretary	**secretar** (m)	[sekre'tar]
personal assistant	**secretar** (m) **personal**	[sekre'tar perso'nal]
businessman	**om** (m) **de afaceri**	[om de a'fatʃerʲ]
entrepreneur	**întreprinzător** (m)	[ɨntreprinzə'tor]
founder	**fondator** (m)	[fonda'tor]
to found (vt)	**a fonda**	[a fon'da]
incorporator	**fondator** (m)	[fonda'tor]
partner	**partener** (m)	[parte'ner]
stockholder	**acționar** (m)	[aktsio'nar]
millionaire	**milionar** (m)	[milio'nar]
billionaire	**miliardar** (n)	[miliar'dar]
owner, proprietor	**proprietar** (m)	[proprie'tar]
landowner	**proprietar** (m) **funciar**	[proprie'tar funtʃi'ar]
client	**client** (m)	[kli'ent]
regular client	**client** (m) **fidel**	[kli'ent fi'del]
buyer (customer)	**cumpărător** (m)	[kumpərə'tor]
visitor	**vizitator** (m)	[vizita'tor]
professional (n)	**profesionist** (m)	[profesio'nist]
expert	**expert** (m)	[eks'pert]
specialist	**specialist** (m)	[spetʃia'list]
banker	**bancher** (m)	[ban'ker]
broker	**broker** (m)	['broker]
cashier, teller	**casier** (m)	[ka'sjer]
accountant	**contabil** (f)	[kon'tabil]
security guard	**paznic** (m)	['paznik]
investor	**investitor** (m)	[investi'tor]
debtor	**datornic** (m)	[da'tornik]
creditor	**creditor** (m)	[kredi'tor]
borrower	**datornic** (m)	[da'tornik]
importer	**importator** (m)	[importa'tor]
exporter	**exportator** (m)	[eksporta'tor]
manufacturer	**producător** (m)	[produkə'tor]
distributor	**distribuitor** (m)	[distribui'tor]
middleman	**intermediar** (m)	[intermedi'ar]
consultant	**consultant** (m)	[konsul'tant]
sales representative	**reprezentant** (m)	[reprezen'tant]
agent	**agent** (m)	[a'dʒent]
insurance agent	**agent** (m) **de asigurare**	[a'dʒent de asigu'rare]

125. Service professions

cook	**bucătar** (m)	[bukə'tar]
chef (kitchen chef)	**bucătar-şef** (m)	[bukə'tar 'ʃəf]
baker	**brutar** (m)	[bru'tar]
bartender	**barman** (m)	['barman]
waiter	**chelner** (m)	['kelner]
waitress	**chelneriță** (f)	[kelne'ritsə]
lawyer, attorney	**avocat** (m)	[avo'kat]
lawyer (legal expert)	**jurist** (m)	[ʒu'rist]
notary public	**notar** (m)	[no'tar]
electrician	**electrician** (m)	[elektritʃi'an]
plumber	**instalator** (m)	[instala'tor]
carpenter	**dulgher** (m)	[dul'ger]
masseur	**masor** (m)	[ma'sor]
masseuse	**maseză** (f)	[ma'sezə]
doctor	**medic** (m)	['medik]
taxi driver	**taximetrist** (m)	[taksime'trist]
driver	**şofer** (m)	[ʃo'fer]
delivery man	**curier** (m)	[ku'rjer]
chambermaid	**femeie** (f) **de serviciu**	[fe'mee de ser'vitʃiu]
security guard	**paznic** (m)	['paznik]
flight attendant (fem.)	**stewardesă** (f)	[stjuar'desə]
schoolteacher	**profesor** (m)	[pro'fesor]
librarian	**bibliotecar** (m)	[bibliote'kar]
translator	**traducător** (m)	[tradukə'tor]
interpreter	**interpret** (m)	[inter'pret]
guide	**ghid** (m)	[gid]
hairdresser	**frizer** (m)	[fri'zer]
mailman	**poştaş** (m)	[poʃ'taʃ]
salesman (store staff)	**vânzător** (m)	[vinzə'tor]
gardener	**grădinar** (m)	[grədi'nar]
domestic servant	**servitor** (m)	[servi'tor]
maid (female servant)	**servitoare** (f)	[servito'are]
cleaner (cleaning lady)	**femeie** (f) **de serviciu**	[fe'mee de ser'vitʃiu]

126. Military professions and ranks

private	**soldat** (m)	[sol'dat]
sergeant	**sergent** (m)	[ser'dʒent]

lieutenant	**locotenent** (m)	[lokote'nent]
captain	**căpitan** (m)	[kəpi'tan]
major	**maior** (m)	[ma'jor]
colonel	**colonel** (m)	[kolo'nel]
general	**general** (m)	[ʤene'ral]
marshal	**mareşal** (m)	[mare'ʃal]
admiral	**amiral** (m)	[ami'ral]
military (n)	**militar** (m)	[mili'tar]
soldier	**soldat** (m)	[sol'dat]
officer	**ofiţer** (m)	[ofi'ʦer]
commander	**comandant** (m)	[koman'dant]
border guard	**grănicer** (m)	[grəni'ʧer]
radio operator	**radist** (m)	[ra'dist]
scout (searcher)	**cercetaş** (m)	[ʧerʧe'taʃ]
pioneer (sapper)	**genist** (m)	[ʤe'nist]
marksman	**trăgător** (m)	[trəgə'tor]
navigator	**navigator** (m)	[naviga'tor]

127. Officials. Priests

king	**rege** (m)	['reʤe]
queen	**regină** (f)	[re'ʤinə]
prince	**prinţ** (m)	[prinʦ]
princess	**prinţesă** (f)	[prin'ʦesə]
czar	**ţar** (m)	[ʦar]
czarina	**ţarină** (f)	[ʦa'rinə]
president	**preşedinte** (m)	[preʃə'dinte]
Secretary (minister)	**ministru** (m)	[mi'nistru]
prime minister	**prim-ministru** (m)	['prim mi'nistru]
senator	**senator** (m)	[sena'tor]
diplomat	**diplomat** (m)	[diplo'mat]
consul	**consul** (m)	['konsul]
ambassador	**ambasador** (m)	[ambasa'dor]
counselor (diplomatic officer)	**consilier** (m)	[konsi'ljer]
official, functionary (civil servant)	**funcţionar** (m)	[funkʦio'nar]
prefect	**prefect** (m)	[pre'fekt]
mayor	**primar** (m)	[pri'mar]
judge	**judecător** (m)	[ʒudekə'tor]
prosecutor (e.g., district attorney)	**procuror** (m)	[proku'ror]

missionary	**misionar** (m)	[misio'nar]
monk	**călugăr** (m)	[kə'lugər]
abbot	**abate** (m)	[a'bate]
rabbi	**rabin** (m)	[ra'bin]
vizier	**vizir** (m)	[vi'zir]
shah	**şah** (m)	[ʃah]
sheikh	**şeic** (m)	['ʃejk]

128. Agricultural professions

beekeeper	**apicultor** (m)	[apikul'tor]
herder, shepherd	**păstor** (m)	[pəs'tor]
agronomist	**agronom** (m)	[agro'nom]
cattle breeder	**zootehnician** (m)	[zootehnitʃi'an]
veterinarian	**veterinar** (m)	[veteri'nar]
farmer	**fermier** (m)	[fer'mjer]
winemaker	**vinificator** (m)	[vinifika'tor]
zoologist	**zoolog** (m)	[zoo'log]
cowboy	**cowboy** (m)	['kauboj]

129. Art professions

actor	**actor** (m)	[ak'tor]
actress	**actriță** (f)	[ak'tritsə]
singer (masc.)	**cântăreț** (m)	[kɨntə'rets]
singer (fem.)	**cântăreață** (f)	[kɨntə'rʲatsə]
dancer (masc.)	**dansator** (m)	[dansa'tor]
dancer (fem.)	**dansatoare** (f)	[dansato'are]
performer (masc.)	**artist** (m)	[ar'tist]
performer (fem.)	**artistă** (f)	[ar'tistə]
musician	**muzician** (m)	[muzitʃi'an]
pianist	**pianist** (m)	[pia'nist]
guitar player	**chitarist** (m)	[kita'rist]
conductor (orchestra ~)	**dirijor** (m)	[diri'ʒor]
composer	**compozitor** (m)	[kompo'zitor]
impresario	**impresar** (m)	[impre'sar]
film director	**regizor** (m)	[re'dʒizor]
producer	**producător** (m)	[produkə'tor]
scriptwriter	**scenarist** (m)	[stʃena'rist]
critic	**critic** (m)	['kritik]

writer	**scriitor** (m)	[skrii'tor]
poet	**poet** (m)	[po'et]
sculptor	**sculptor** (m)	['skulptor]
artist (painter)	**pictor** (m)	['piktor]
juggler	**jongler** (m)	[ʒon'gler]
clown	**clovn** (m)	[klovn]
acrobat	**acrobat** (m)	[akro'bat]
magician	**magician** (m)	[madʒitʃi'an]

130. Various professions

doctor	**medic** (m)	['medik]
nurse	**asistentă** (f) **medicală**	[asis'tentə medi'kalə]
psychiatrist	**psihiatru** (m)	[psihi'atru]
dentist	**stomatolog** (m)	[stomato'log]
surgeon	**chirurg** (m)	[ki'rurg]
astronaut	**astronaut** (m)	[astrona'ut]
astronomer	**astronom** (m)	[astro'nom]
pilot	**pilot** (m)	[pi'lot]
driver (of taxi, etc.)	**şofer** (m)	[ʃo'fer]
engineer (train driver)	**maşinist** (m)	[maʃi'nist]
mechanic	**mecanic** (m)	[me'kanik]
miner	**miner** (m)	[mi'ner]
worker	**muncitor** (m)	[muntʃi'tor]
locksmith	**lăcătuş** (m)	[ləkə'tuʃ]
joiner (carpenter)	**tâmplar** (m)	[tɨm'plar]
turner (lathe operator)	**strungar** (m)	[strun'gar]
construction worker	**constructor** (m)	[kon'struktor]
welder	**sudor** (m)	[su'dor]
professor (title)	**profesor** (m)	[pro'fesor]
architect	**arhitect** (m)	[arhi'tekt]
historian	**istoric** (m)	[is'torik]
scientist	**savant** (m)	[sa'vant]
physicist	**fizician** (m)	[fizitʃi'an]
chemist (scientist)	**chimist** (m)	[ki'mist]
archeologist	**arheolog** (m)	[arheo'log]
geologist	**geolog** (m)	[dʒeo'log]
researcher (scientist)	**cercetător** (m)	[tʃertʃetə'tor]
babysitter	**dădacă** (f)	[də'dakə]
teacher, educator	**pedagog** (m)	[peda'gog]
editor	**redactor** (m)	[re'daktor]
editor-in-chief	**redactor-şef** (m)	[re'daktor 'ʃef]

correspondent	**corespondent** (m)	[korespon'dent]
typist (fem.)	**dactilografă** (f)	[daktilo'grafə]
designer	**designer** (m)	[di'zajner]
computer expert	**operator** (m)	[opera'tor]
programmer	**programator** (m)	[programa'tor]
engineer (designer)	**inginer** (m)	[indʒi'ner]
sailor	**marinar** (m)	[mari'nar]
seaman	**marinar** (m)	[mari'nar]
rescuer	**salvator** (m)	[salva'tor]
fireman	**pompier** (m)	[pom'pjer]
police officer	**polițist** (m)	[poli'tsist]
watchman	**paznic** (m)	['paznik]
detective	**detectiv** (m)	[detek'tiv]
customs officer	**vameş** (m)	['vameʃ]
bodyguard	**gardă** (f) **de corp**	['gardə de 'korp]
prison guard	**supraveghetor** (m)	[supravege'tor]
inspector	**inspector** (m)	[in'spektor]
sportsman	**sportiv** (m)	[spor'tiv]
trainer, coach	**antrenor** (m)	[antre'nor]
butcher	**măcelar** (m)	[mətʃe'lar]
cobbler (shoe repairer)	**cizmar** (m)	[tʃiz'mar]
merchant	**comerciant** (m)	[komertʃi'ant]
loader (person)	**hamal** (m)	[ha'mal]
fashion designer	**modelier** (n)	[mode'ljer]
model (fem.)	**model** (n)	[mo'del]

131. Occupations. Social status

schoolboy	**elev** (m)	[e'lev]
student (college ~)	**student** (m)	[stu'dent]
philosopher	**filozof** (m)	[filo'zof]
economist	**economist** (m)	[ekono'mist]
inventor	**inventator** (m)	[inventa'tor]
unemployed (n)	**şomer** (m)	[ʃo'mer]
retiree	**pensionar** (m)	[pensio'nar]
spy, secret agent	**spion** (m)	[spi'on]
prisoner	**arestat** (m)	[ares'tat]
striker	**grevist** (m)	[gre'vist]
bureaucrat	**birocrat** (m)	[biro'krat]
traveler (globetrotter)	**călător** (m)	[kələ'tor]
gay, homosexual (n)	**homosexual** (m)	[homoseksu'al]

hacker	**hacker** (m)	['haker]
bandit	**bandit** (m)	[ban'dit]
hit man, killer	**asasin** (m) **plătit**	[asa'sin plə'tit]
drug addict	**narcoman** (m)	[narko'man]
drug dealer	**vânzător** (m) **de droguri**	[vinzə'tor de 'drogurʲ]
prostitute (fem.)	**prostituată** (f)	[prostitu'atə]
pimp	**proxenet** (m)	[prokse'net]
sorcerer	**vrăjitor** (m)	[vrəʒi'tor]
sorceress (evil ~)	**vrăjitoare** (f)	[vrəʒito'are]
pirate	**pirat** (m)	[pi'rat]
slave	**rob** (m)	[rob]
samurai	**samurai** (m)	[samu'raj]
savage (primitive)	**sălbatic** (m)	[səl'batik]

Sports

132. Kinds of sports. Sportspersons

sportsman	**sportiv** (m)	[spor'tiv]
kind of sports	**gen** (n) **de sport**	['ʤen de 'sport]
basketball	**baschet** (n)	['basket]
basketball player	**baschetbalist** (m)	[basketba'list]
baseball	**base-ball** (n)	['bejsbol]
baseball player	**jucător** (m) **de base-ball**	[ʒukə'tor de 'bejsbol]
soccer	**fotbal** (n)	['fotbal]
soccer player	**fotbalist** (m)	[fotba'list]
goalkeeper	**portar** (m)	[por'tar]
hockey	**hochei** (n)	['hokej]
hockey player	**hocheist** (m)	[hoke'ist]
volleyball	**volei** (n)	['volej]
volleyball player	**voleibalist** (m)	[volejba'list]
boxing	**box** (n)	[boks]
boxer	**boxer** (m)	[bok'ser]
wrestling	**luptă** (f)	['luptə]
wrestler	**luptător** (m)	[luptə'tor]
karate	**carate** (n)	[ka'rate]
karate fighter	**karatist** (m)	[kara'tist]
judo	**judo** (n)	['ʤudo]
judo athlete	**judocan** (m)	[ʤudo'kan]
tennis	**tenis** (n)	['tenis]
tennis player	**tenisman** (m)	[tenis'man]
swimming	**înot** (n)	[i'not]
swimmer	**înotător** (m)	[inotə'tor]
fencing	**scrimă** (f)	['skrimə]
fencer	**jucător** (m) **de scrimă**	[ʒukə'tor de 'skrimə]
chess	**şah** (n)	[ʃah]
chess player	**şahist** (m)	[ʃa'hist]

alpinism	**alpinism** (n)	[alpi'nizm]
alpinist	**alpinist** (m)	[alpi'nist]
running	**alergare** (f)	[aler'gare]
runner	**alergător** (m)	[alergə'tor]
athletics	**atletism** (n)	[atle'tizm]
athlete	**atlet** (m)	[at'let]
horseback riding	**hipism** (n)	[hi'pism]
horse rider	**călăreț** (m)	[kələ'rets]
figure skating	**patinaj** (n) **artistic**	[pati'naʒ ar'tistik]
figure skater (masc.)	**patinator** (m) **artistic**	[patina'tor ar'tistik]
figure skater (fem.)	**patinatore** (f) **artistică**	[patinato'are ar'tistikə]
powerlifting	**atletică** (f) **grea**	[at'letikə grʲa]
powerlifter	**halterofil** (m)	[haltero'fil]
car racing	**raliu** (n)	[ra'liu]
racer (driver)	**pilot** (m) **de curse**	[pi'lot de 'kurse]
cycling	**ciclism** (n)	[tʃi'klizm]
cyclist	**ciclist** (m)	[tʃi'klist]
broad jump	**sărituri** (f pl) **în lungime**	[səri'turʲ ɨn lun'dʒime]
pole vault	**săritură** (f) **cu prăjina**	[səri'turə ku prə'ʒina]
jumper	**săritor** (m)	[səri'tor]

133. Kinds of sports. Miscellaneous

football	**fotbal** (n) **american**	['fotbal ameri'kan]
badminton	**badminton** (n)	[bedmin'ton]
biathlon	**biatlon** (n)	[biat'lon]
billiards	**biliard** (n)	[bi'ljard]
bobsled	**bob** (n)	[bob]
bodybuilding	**culturism** (n)	[kultu'rism]
water polo	**polo** (n) **pe apă**	['polo pe 'apə]
handball	**handbal** (n)	['handbal]
golf	**golf** (n)	[golf]
rowing, crew	**canotaj** (n)	[kano'taʒ]
scuba diving	**scufundare** (f)	[skufun'dare]
cross-country skiing	**concurs** (n) **de schi**	[ko'nkurs de 'ski]
table tennis (ping-pong)	**tenis** (n) **de masă**	['tenis de 'masə]
sailing	**iahting** (n)	['jahting]
rally racing	**raliu** (n)	[ra'liu]
rugby	**rugby** (n)	['regbi]

snowboarding	**snowboard** (n)	[snou'bord]
archery	**tragere** (f) **cu arcul**	['tradʒere 'ku 'arkul]

134. Gym

barbell	**halteră** (f)	[hal'terə]
dumbbells	**haltere** (f pl)	['haltere]
training machine	**dispozitiv** (n) **pentru antrenament**	[dispozi'tiv 'pentru antrena'ment]
exercise bicycle	**bicicletă** (f)	[bitʃi'kletə]
treadmill	**pistă** (f) **de alergare**	['pistə de aler'gare]
horizontal bar	**bară** (f)	['barə]
parallel bars	**bare** (f pl)	['bare]
vault (vaulting horse)	**cal** (m) **de gimnastică**	['kal de dʒim'nastikə]
mat (exercise ~)	**saltea** (f)	[sal'tʲa]
jump rope	**coardă** (f)	[ko'ardə]
aerobics	**aerobică** (f)	[ae'robikə]
yoga	**yoga** (f)	['joga]

135. Hockey

hockey	**hochei** (n)	['hokej]
hockey player	**hocheist** (m)	[hoke'ist]
to play hockey	**a juca hochei**	[a ʒu'ka 'hokej]
ice	**gheață** (f)	['gʲatsə]
puck	**puc** (n)	[puk]
hockey stick	**crosă** (f)	['krosə]
ice skates	**patine** (f pl)	[pa'tine]
board (ice hockey rink ~)	**bandă** (f)	['bandə]
shot	**lovitură** (f)	[lovi'turə]
goaltender	**portar** (m)	[por'tar]
goal (score)	**gol** (n)	[gol]
to score a goal	**a marca un gol**	[a mar'ka un gol]
period	**repriză** (f)	[re'prizə]
substitutes bench	**bancă** (f) **de rezervă**	['bankə de re'zervə]

136. Soccer

soccer	**fotbal** (n)	['fotbal]
soccer player	**fotbalist** (m)	[fotba'list]

to play soccer	**a juca fotbal**	[a ʒu'ka 'fotbal]
major league	**ligă** (f) **superioară**	['ligə superio'arə]
soccer club	**club** (n) **de fotbal**	['klub de 'fotbal]
coach	**antrenor** (m)	[antre'nor]
owner, proprietor	**proprietar** (m)	[proprie'tar]
team	**echipă** (f)	[e'kipə]
team captain	**căpitanul** (m) **echipei**	[kəpi'tanul e'kipej]
player	**jucător** (m)	[ʒukə'tor]
substitute	**jucător** (m) **de rezervă**	[ʒukə'tor de re'zervə]
forward	**atacant** (m)	[ata'kant]
center forward	**atacant** (m) **la centru**	[ata'kant la 'ʧentru]
scorer	**golgheter** (m)	[gol'geter]
defender, back	**apărător** (m)	[apərə'tor]
midfielder, halfback	**mijlocaş** (m)	[miʒlo'kaʃ]
match	**meci** (n)	['meʧi]
to meet (vi, vt)	**a se întâlni**	[a se ɨntɨl'ni]
final	**finală** (f)	[fi'nalə]
semi-final	**semifinală** (f)	[semifi'nalə]
championship	**campionat** (n)	[kampio'nat]
period, half	**repriză** (f)	[re'prizə]
first period	**prima repriză** (f)	['prima re'prizə]
half-time	**pauză** (f)	['pauzə]
goal	**poartă** (f)	[po'artə]
goalkeeper	**portar** (m)	[por'tar]
goalpost	**bară** (f)	['barə]
crossbar	**bară** (f) **transversală**	['barə transver'salə]
net	**plasă** (f)	['plasə]
to concede a goal	**a rata gol**	[a rə'ta gol]
ball	**minge** (f)	['minʤe]
pass	**pasă** (f)	['pasə]
kick	**lovitură** (f)	[lovi'turə]
to kick (~ the ball)	**a da o lovitură**	[a da o lovi'turə]
free kick (direct ~)	**lovitură** (f) **de pedeapsă**	[lovi'turə de pe'dʲapsə]
corner kick	**lovitură** (f) **de colț**	[lovi'turə de 'kolʦ]
attack	**atac** (n)	[a'tak]
counterattack	**contraatac** (n)	[kontraa'tak]
combination	**combinație** (f)	[kombi'naʦie]
referee	**arbitru** (m)	[ar'bitru]
to blow the whistle	**a fluiera**	[a flue'ra]
whistle (sound)	**fluier** (n)	['flujer]
foul, misconduct	**încălcare** (f)	[ɨnkəl'kare]
to commit a foul	**a încălca**	[a ɨnkəl'ka]
to send off	**a elimina de pe teren**	[a elimi'na de pe te'ren]
yellow card	**cartonaş** (n) **galben**	[karto'naʃ 'galben]

red card	**cartonaş** (n) **roşu**	[karto'naʃ 'roʃu]
disqualification	**descalificare** (f)	[deskalifi'kare]
to disqualify (vt)	**a descalifica**	[a deskalifi'ka]
penalty kick	**penalti** (n)	[pe'nalti]
wall	**perete** (m)	[pe'rete]
to score (vi, vt)	**a marca**	[a mar'ka]
goal (score)	**gol** (n)	[gol]
to score a goal	**a marca un gol**	[a mar'ka un gol]
substitution	**înlocuire** (f)	[ɨnloku'ire]
to replace (a player)	**a înlocui**	[a ɨnloku'i]
rules	**reguli** (f pl)	['regulʲ]
tactics	**tactică** (f)	['taktikə]
stadium	**stadion** (n)	[stadi'on]
stand (bleachers)	**tribună** (f)	[tri'bunə]
fan, supporter	**suporter** (m)	[su'porter]
to shout (vi)	**a striga**	[a stri'ga]
scoreboard	**tablă** (f)	['tablə]
score	**scor** (n)	[skor]
defeat	**înfrângere** (f)	[ɨn'frɨnʤere]
to lose (not win)	**a pierde**	[a 'pjerde]
tie	**egalitate** (f)	[egali'tate]
to tie (vi)	**a juca la egalitate**	[a ʒu'ka la egali'tate]
victory	**victorie** (f)	[vik'torie]
to win (vi, vt)	**a învinge**	[a ɨn'vinʤe]
champion	**campion** (m)	[kampi'on]
best (adj)	**cel mai bun**	[ʧel maj bun]
to congratulate (vt)	**a felicita**	[a feliʧi'ta]
commentator	**comentator** (m)	[komenta'tor]
to commentate (vt)	**a comenta**	[a komen'ta]
broadcast	**transmisiune** (f)	[trans'misjune]

137. Alpine skiing

skis	**schiuri** (n)	['skjurʲ]
to ski (vi)	**a schia**	[a ski'a]
mountain-ski resort	**stațiune** (f) **de schi montan**	[staʦi'une de ski mon'tan]
ski lift	**ascensor** (m)	[asʧen'sor]
ski poles	**bețe** (n pl)	['beʦe]
slope	**pantă** (f)	['pantə]
slalom	**slalom** (n)	['slalom]

138. Tennis. Golf

golf	**golf** (n)	[golf]
golf club	**club** (n) **de golf**	['klub de 'golf]
golfer	**jucător** (m) **de golf**	[ʒukə'tor de 'golf]
hole	**gaură** (f)	['gaurə]
club	**crosă** (f)	['krosə]
golf trolley	**cărucior** (n) **pentru crose**	[kəru'tʃior 'pentru 'krose]
tennis	**tenis** (n)	['tenis]
tennis court	**teren** (n) **de tenis**	[te'ren de 'tenis]
serve	**serviciu** (n)	[ser'vitʃiu]
to serve (vt)	**a servi**	[a ser'vi]
racket	**paletă** (f)	[pa'letə]
net	**plasă** (f)	['plasə]
ball	**minge** (f)	['mindʒe]

139. Chess

chess	**şah** (n)	[ʃah]
chessmen	**piese** (f pl)	['pjese]
chess player	**şahist** (m)	[ʃa'hist]
chessboard	**tablă** (f) **de şah**	['tablə de ʃah]
chessman	**piesă** (f)	['pjesə]
White (white pieces)	**piese** (f pl) **albe**	['pjese 'albe]
Black (black pieces)	**piese** (f pl) **negre**	['pjese 'negre]
pawn	**pion** (m)	[pi'on]
bishop	**nebun** (m)	[ne'bun]
knight	**cal** (m)	[kal]
rook	**turn** (n)	[turn]
queen	**regină** (f)	[re'dʒinə]
king	**rege** (m)	['redʒe]
move	**mutare** (f)	[mu'tare]
to move (vi, vt)	**a muta**	[a mu'ta]
to sacrifice (vt)	**a sacrifica**	[a sakrifi'ka]
castling	**rocadă** (f)	[ro'kadə]
check	**şah** (n)	[ʃah]
checkmate	**mat** (n)	[mat]
chess tournament	**turneu** (n) **de şah**	[tur'neu de ʃah]
Grand Master	**mare maestru** (m)	['mare ma'estru]
combination	**combinaţie** (f)	[kombi'natsie]
game (in chess)	**partidă** (f)	[par'tidə]
checkers	**joc** (n) **de dame**	[ʒok de 'dame]

140. Boxing

boxing	**box** (n)	[boks]
fight (bout)	**luptă** (f)	['luptə]
boxing match	**duel** (n)	[du'el]
round (in boxing)	**rundă** (f)	['rundə]
ring	**ring** (n)	[ring]
gong	**gong** (n)	[gong]
punch	**lovitură** (f)	[lovi'turə]
knockdown	**cnocdaun** (n)	['knokdaun]
knockout	**cnocaut** (n)	['knokaut]
to knock out	**a face cnocaut**	[a 'fatʃe 'knokaut]
boxing glove	**mănuşă** (f) **de box**	[mə'nuʃə de 'boks]
referee	**arbitru** (m)	[ar'bitru]
lightweight	**categorie** (f) **uşoară**	[katego'rie uʃo'arə]
middleweight	**categorie** (f) **mijlocie**	[katego'rie miʒlo'tʃie]
heavyweight	**categorie** (f) **grea**	[katego'rie grʲa]

141. Sports. Miscellaneous

Olympic Games	**Jocuri** (n pl) **Olimpice**	['ʒokurʲ o'limpitʃe]
winner	**învingător** (m)	[ɨnvingə'tor]
to be winning	**a învinge**	[a ɨn'vindʒe]
to win (vi)	**a câştiga**	[a kɨʃti'ga]
leader	**lider** (m)	['lider]
to lead (vi)	**a fi în fruntea**	[a fi ɨn 'fruntʲa]
first place	**primul loc** (n)	['primul lok]
second place	**al doilea loc** (n)	[al 'dojlʲa lok]
third place	**al treilea loc** (n)	[al 'trejlʲa lok]
medal	**medalie** (f)	[me'dalie]
trophy	**trofeu** (n)	[tro'feu]
prize cup (trophy)	**cupă** (f)	['kupə]
prize (in game)	**premiu** (n)	['premju]
main prize	**premiul** (n) **principal**	['premjul printʃi'pal]
record	**record** (n)	[re'kord]
to set a record	**a bate recordul**	[a 'bate re'kordul]
final	**finală** (f)	[fi'nalə]
final (adj)	**final**	[fi'nal]
champion	**campion** (m)	[kampi'on]
championship	**campionat** (n)	[kampio'nat]

stadium	**stadion** (n)	[stadi'on]
stand (bleachers)	**tribună** (f)	[tri'bunə]
fan, supporter	**suporter** (m)	[su'porter]
opponent, rival	**adversar** (m)	[adver'sar]
start (start line)	**start** (n)	[start]
finish line	**finiş** (n)	['finiʃ]
defeat	**înfrângere** (f)	[ɨn'frɨndʒere]
to lose (not win)	**a pierde**	[a 'pjerde]
referee	**arbitru** (m)	[ar'bitru]
jury (judges)	**juriu** (n)	['ʒurju]
score	**scor** (n)	[skor]
tie	**egalitate** (f)	[egali'tate]
to tie (vi)	**a juca la egalitate**	[a ʒu'ka la egali'tate]
point	**punct** (n)	[punkt]
result (final score)	**rezultat** (n)	[rezul'tat]
period	**repriză** (f)	[re'prizə]
half-time	**pauză** (f)	['pauzə]
doping	**dopaj** (n)	[do'paʒ]
to penalize (vt)	**a penaliza**	[a penali'za]
to disqualify (vt)	**a descalifica**	[a deskalifi'ka]
apparatus	**aparat** (n)	[apa'rat]
javelin	**suliță** (f)	['sulitsə]
shot (metal ball)	**greutate** (f)	[greu'tate]
ball (snooker, etc.)	**bilă** (f)	['bilə]
aim (target)	**țintă** (f)	['tsintə]
target	**țintă** (f)	['tsintə]
to shoot (vi)	**a trage**	[a 'tradʒə]
accurate (~ shot)	**exact**	[e'gzakt]
trainer, coach	**antrenor** (m)	[antre'nor]
to train (sb)	**a antrena**	[a antre'na]
to train (vi)	**a se antrena**	[a se antre'na]
training	**antrenament** (n)	[antrena'ment]
gym	**sală** (f) **de sport**	['salə de sport]
exercise (physical)	**exercițiu** (n)	[egzer'tʃitsju]
warm-up (athlete ~)	**încălzire** (f)	[ɨnkəl'zire]

Education

142. School

school	**şcoală** (f)	[ʃko'alə]
principal (headmaster)	**director** (m)	[di'rektor]
pupil (boy)	**elev** (m)	[e'lev]
pupil (girl)	**elevă** (f)	[e'levə]
schoolboy	**elev** (m)	[e'lev]
schoolgirl	**elevă** (f)	[e'levə]
to teach (sb)	**a învăţa**	[a ɨnvə'ʦa]
to learn (language, etc.)	**a învăţa**	[a ɨnvə'ʦa]
to learn by heart	**a învăţa pe de rost**	[a ɨnvə'ʦa pe de rost]
to learn (~ to count, etc.)	**a învăţa**	[a ɨnvə'ʦa]
to be in school	**a merge la şcoală**	[a 'merʤe la ʃko'alə]
to go to school	**a merge la şcoală**	[a 'merʤe la ʃko'alə]
alphabet	**alfabet** (n)	[alfa'bet]
subject (at school)	**disciplină** (f)	[disʧi'plinə]
classroom	**clasă** (f)	['klasə]
lesson	**lecţie** (f)	['lekʦie]
recess	**recreaţie** (f)	[rekre'aʦie]
school bell	**sunet** (n)	['sunet]
school desk	**bancă** (f)	['bankə]
chalkboard	**tablă** (f)	['tablə]
grade	**notă** (f)	['notə]
good grade	**notă** (f) **bună**	['notə 'bunə]
bad grade	**notă** (f) **rea**	['notə rʲa]
to give a grade	**a pune notă**	[a 'pune 'notə]
mistake, error	**greşeală** (f)	[gre'ʃalə]
to make mistakes	**a greşi**	[a gre'ʃi]
to correct (an error)	**a corecta**	[a korek'ta]
cheat sheet	**fiţuică** (f)	[fi'ʦujkə]
homework	**temă** (f) **pentru acasă**	['temə 'pentru a'kasə]
exercise (in education)	**exerciţiu** (n)	[egzer'ʧiʦju]
to be present	**a fi prezent**	[a fi pre'zent]
to be absent	**a lipsi**	[a lip'si]
to punish (vt)	**a pedepsi**	[a pedep'si]

punishment	**pedeapsă** (f)	[pe'dʲapsə]
conduct (behavior)	**comportament** (n)	[komporta'ment]
report card	**agendă** (f)	[a'dʒendə]
pencil	**creion** (n)	[kre'jon]
eraser	**radieră** (f)	[radi'erə]
chalk	**cretă** (f)	['kretə]
pencil case	**penar** (n)	[pe'nar]
schoolbag	**ghiozdan** (n)	[goz'dan]
pen	**pix** (n)	[piks]
school notebook	**caiet** (n)	[ka'et]
textbook	**manual** (n)	[manu'al]
drafting compass	**compas** (n)	[kom'pas]
to make technical drawings	**a schița**	[a ski'ʦa]
technical drawing	**plan** (n)	[plan]
poem	**poezie** (f)	[poe'zie]
by heart (adv)	**pe de rost**	[pe de rost]
to learn by heart	**a învăța pe de rost**	[a ɨnvə'ʦa pe de rost]
school vacation	**vacanță** (f)	[va'kanʦə]
to be on vacation	**a fi în vacanță**	[a fi ɨn va'kanʦə]
test (written math ~)	**lucrare** (f) **de control**	[lu'krare de kon'trol]
essay (composition)	**compunere** (f)	[kom'punere]
dictation	**dictare** (f)	[dik'tare]
exam (examination)	**examen** (n)	[e'gzamen]
to take an exam	**a da examene**	[a da e'gzamene]
experiment (e.g., chemistry ~)	**experiment** (f)	[eksperi'ment]

143. College. University

academy	**academie** (f)	[akade'mie]
university	**universitate** (f)	[universi'tate]
faculty (e.g., ~ of Medicine)	**facultate** (f)	[fakul'tate]
student (masc.)	**student** (m)	[stu'dent]
student (fem.)	**studentă** (f)	[stu'dentə]
lecturer (teacher)	**profesor** (m)	[pro'fesor]
lecture hall, room	**aulă** (f)	[a'ulə]
graduate	**absolvent** (m)	[absol'vent]
diploma	**diplomă** (f)	['diplomə]
dissertation	**disertație** (f)	[diser'taʦie]
study (report)	**cercetare** (f)	[ʧerʧe'tare]

laboratory	**laborator** (n)	[labora'tor]
lecture	**prelegere** (f)	[pre'ledʒere]
coursemate	**coleg** (m) **de an**	[ko'leg de an]
scholarship	**bursă** (f)	['bursə]
academic degree	**titlu** (n) **științific**	['titlu ʃtiin'ʦifik]

144. Sciences. Disciplines

mathematics	**matematică** (f)	[mate'matikə]
algebra	**algebră** (f)	[al'dʒebrə]
geometry	**geometrie** (f)	[dʒeome'trie]
astronomy	**astronomie** (f)	[astrono'mie]
biology	**biologie** (f)	[biolo'dʒie]
geography	**geografie** (f)	[dʒeogra'fie]
geology	**geologie** (f)	[dʒeolo'dʒie]
history	**istorie** (f)	[is'torie]
medicine	**medicină** (f)	[medi'ʧinə]
pedagogy	**pedagogie** (f)	[pedago'dʒie]
law	**drept** (n)	[drept]
physics	**fizică** (f)	['fizikə]
chemistry	**chimie** (f)	[ki'mie]
philosophy	**filozofie** (f)	[filozo'fie]
psychology	**psihologie** (f)	[psiholo'dʒie]

145. Writing system. Orthography

grammar	**gramatică** (f)	[gra'matikə]
vocabulary	**lexic** (n)	['leksik]
phonetics	**fonetică** (f)	[fo'netikə]
noun	**substantiv** (n)	[substan'tiv]
adjective	**adjectiv** (n)	[adʒek'tiv]
verb	**verb** (n)	[verb]
adverb	**adverb** (n)	[ad'verb]
pronoun	**pronume** (n)	[pro'nume]
interjection	**interjecție** (f)	[inter'ʒekʦie]
preposition	**prepoziție** (f)	[prepo'ziʦie]
root	**rădăcina** (f) **cuvântului**	[rədə'ʧina ku'vintuluj]
ending	**terminație** (f)	[termi'naʦie]
prefix	**prefix** (n)	[pre'fiks]
syllable	**silabă** (f)	[si'labə]
suffix	**sufix** (n)	[su'fiks]
stress mark	**accent** (n)	[ak'ʧent]

apostrophe	**apostrof** (n)	[apo'strof]
period, dot	**punct** (n)	[punkt]
comma	**virgulă** (f)	['virgulə]
semicolon	**punct** (n) **şi virgulă**	[punkt ʃi 'virgulə]
colon	**două puncte** (n pl)	['dowə 'punkte]
ellipsis	**puncte-puncte** (n pl)	['punkte 'punkte]
question mark	**semn** (n) **de întrebare**	[semn de ɨntre'bare]
exclamation point	**semn** (n) **de exclamare**	[semn de ekskla'mare]
quotation marks	**ghilimele** (f pl)	[gili'mele]
in quotation marks	**în ghilimele**	[ɨn gili'mele]
parenthesis	**paranteze** (f pl)	[paran'teze]
in parenthesis	**în paranteze**	[ɨn paran'teze]
hyphen	**cratimă** (f)	['kratimə]
dash	**cratimă** (f)	['kratimə]
space (between words)	**spațiu** (n) **liber**	['spatsju 'liber]
letter	**literă** (f)	['literə]
capital letter	**majusculă** (f)	[ma'ʒuskulʲa]
vowel (n)	**vocală** (f)	[vo'kalə]
consonant (n)	**consoană** (f)	[konso'anə]
sentence	**prepoziție** (f)	[prepo'zitsie]
subject	**subiect** (n)	[su'bjekt]
predicate	**predicat** (n)	[predi'kat]
line	**rând** (n)	[rɨnd]
on a new line	**alineat**	[aline'at]
paragraph	**paragraf** (n)	[para'graf]
word	**cuvânt** (n)	[ku'vɨnt]
group of words	**îmbinare** (f) **de cuvinte**	[ɨmbi'nare de ku'vinte]
expression	**expresie** (f)	[eks'presie]
synonym	**sinonim** (n)	[sino'nim]
antonym	**antonim** (n)	[anto'nim]
rule	**regulă** (f)	['regulə]
exception	**excepție** (f)	[eks'tʃeptsie]
correct (adj)	**corect**	[ko'rekt]
conjugation	**conjugare** (f)	[konʒu'gare]
declension	**declinare** (f)	[dekli'nare]
nominal case	**caz** (n)	[kaz]
question	**întrebare** (f)	[ɨntre'bare]
to underline (vt)	**a sublinia**	[a sublini'a]
dotted line	**linie** (f) **punctată**	['linie punk'tatə]

146. Foreign languages

language	**limbă** (f)	['limbə]
foreign (adj)	**străin**	[strə'in]
foreign language	**limbă** (f) **străină**	['limbə strə'inə]
to study (vt)	**a studia**	[a studi'a]
to learn (language, etc.)	**a învăța**	[a ɨnvə'tsa]
to read (vi, vt)	**a citi**	[a tʃi'ti]
to speak (vi, vt)	**a vorbi**	[a vor'bi]
to understand (vt)	**a înțelege**	[a ɨntse'ledʒe]
to write (vt)	**a scrie**	[a 'skrie]
fast (adv)	**repede**	['repede]
slowly (adv)	**încet**	[ɨn'tʃet]
fluently (adv)	**liber**	['liber]
rules	**reguli** (f pl)	['regulʲ]
grammar	**gramatică** (f)	[gra'matikə]
vocabulary	**lexic** (n)	['leksik]
phonetics	**fonetică** (f)	[fo'netikə]
textbook	**manual** (n)	[manu'al]
dictionary	**dicționar** (n)	[diktsio'nar]
teach-yourself book	**manual** (n) **autodidactic**	[manu'al autodi'daktik]
phrasebook	**ghid** (n) **de conversație**	[gid de konver'satsie]
cassette, tape	**casetă** (f)	[ka'setə]
videotape	**casetă** (f) **video**	[ka'setə 'video]
CD, compact disc	**CD** (n)	[si'di]
DVD	**DVD** (n)	[divi'di]
alphabet	**alfabet** (n)	[alfa'bet]
to spell (vt)	**a spune pe litere**	[a vor'bi pe 'litere]
pronunciation	**pronunție** (f)	[pro'nuntsie]
accent	**accent** (n)	[ak'tʃent]
with an accent	**cu accent**	['ku ak'tʃent]
without an accent	**fără accent**	['fərə ak'tʃent]
word	**cuvânt** (n)	[ku'vɨnt]
meaning	**sens** (n)	[sens]
course (e.g., a French ~)	**cursuri** (n)	['kursurʲ]
to sign up	**a se înscrie**	[a se ɨn'skrie]
teacher	**profesor** (m)	[pro'fesor]
translation (process)	**traducere** (f)	[tra'dutʃere]
translation (text, etc.)	**traducere** (f)	[tra'dutʃere]
translator	**traducător** (m)	[tradukə'tor]
interpreter	**translator** (m)	[trans'lator]

polyglot	**poliglot** (m)	[poli'glot]
memory	**memorie** (f)	[me'morie]

147. Fairy tale characters

Santa Claus	**Santa Claus** (m)	['santa 'klaus]
Cinderella	**Cenuşăreasa** (f)	[ʧenuʃə'rʲasə]
mermaid	**sirenă** (f)	[si'renə]
Neptune	**Neptun** (m)	[nep'tun]
magician, wizard	**vrăjitor** (m)	[vrəʒi'tor]
fairy	**vrăjitoare** (f)	[vrəʒito'are]
magic (adj)	**miraculos**	[miraku'los]
magic wand	**baghetă** (f) **magică**	[ba'getə 'madʒikə]
fairy tale	**poveste** (f)	[po'veste]
miracle	**minune** (f)	[mi'nune]
dwarf	**gnom** (m)	[gnom]
to turn into ...	**a se preface în ...**	[a se pre'faʧe ɨn]
ghost	**stafie** (f)	[sta'fie]
phantom	**fantomă** (f)	[fan'tomə]
monster	**monstru** (m)	['monstru]
dragon	**dragon** (m)	[dra'gon]
giant	**uriaş** (m)	[uri'aʃ]

148. Zodiac Signs

Aries	**Berbec** (m)	[ber'bek]
Taurus	**Taur** (m)	['taur]
Gemini	**Gemeni** (m pl)	['dʒemenʲ]
Cancer	**Rac** (m)	[rak]
Leo	**Leu** (m)	['leu]
Virgo	**Fecioară** (f)	[feʧio'arə]
Libra	**Balanță** (f)	[ba'lantsə]
Scorpio	**Scorpion** (m)	[skorpi'on]
Sagittarius	**Săgetător** (m)	[sədʒetə'tor]
Capricorn	**Capricorn** (m)	[kapri'korn]
Aquarius	**Vărsător** (m)	[vərsə'tor]
Pisces	**Peşti** (m pl)	[peʃtʲ]
character	**caracter** (m)	[karak'ter]
character traits	**trăsături** (f pl) **de caracter**	[trəsə'turʲ de karak'ter]
behavior	**comportament** (n)	[komporta'ment]
to tell fortunes	**a prezice**	[a pre'ziʧe]
fortune-teller	**prezicătoare** (f)	[prezikəto'are]
horoscope	**horoscop** (n)	[horo'skop]

Arts

149. Theater

theater	**teatru** (n)	[te'atru]
opera	**operă** (f)	['operə]
operetta	**operetă** (f)	[ope'retə]
ballet	**balet** (n)	[ba'let]
theater poster	**afiş** (n)	[a'fiʃ]
troupe (theatrical company)	**trupă** (f)	['trupə]
tour	**turneu** (n)	[tur'neu]
to be on tour	**a juca în turneu**	[a ʒu'ka ɨn tur'neu]
to rehearse (vi, vt)	**a repeta**	[a repe'ta]
rehearsal	**repetiție** (f)	[repe'tiʦie]
repertoire	**repertoriu** (n)	[reper'torju]
performance	**reprezentație** (f)	[rəprəzən'tatje]
theatrical show	**spectacol** (n)	[spekta'kol]
play	**piesă** (f) **de teatru**	['pjesə de te'atru]
ticket	**bilet** (n)	[bi'let]
box office (ticket booth)	**casă** (f) **de bilete**	['kasə de bi'lete]
lobby, foyer	**hol** (n)	[hol]
coat check (cloakroom)	**garderobă** (f)	[garde'robə]
coat check tag	**număr** (n)	['numər]
binoculars	**binoclu** (n)	[bi'noklu]
usher	**controlor** (m)	[kontro'lor]
orchestra seats	**parter** (n)	[par'ter]
balcony	**balcon** (n)	[bal'kon]
dress circle	**mezanin** (n)	[meza'nin]
box	**lojă** (f)	['loʒə]
row	**rând** (n)	[rɨnd]
seat	**loc** (n)	[lok]
audience	**public** (n)	['publik]
spectator	**spectator** (m)	[spekta'tor]
to clap (vi, vt)	**a aplauda**	[a aplau'da]
applause	**aplauze** (f pl)	[ap'lauze]
ovation	**ovații** (f pl)	[o'vaʦij]
stage	**scenă** (f)	['sʧenə]
curtain	**cortină** (f)	[kor'tinə]
scenery	**decor** (n)	[de'kor]

backstage	**culise** (f)	[ku'lise]
scene (e.g., the last ~)	**scenă** (f)	['sʧenə]
act	**act** (n)	[akt]
intermission	**antract** (n)	[an'trakt]

150. Cinema

actor	**actor** (m)	[ak'tor]
actress	**actriță** (f)	[ak'tritsə]
movies (industry)	**cinema** (n)	[ʧine'ma]
movie	**film** (n)	[film]
episode	**serie** (f)	['serie]
detective movie	**detectiv** (n)	[detek'tiv]
action movie	**film** (n) **de acțiune**	['film de aktsi'une]
adventure movie	**film** (n) **de aventură**	['film de aven'turə]
sci-fi movie	**film** (n) **fantastic**	['film fan'tastik]
horror movie	**film** (m) **de groază**	['film de gro'azə]
comedy movie	**comedie** (f)	[kome'die]
melodrama	**melodramă** (f)	[melo'dramə]
drama	**dramă** (f)	['dramə]
fictional movie	**film** (n) **artistic**	[film ar'tistik]
documentary	**film** (n) **documentar**	[film dokumen'tar]
cartoon	**desene** (n) **animate**	[de'sene ani'mate]
silent movies	**film** (n) **mut**	[film mut]
role (part)	**rol** (n)	[rol]
leading role	**rolul** (n) **principal**	['rolul prinʧi'pal]
to play (vi, vt)	**a juca**	[a ʒu'ka]
movie star	**stea** (f) **de cinema**	[st'a de ʧine'ma]
well-known (adj)	**cunoscut**	[kunos'kut]
famous (adj)	**vestit**	[ves'tit]
popular (adj)	**popular**	[popu'lar]
script (screenplay)	**scenariu** (n)	[sʧe'narju]
scriptwriter	**scenarist** (m)	[sʧena'rist]
movie director	**regizor** (m)	[re'ʤizor]
producer	**producător** (m)	[produkə'tor]
assistant	**asistent** (m)	[asis'tent]
cameraman	**operator** (m)	[opera'tor]
stuntman	**cascador** (m)	[kaska'dor]
double (stand-in)	**dublură** (f)	[du'blurə]
to shoot a movie	**a turna un film**	[a tur'na un film]
audition, screen test	**probe** (f pl)	['probe]
shooting	**filmări** (f pl)	[filmərʲ]

movie crew	**echipă** (f) **de filmare**	[e'kipə de fil'mare]
movie set	**teren** (n) **de filmare**	[te'ren de fil'mare]
camera	**cameră** (f) **de luat vederi**	['kamerə de lu'at ve'derʲ]
movie theater	**cinematograf** (n)	[ʧinemato'graf]
screen (e.g., big ~)	**ecran** (n)	[e'kran]
to show a movie	**a prezenta un film**	[a prezen'ta 'un 'film]
soundtrack	**linie** (f) **sonoră**	['linie so'norə]
special effects	**efecte** (n pl) **speciale**	[e'fekte speʧi'ale]
subtitles	**subtitluri** (n pl)	[sub'titlurʲ]
credits	**titrări** (f pl)	[tit'rərʲ]
translation	**traducere** (f)	[tra'duʧere]

151. Painting

art	**artă** (f)	['artə]
fine arts	**arte** (f pl) **frumoase**	['arte frumo'ase]
art gallery	**galerie** (f)	[gale'rie]
art exhibition	**expoziție** (f) **de tablouri**	[ekspo'zitsie de tab'lourʲ]
painting (art)	**pictură** (f)	[pik'turə]
graphic art	**grafică** (f)	['grafikə]
abstract art	**abstracționism** (n)	[abstraktsio'nism]
impressionism	**impresionism** (n)	[impresio'nism]
picture (painting)	**tablou** (n)	[tab'lou]
drawing	**desen** (n)	[de'sen]
poster	**afiş** (n)	[a'fiʃ]
illustration (picture)	**ilustrație** (f)	[ilus'tratsie]
miniature	**miniatură** (f)	[minia'turə]
copy (of painting, etc.)	**copie** (f)	['kopie]
reproduction	**reproducere** (f)	[repro'duʧere]
mosaic	**mozaic** (n)	[moza'ik]
stained glass window	**vitraliu** (n)	[vi'tralju]
fresco	**frescă** (f)	['freskə]
engraving	**gravură** (f)	[gra'vurə]
bust (sculpture)	**bust** (n)	[bust]
sculpture	**sculptură** (f)	[skulp'turə]
statue	**statuie** (f)	[sta'tue]
plaster of Paris	**ghips** (n)	[gips]
plaster (as adj)	**de, din ghips**	[de, din gips]
portrait	**portret** (n)	[por'tret]
self-portrait	**autoportret** (n)	[autopor'tret]
landscape painting	**peisaj** (n)	[pej'saʒ]
still life	**natură** (f) **moartă**	[na'turə mo'artə]

caricature	**caricatură** (f)	[karika'turə]
paint	**vopsea** (f)	[vop'sja]
watercolor paint	**acuarelă** (f)	[akua'relə]
oil (paint)	**ulei** (n)	[u'lej]
pencil	**creion** (n)	[kre'jon]
India ink	**tuş** (n)	[tuʃ]
charcoal	**cărbune** (m)	[kər'bune]
to draw (vi, vt)	**a schița**	[a ski'ʦa]
to paint (vi, vt)	**a schița**	[a ski'ʦa]
to pose (vi)	**a poza**	[a po'za]
artist's model (masc.)	**naturist** (m)	[natu'rist]
artist's model (fem.)	**naturistă** (f)	[natu'ristə]
artist (painter)	**pictor** (m)	['piktor]
work of art	**operă** (f)	['operə]
masterpiece	**capodoperă** (f)	[kapo'doperə]
studio (artist's workroom)	**atelier** (n)	[ate'ljer]
canvas (cloth)	**pânză** (f)	['pɨnzə]
easel	**şevalet** (n)	[ʃəva'let]
palette	**paletă** (f)	[pa'letə]
frame (picture ~, etc.)	**ramă** (f)	['ramə]
restoration	**restaurare** (f)	[restau'rare]
to restore (vt)	**a restaura**	[a restau'ra]

152. Literature & Poetry

literature	**literatură** (f)	[litera'turə]
author (writer)	**autor** (m)	[au'tor]
pseudonym	**pseudonim** (n)	[pseudo'nim]
book	**carte** (f)	['karte]
volume	**volum** (n)	[vo'lum]
table of contents	**cuprins** (n)	[ku'prins]
page	**pagină** (f)	['paʤinə]
main character	**erou** (m) **principal**	[e'rou prinʧi'pal]
autograph	**autograf** (n)	[auto'graf]
short story	**povestire** (f)	[poves'tire]
story (novella)	**nuvelă** (f)	[nu'velə]
novel	**roman** (n)	[ro'man]
work (writing)	**compunere** (f)	[kom'punere]
fable	**fabulă** (f)	['fabulə]
detective novel	**detectiv** (m)	[detek'tiv]
poem (verse)	**poezie** (f)	[poe'zie]
poetry	**poezie** (f)	[poe'zie]
poem (epic, ballad)	**poem** (n)	[po'em]

poet	**poet** (m)	[po'et]
fiction	**literatură** (f) **artistică**	[litera'turə ar'tistikə]
science fiction	**science fiction** (n)	['saens 'fikʃn]
adventures	**aventură** (f)	[aven'turə]
educational literature	**literatură** (f) **ştiinţifică**	[litera'turə ʃtiin'ʦifikə]
children's literature	**literatură** (f) **pentru copii**	[litera'turə 'pentru ko'pij]

153. Circus

circus	**circ** (n)	[ʧirk]
traveling circus	**circ** (n) **pe roţi**	[ʧirk pe 'roʦ]
program	**program** (n)	[pro'gram]
performance	**spectacol** (n)	[spekta'kol]
act (circus ~)	**număr** (n)	['numər]
circus ring	**arenă** (f)	[a'renə]
pantomime (act)	**pantomimă** (f)	[panto'mimə]
clown	**clovn** (m)	[klovn]
acrobat	**acrobat** (m)	[akro'bat]
acrobatics	**acrobatică** (f)	[akro'batikə]
gymnast	**gimnast** (m)	[dʒim'nast]
acrobatic gymnastics	**gimnastică** (f)	[dʒim'nastikə]
somersault	**tumbă** (f)	['tumbə]
athlete (strongman)	**atlet** (m)	[at'let]
tamer (e.g., lion ~)	**îmblânzitor** (m)	[imblɨnzi'tor]
rider (circus horse ~)	**călăreţ** (m)	[kələ'reʦ]
assistant	**asistent** (m)	[asis'tent]
stunt	**truc** (n)	[truk]
magic trick	**scamatorie** (f)	[skama'torie]
conjurer, magician	**scamator** (m)	[skama'tor]
juggler	**jongler** (m)	[ʒon'gler]
to juggle (vi, vt)	**a jongla**	[a ʒon'gla]
animal trainer	**dresor** (m)	[dre'sor]
animal training	**dresare** (f)	[dre'sare]
to train (animals)	**a dresa**	[a dre'sa]

154. Music. Pop music

music	**muzică** (f)	['muzikə]
musician	**muzician** (m)	[muziʧi'an]
musical instrument	**instrument** (n) **muzical**	[instru'ment muzi'kal]
to play ...	**a cânta la ...**	[a kin'ta 'la]
guitar	**chitară** (f)	[ki'tarə]

violin	**vioară** (f)	[vio'arə]
cello	**violoncel** (n)	[violon'ʧel]
double bass	**contrabas** (n)	[kontra'bas]
harp	**harpă** (f)	['harpə]
piano	**pianină** (f)	[pia'nino]
grand piano	**pian** (n) **cu coadă**	['pjan ku ku'ado]
organ	**orgă** (f)	['orgə]
wind instruments	**instrumente** (n pl) **de suflat**	[instru'mente de suf'lat]
oboe	**oboi** (m)	[o'boj]
saxophone	**saxofon** (n)	[sakso'fon]
clarinet	**clarinet** (n)	[klari'net]
flute	**flaut** (n)	['flaut]
trumpet	**trompetă** (f)	[trom'petə]
accordion	**acordeon** (n)	[akorde'on]
drum	**tobă** (f)	['tobə]
duo	**duet** (n)	[du'et]
trio	**trio** (n)	['trio]
quartet	**cvartet** (n)	[kvar'tet]
choir	**cor** (n)	[kor]
orchestra	**orchestră** (f)	[or'kestrə]
pop music	**muzică** (f) **pop**	['muzikə pop]
rock music	**muzică** (f) **rock**	['muzikə rok]
rock group	**formație** (n) **rock**	[for'maʦie rok]
jazz	**jazz** (n)	[ʤaz]
idol	**idol** (m)	['idol]
admirer, fan	**fan** (m)	[fan]
concert	**concert** (n)	[kon'ʧert]
symphony	**simfonie** (f)	[simfo'nie]
composition	**operă** (f)	['operə]
to compose (write)	**a compune**	[a kom'pune]
singing (n)	**cântare** (f)	[kɨn'tare]
song	**cântec** (n)	['kɨntek]
tune (melody)	**melodie** (f)	[melo'die]
rhythm	**ritm** (n)	[ritm]
blues	**blues** (n)	[bluz]
sheet music	**note** (f pl)	['note]
baton	**baghetă** (f)	[ba'getə]
bow	**arcuş** (n)	[ar'kuʃ]
string	**coardă** (f)	[ko'ardə]
case (e.g., guitar ~)	**husă** (f)	['husə]

Rest. Entertainment. Travel

155. Trip. Travel

tourism, travel	**turism** (n)	[tu'rism]
tourist	**turist** (m)	[tu'rist]
trip, voyage	**călătorie** (f)	[kələto'rie]
adventure	**aventură** (f)	[aven'turə]
trip, journey	**voiaj** (n)	[vo'jaʒ]
vacation	**concediu** (n)	[kon'ʧedju]
to be on vacation	**a fi în concediu**	[a fi ɨn kon'ʧedju]
rest	**odihnă** (f)	[o'dihnə]
train	**tren** (n)	[tren]
by train	**cu trenul**	[ku 'trenul]
airplane	**avion** (n)	[a'vjon]
by airplane	**cu avionul**	[ku a'vjonul]
by car	**cu automobilul**	[ku automo'bilul]
by ship	**cu vaporul**	[ku va'porul]
luggage	**bagaj** (n)	[ba'gaʒ]
suitcase	**valiză** (f)	[va'lizə]
luggage cart	**cărucior** (n) **pentru bagaj**	[kəru'ʧior 'pentru ba'gaʒ]
passport	**paşaport** (n)	[paʃa'port]
visa	**viză** (f)	['vizə]
ticket	**bilet** (n)	[bi'let]
air ticket	**bilet** (n) **de avion**	[bi'let de a'vjon]
guidebook	**ghid** (m)	[gid]
map (tourist ~)	**hartă** (f)	['hartə]
area (rural ~)	**localitate** (f)	[lokali'tate]
place, site	**loc** (n)	[lok]
exotica (n)	**exotism** (n)	[egzo'tism]
exotic (adj)	**exotic**	[e'gzotik]
amazing (adj)	**uimitor**	[ujmi'tor]
group	**grup** (n)	[grup]
excursion, sightseeing tour	**excursie** (f)	[eks'kursie]
guide (person)	**ghid** (m)	[gid]

156. Hotel

hotel	**hotel** (n)	[ho'tel]
motel	**motel** (n)	[mo'tel]
three-star (~ hotel)	**trei stele**	[trej 'stele]
five-star	**cinci stele**	[ʧinʧ 'stele]
to stay (in a hotel, etc.)	**a se opri**	[a se o'pri]
room	**cameră** (f)	['kamerə]
single room	**cameră pentru o persoană** (n)	['kamerə 'pentru o perso'anə]
double room	**cameră pentru două persoane** (n)	['kamerə 'pentru 'dowə perso'ane]
to book a room	**a rezerva o cameră**	[a rezer'va o 'kamerə]
half board	**demipensiune** (f)	[demipensi'une]
full board	**pensiune** (f)	[pensi'une]
with bath	**cu baie**	[ku 'bae]
with shower	**cu duş**	[ku duʃ]
satellite television	**televiziune** (f) **prin satelit**	[televizi'une 'prin sate'lit]
air-conditioner	**aer** (n) **condiționat**	['aer kondiʦio'nat]
towel	**prosop** (n)	[pro'sop]
key	**cheie** (f)	['kee]
administrator	**administrator** (m)	[adminis'trator]
chambermaid	**femeie** (f) **de serviciu**	[fe'mee de ser'viʧiu]
porter, bellboy	**hamal** (m)	[ha'mal]
doorman	**portar** (m)	[por'tar]
restaurant	**restaurant** (n)	[restau'rant]
pub, bar	**bar** (n)	[bar]
breakfast	**micul dejun** (n)	['mikul de'ʒun]
dinner	**cină** (f)	['ʧinə]
buffet	**masă suedeză** (f)	['masə sue'dezə]
lobby	**vestibul** (n)	[vesti'bul]
elevator	**lift** (n)	[lift]
DO NOT DISTURB	**NU DERANJAȚI!**	[nu deran'ʒaʦ]
NO SMOKING	**NU FUMAȚI!**	[nu fu'maʦ]

157. Books. Reading

book	**carte** (f)	['karte]
author	**autor** (m)	[au'tor]
writer	**scriitor** (m)	[skrii'tor]
to write (~ a book)	**a scrie**	[a 'skrie]

reader	**cititor** (m)	[ʧiti'tor]
to read (vi, vt)	**a citi**	[a ʧi'ti]
reading (activity)	**lectură** (f)	[lek'turə]
silently (to oneself)	**în gând**	[ɨn gɨnd]
aloud (adv)	**cu voce tare**	[ku 'voʧe 'tare]
to publish (vt)	**a publica**	[a publi'ka]
publishing (process)	**ediție** (f)	[e'diʦie]
publisher	**editor** (m)	[edi'tor]
publishing house	**editură** (f)	[edi'turə]
to come out (be released)	**a apărea**	[a apə'rʲa]
release (of a book)	**publicare** (f)	[publi'kare]
print run	**tiraj** (n)	[ti'raʒ]
bookstore	**librărie** (f)	[librə'rie]
library	**bibliotecă** (f)	[biblio'tekə]
story (novella)	**nuvelă** (f)	[nu'velə]
short story	**povestire** (f)	[poves'tire]
novel	**roman** (n)	[ro'man]
detective novel	**detectiv** (n)	[detek'tiv]
memoirs	**memorii** (n pl)	[me'morij]
legend	**legendă** (f)	[le'ʤendə]
myth	**mit** (n)	[mit]
poetry, poems	**versuri** (n pl)	['versurʲ]
autobiography	**autobiografie** (f)	[autobiogra'fie]
selected works	**opere** (f pl) **alese**	['opere a'lese]
science fiction	**fantastică** (f)	[fan'tastikə]
title	**denumire** (f)	[denu'mire]
introduction	**prefață** (f)	[pre'faʦə]
title page	**foaie** (f) **de titlu**	[fo'ae de 'titlu]
chapter	**capitol** (n)	[ka'pitol]
extract	**fragment** (n)	[frag'ment]
episode	**episod** (n)	[epi'zod]
plot (storyline)	**subiect** (n)	[su'bjekt]
contents	**cuprins** (n)	[ku'prins]
table of contents	**cuprins** (n)	[ku'prins]
main character	**erou** (m) **principal**	[e'rou prinʧi'pal]
volume	**volum** (n)	[vo'lum]
cover	**copertă** (f)	[ko'pertə]
binding	**copertă** (f)	[ko'pertə]
bookmark	**semn** (n) **de carte**	[semn de 'karte]
page	**pagină** (f)	['paʤinə]
to page through	**a răsfoi**	[a rəsfo'i]

margins	**margine** (f)	['mardʒine]
annotation (marginal note, etc.)	**notă** (f) **marginală**	['notə mardʒi'nalə]
footnote	**însemnare** (f)	[ɨnsem'nare]
text	**text** (n)	[tekst]
type, font	**caracter** (n)	[karak'ter]
misprint, typo	**greşeală** (f) **de tipar**	[gre'ʃalə de ti'par]
translation	**traducere** (f)	[tra'dutʃere]
to translate (vt)	**a traduce**	[a tra'dutʃe]
original (n)	**original** (n)	[oridʒi'nal]
famous (adj)	**vestit**	[ves'tit]
unknown (not famous)	**necunoscut**	[nekunos'kut]
interesting (adj)	**interesant**	[intere'sant]
bestseller	**best seller** (n)	[best 'seler]
dictionary	**dicționar** (n)	[diktsio'nar]
textbook	**manual** (n)	[manu'al]
encyclopedia	**enciclopedie** (f)	[entʃiklope'die]

158. Hunting. Fishing

hunting	**vânătoare** (f)	[vɨnəto'are]
to hunt (vi, vt)	**a vâna**	[a vɨ'na]
hunter	**vânător** (m)	[vɨnə'tor]
to shoot (vi)	**a trage**	[a 'tradʒə]
rifle	**armă** (f)	['armə]
bullet (shell)	**cartuş** (n)	[kar'tuʃ]
shot (lead balls)	**alice** (f)	[a'litʃe]
steel trap	**capcană** (f)	[kap'kanə]
snare (for birds, etc.)	**cursă** (f)	['kursə]
to lay a steel trap	**a pune capcană**	[a 'pune kap'kanə]
poacher	**braconier** (m)	[brako'njer]
game (in hunting)	**vânat** (n)	[vɨ'nat]
hound dog	**câine** (m) **de vânătoare**	['kɨne de vɨnəto'are]
safari	**safari** (n)	[sa'fari]
mounted animal	**animal** (n) **împăiat**	[ani'mal ɨmpə'jat]
fisherman, angler	**pescar** (m)	[pes'kar]
fishing (angling)	**pescuit** (n)	[pesku'it]
to fish (vi)	**a pescui**	[a pesku'i]
fishing rod	**undiță** (f)	['unditsə]
fishing line	**sfoara** (f) **undiței**	[sfo'ara 'unditsej]
hook	**cârlig** (n)	[kɨr'lig]

float, bobber	**plută** (f)	['plutə]
bait	**momeală** (f)	[mo'mʲalə]
to cast a line	**a arunca undița**	[a arun'ka 'unditsa]
to bite (ab. fish)	**a trage la undiță**	[a 'tradʒe la 'unditsə]
catch (of fish)	**pescuit** (n)	[pesku'it]
ice-hole	**copcă** (f)	['kopkə]
fishing net	**plasă** (f)	['plasə]
boat	**barcă** (f)	['barkə]
to net (to fish with a net)	**a prinde cu plasa**	[a 'prinde 'ku 'plasa]
to cast[throw] the net	**a arunca plasa**	[a arun'ka 'plasa]
to haul the net in	**a scoate plasa**	[a sko'ate 'plasa]
whaler (person)	**vânător** (m) **de balene**	[vanə'tor də 'balenə]
whaleboat	**balenieră** (f)	[bale'njerə]
harpoon	**harpon** (n)	[har'pon]

159. Games. Billiards

billiards	**biliard** (n)	[bi'ljard]
billiard room, hall	**sală** (f) **de biliard**	['salə de bi'ljard]
ball (snooker, etc.)	**bilă** (f)	['bilə]
to pocket a ball	**a băga bila**	[a bə'ga 'bila]
cue	**tac** (n)	[tak]
pocket	**gaură** (f) **de biliard**	['gaurə de bi'ljard]

160. Games. Playing cards

diamonds	**tobă** (f)	['tobə]
spades	**pică** (f)	['pikə]
hearts	**cupă** (f)	['kupə]
clubs	**treflă** (f)	['treflə]
ace	**as** (m)	[as]
king	**rege** (m)	['redʒe]
queen	**damă** (f)	['damə]
jack, knave	**valet** (m)	[va'let]
playing card	**carte** (f) **de joc**	['karte de ʒok]
cards	**cărți** (f pl) **de joc**	[kərtsʲ de ʒok]
trump	**atu** (n)	[a'tu]
deck of cards	**pachet** (n) **de cărți de joc**	[pa'ket de kərts de ʒok]
point	**punct** (n)	[punkt]
to deal (vi, vt)	**a împărți**	[a ɨmpər'tsi]

to shuffle (cards)	**a amesteca**	[a ameste'ka]
lead, turn (n)	**rând** (n)	[rɨnd]
cardsharp	**trişor** (m)	[tri'ʃor]

161. Casino. Roulette

casino	**cazinou** (n)	[kazi'nou]
roulette (game)	**ruletă** (f)	[ru'letə]
bet	**miză** (f)	['mizə]
to place bets	**a miza**	[a mi'za]
red	**roşu** (m)	['roʃu]
black	**negru** (m)	['negru]
to bet on red	**a miza pe roşu**	[a mi'za pe 'roʃu]
to bet on black	**a miza pe negru**	[a mi'za pe 'negru]
croupier (dealer)	**crupier** (m)	[kru'pjer]
to spin the wheel	**a învârti ruleta**	[a ɨnvɨr'ti ru'leta]
rules (of game)	**reguli** (f pl) **de joc**	['regulʲ de ʒok]
chip	**fisă** (f)	['fisə]
to win (vi, vt)	**a câştiga**	[a kɨʃti'ga]
win (winnings)	**câştig** (n)	[kɨʃ'tig]
to lose (~ 100 dollars)	**a pierde**	[a 'pjerde]
loss (losses)	**pierdere** (f)	['perdere]
player	**jucător** (m)	[ʒukə'tor]
blackjack (card game)	**Black Jack** (m)	[blək dʒek]
craps (dice game)	**table** (f pl)	['table]
dice (a pair of ~)	**zaruri** (n pl)	['zarurʲ]
slot machine	**joc** (n) **mecanic**	[ʒok me'kanik]

162. Rest. Games. Miscellaneous

to stroll (vi, vt)	**a se plimba**	[a se plim'ba]
stroll (leisurely walk)	**plimbare** (f)	[plim'bare]
car ride	**excursie** (f)	[eks'kursie]
adventure	**aventură** (f)	[aven'turə]
picnic	**picnic** (n)	['piknik]
game (chess, etc.)	**joc** (n)	[ʒok]
player	**jucător** (m)	[ʒukə'tor]
game (one ~ of chess)	**partidă** (f)	[par'tidə]
collector (e.g., philatelist)	**colecţionar** (m)	[kolektsio'nar]
to collect (stamps, etc.)	**a colecţiona**	[a kolektsio'na]
collection	**colecţie** (f)	[ko'lektsie]

crossword puzzle	**rebus** (n)	['rebus]
racetrack (horse racing venue)	**hipodrom** (n)	[hipo'drom]
disco (discotheque)	**discotecă** (f)	[disko'tekə]
sauna	**saună** (f)	['saunə]
lottery	**loterie** (f)	[lote'rie]
camping trip	**camping** (n)	['kemping]
camp	**tabără** (f)	['tabərə]
tent (for camping)	**cort** (n)	[kort]
compass	**busolă** (f)	[bu'solə]
camper	**turist** (m)	[tu'rist]
to watch (movie, etc.)	**a se uita**	[a se uj'ta]
viewer	**telespectator** (m)	[telespekta'tor]
TV show (TV program)	**emisiune** (f) **televizată**	[emisi'une televi'zatə]

163. Photography

camera (photo)	**aparat** (n) **foto**	[apa'rat 'foto]
photo, picture	**fotografie** (f)	[fotogra'fie]
photographer	**fotograf** (m)	[foto'graf]
photo studio	**studio** (n) **foto**	[stu'djo 'foto]
photo album	**album** (n) **foto**	[al'bum 'foto]
camera lens	**obiectiv** (n)	[objek'tiv]
telephoto lens	**teleobiectiv** (n)	[teleobjek'tiv]
filter	**filtru** (n)	['filtru]
lens	**lentilă** (f)	[len'tilə]
optics (high-quality ~)	**optică** (f)	['optikə]
diaphragm (aperture)	**diafragmă** (f)	[dia'fragmə]
exposure time (shutter speed)	**timp** (m) **de expunere**	['timp de eks'punere]
viewfinder	**vizor** (n)	[vi'zor]
digital camera	**cameră** (f) **digitală**	['kamerə didʒi'talə]
tripod	**suport** (n)	[su'port]
flash	**blitz** (n)	[blits]
to photograph (vt)	**a fotografia**	[a fotografi'ja]
to take pictures	**a fotografia**	[a fotografi'ja]
to have one's picture taken	**a se fotografia**	[a se fotografi'ja]
focus	**claritate** (f)	[klari'tate]
to focus	**a îndrepta**	[a indrep'ta]
sharp, in focus (adj)	**clar**	[klar]
sharpness	**claritatea** (f) **imaginii**	[klari'tatʲa i'madʒinij]

contrast	**contrast** (n)	[kon'trast]
contrast (as adj)	**de contrast**	[de kon'trast]
picture (photo)	**fotografie** (f)	[fotogra'fie]
negative (n)	**negativ** (n)	[nega'tiv]
film (a roll of ~)	**film** (n)	[film]
frame (still)	**cadru** (n)	['kadru]
to print (photos)	**a tipări**	[a tipə'ri]

164. Beach. Swimming

beach	**plajă** (f)	['plaʒə]
sand	**nisip** (n)	[ni'sip]
deserted (beach)	**pustiu**	[pus'tiu]
suntan	**bronz** (n)	[bronz]
to get a tan	**a se bronza**	[a se bron'za]
tan (adj)	**bronzat**	[bron'zat]
sunscreen	**cremă** (f) **pentru bronzat**	['kremə 'pentru bron'zat]
bikini	**bikini** (n)	[bi'kini]
bathing suit	**costum** (n) **de baie**	[kos'tum de 'bae]
swim trunks	**slipi** (m pl)	[slip^j]
swimming pool	**bazin** (n)	[ba'zin]
to swim (vi)	**a înota**	[a ɨno'ta]
shower	**duş** (n)	[duʃ]
to change (one's clothes)	**a se schimba**	[a se skim'ba]
towel	**prosop** (n)	[pro'sop]
boat	**barcă** (f)	['barkə]
motorboat	**cuter** (n)	['kuter]
water ski	**schiuri** (n pl) **pe apă**	['skjur^j pe 'apə]
paddle boat	**bicicletă** (f) **pe apă**	[bitʃi'kletə pe 'apə]
surfing	**surfing** (n)	['serfing]
surfer	**surfer** (m)	['serfer]
scuba set	**acvalang** (n)	[akva'lang]
flippers (swim fins)	**labe** (f pl) **de înot**	['labe de ɨ'not]
mask (diving ~)	**mască** (f)	['maskə]
diver	**scufundător** (m)	[skufundə'tor]
to dive (vi)	**a se scufunda**	[a se skufun'da]
underwater (adv)	**sub apă**	[sub 'apə]
beach umbrella	**umbrelă** (f)	[um'brelə]
sunbed (lounger)	**şezlong** (n)	[ʃəz'long]
sunglasses	**ochelari** (m pl)	[oke'lar^j]
air mattress	**saltea** (f) **de înot**	[sal'tʲa de ɨ'not]
to play (amuse oneself)	**a juca**	[a ʒu'ka]

to go for a swim	**a se scălda**	[a se skəl'da]
beach ball	**minge** (f)	['mindʒe]
to inflate (vt)	**a umfla**	[a um'fla]
inflatable, air (adj)	**pneumatic**	[pneu'matik]
wave	**val** (n)	[val]
buoy (line of ~s)	**baliză** (f)	[ba'lizə]
to drown (ab. person)	**a se îneca**	[a se ɨne'ka]
to save, to rescue	**a salva**	[a sal'va]
life vest	**vestă** (f) **de salvare**	['vestə de sal'vare]
to observe, to watch	**a observa**	[a obser'va]
lifeguard	**salvator** (m)	[salva'tor]

TECHNICAL EQUIPMENT. TRANSPORTATION

Technical equipment

165. Computer

computer	**calculator** (n)	[kalkula'tor]
notebook, laptop	**laptop** (n)	[ləp'top]
to turn on	**a deschide**	[a des'kide]
to turn off	**a închide**	[a ɨ'nkide]
keyboard	**tastatură** (f)	[tasta'turə]
key	**tastă** (f)	['tastə]
mouse	**mouse** (n)	['maus]
mouse pad	**mousepad** (n)	[maus'pad]
button	**tastă** (f)	['tastə]
cursor	**cursor** (m)	[kur'sor]
monitor	**monitor** (n)	[moni'tor]
screen	**ecran** (n)	[e'kran]
hard disk	**hard disc** (n)	[hard disk]
hard disk capacity	**capacitatea** (f) **hard discului**	[kapatʃi'tatʲa 'hard 'diskuluj]
memory	**memorie** (f)	[me'morie]
random access memory	**memorie** (f) **operativă**	[me'morie opera'tivə]
file	**fişier** (n)	[fiʃi'er]
folder	**document** (n)	[doku'ment]
to open (vt)	**a deschide**	[a des'kide]
to close (vt)	**a închide**	[a ɨ'nkide]
to save (vt)	**a păstra**	[a pəs'tra]
to delete (vt)	**a şterge**	[a 'ʃterdʒe]
to copy (vt)	**a copia**	[a kopi'ja]
to sort (vt)	**a sorta**	[a sor'ta]
to transfer (copy)	**a copia**	[a kopi'ja]
program	**program** (n)	[pro'gram]
software	**programe** (n) **de aplicaţie**	[pro'grame de apli'katsie]
programmer	**programator** (m)	[programa'tor]
to program (vt)	**a programa**	[a progra'ma]

hacker	**hacker** (m)	['haker]
password	**parolă** (f)	[pa'rolə]
virus	**virus** (m)	['virus]
to find, to detect	**a găsi**	[a gə'si]
byte	**bait** (m)	[bajt]
megabyte	**megabyte** (m)	[mega'bajt]
data	**date** (f pl)	['date]
database	**bază** (f) **de date**	['bazə de 'date]
cable (USB, etc.)	**cablu** (n)	['kablu]
to disconnect (vt)	**a deconecta**	[a dekonek'ta]
to connect (sth to sth)	**a conecta**	[a konek'ta]

166. Internet. E-mail

Internet	**internet** (n)	[inter'net]
browser	**browser** (n)	['brauzer]
search engine	**motor** (n) **de căutare**	[mo'tor de kəu'tare]
provider	**cablu** (n)	['kablu]
webmaster	**web master** (m)	[web 'master]
website	**web site** (n)	[web 'sajt]
webpage	**pagină** (f) **web**	['padʒinə web]
address (e-mail ~)	**adresă** (f)	[a'dresə]
address book	**registru** (n) **de adrese**	[re'dʒistru de a'drese]
mailbox	**cutie** (f) **poştală**	[ku'tie poʃ'talə]
mail	**corespondenţă** (f)	[korespon'dentsə]
full (adj)	**plin**	[plin]
message	**mesaj** (n)	[me'saʒ]
incoming messages	**mesaje** (n pl) **primite**	[me'saʒe primite]
outgoing messages	**mesaje** (n pl) **trimise**	[me'saʒe trimise]
sender	**expeditor** (m)	[ekspedi'tor]
to send (vt)	**a expedia**	[a ekspedi'ja]
sending (of mail)	**expediere** (f)	[ekspe'djere]
receiver	**destinatar** (m)	[destina'tar]
to receive (vt)	**a primi**	[a pri'mi]
correspondence	**corespondenţă** (f)	[korespon'dentsə]
to correspond (vi)	**a coresponda**	[a korespon'da]
file	**fişier** (n)	[fiʃi'er]
to download (vt)	**a copia**	[a kopi'ja]
to create (vt)	**a crea**	[a 'krʲa]
to delete (vt)	**a şterge**	[a 'ʃterdʒe]

deleted (adj)	**şters**	[ʃters]
connection (ADSL, etc.)	**conexiune** (f)	[koneksi'une]
speed	**viteză** (f)	[vi'tezə]
modem	**modem** (n)	[mo'dem]
access	**acces** (n)	[ak'ʧes]
port (e.g., input ~)	**port** (n)	[port]
connection (make a ~)	**conectare** (f)	[konek'tare]
to connect to ... (vi)	**a se conecta**	[a se konek'ta]
to select (vt)	**a alege**	[a a'ledʒe]
to search (for ...)	**a căuta**	[a kəu'ta]

167. Electricity

electricity	**electricitate** (f)	[elektriʧi'tate]
electric, electrical (adj)	**electric**	[e'lektrik]
electric power plant	**centrală** (f) **electrică**	[ʧen'tralə e'lektrikə]
energy	**energie** (f)	[ener'dʒie]
electric power	**energie** (f) **electrică**	[ener'dʒie e'lektrikə]
light bulb	**bec** (n)	[bek]
flashlight	**lanternă** (f)	[lan'ternə]
street light	**felinar** (n)	[feli'nar]
light	**lumină** (f)	[lu'minə]
to turn on	**a aprinde**	[a a'prinde]
to turn off	**a stinge**	[a 'stindʒe]
to turn off the light	**a stinge lumina**	[a 'stindʒe lu'mina]
to burn out (vi)	**a arde**	[a 'arde]
short circuit	**scurtcircuit** (n)	['skurtʧirku'it]
broken wire	**ruptură** (f)	[rup'turə]
contact (electrical ~)	**contact** (n)	[kon'takt]
light switch	**întrerupător** (n)	[intrerupə'tor]
wall socket	**priză** (f)	['prizə]
plug	**furcă** (f)	['furkə]
extension cord	**prelungitor** (n)	[prelundʒi'tor]
fuse	**siguranță** (f)	[sigu'rantsə]
cable, wire	**fir** (n) **electric**	[fir e'lektrik]
wiring	**instalație** (f) **electrică**	[insta'latsie e'lektrikə]
ampere	**amper** (m)	[am'per]
amperage	**intensitatea** (f) **curentului**	[intensi'tatʲa ku'rentuluj]
volt	**volt** (m)	[volt]
voltage	**tensiune** (f)	[tensi'une]
electrical device	**aparat** (n) **electric**	[apa'rat e'lektrik]
indicator	**indicator** (n)	[indika'tor]

electrician	**electrician** (m)	[elektriʧi'an]
to solder (vt)	**a lipi**	[a li'pi]
soldering iron	**ciocan** (n) **de lipit**	[ʧio'kan de li'pit]
electric current	**curent** (m)	[ku'rent]

168. Tools

tool, instrument	**instrument** (n)	[instru'ment]
tools	**instrumente** (n pl)	[instru'mente]
equipment (factory ~)	**utilaj** (n)	[uti'laʒ]
hammer	**ciocan** (n)	[ʧio'kan]
screwdriver	**şurubelniță** (f)	[ʃuru'belnitsə]
ax	**topor** (n)	[to'por]
saw	**ferăstrău** (n)	[ferəstrəu]
to saw (vt)	**a tăia cu ferăstrăul**	[a tə'ja 'ku ferəstrəul]
plane (tool)	**rindea** (f)	[rin'dʲa]
to plane (vt)	**a gelui**	[a ʤelu'i]
soldering iron	**ciocan** (n) **de lipit**	[ʧio'kan de li'pit]
to solder (vt)	**a lipi**	[a li'pi]
file (tool)	**pilă** (f)	['pilə]
carpenter pincers	**cleşte** (m)	['kleʃte]
lineman's pliers	**cleşte** (m) **patent**	['kleʃte pa'tent]
chisel	**daltă** (f) **de tâmplărie**	['daltə de timplə'rie]
drill bit	**burghiu** (n)	[bur'gju]
electric drill	**sfredel** (n)	['sfredel]
to drill (vi, vt)	**a sfredeli**	[a sfrede'li]
knife	**cuțit** (n)	[ku'tsit]
pocket knife	**briceag** (n)	[bri'ʧeag]
blade	**lamă** (f)	['lamə]
sharp (blade, etc.)	**ascuțit**	[asku'tsit]
dull, blunt (adj)	**tocit**	[to'ʧit]
to get blunt (dull)	**a se toci**	[a se to'ʧi]
to sharpen (vt)	**a ascuți**	[a asku'tsi]
bolt	**şurub** (n)	[ʃu'rub]
nut	**piuliță** (f)	[pju'litsə]
thread (of a screw)	**filet** (n)	[fi'let]
wood screw	**şurub** (n)	[ʃu'rub]
nail	**cui** (n)	[kuj]
nailhead	**bont** (n)	[bont]
ruler (for measuring)	**linie** (f)	['linie]
tape measure	**ruletă** (f)	[ru'letə]

spirit level	**nivelă** (f)	[ni'vela]
magnifying glass	**lupă** (f)	['lupə]
measuring instrument	**aparat** (n) **de măsurat**	[apa'rat de məsu'rat]
to measure (vt)	**a măsura**	[a məsu'ra]
scale (of thermometer, etc.)	**scală** (f)	['skalə]
readings	**indicații** (f pl)	[indi'katsij]
compressor	**compresor** (n)	[kompre'sor]
microscope	**microscop** (n)	[mikro'skop]
pump (e.g., water ~)	**pompă** (f)	['pompə]
robot	**robot** (m)	[ro'bot]
laser	**laser** (n)	['laser]
wrench	**cheie** (f) **franceză**	['kee fran'tʃezə]
adhesive tape	**bandă** (f) **izolatoare**	['bandə izolato'are]
glue	**clei** (n)	[klej]
sandpaper	**hârtie** (f) **abrazivă**	[hɨr'tie abra'zivə]
spring	**arc** (n)	[ark]
magnet	**magnet** (m)	[mag'net]
gloves	**mănuşi** (f pl)	[mə'nuʃ]
rope	**funie** (f)	['funie]
cord	**şnur** (n)	[ʃnur]
wire (e.g., telephone ~)	**fir** (n) **electric**	[fir e'lektrik]
cable	**cablu** (n)	['kablu]
sledgehammer	**baros** (m)	[ba'ros]
prybar	**rangă** (f)	['rangə]
ladder	**scară** (f)	['skarə]
stepladder	**scară** (f) **de frânghie**	['skarə de frɨn'gie]
to screw (tighten)	**a înşuruba**	[a ɨnʃuru'ba]
to unscrew (lid, filter, etc.)	**a deşuruba**	[a deʃuru'ba]
to tighten (e.g., with a clamp)	**a strânge**	[a 'strɨndʒe]
to glue, to stick	**a lipi**	[a li'pi]
to cut (vt)	**a tăia**	[a tə'ja]
malfunction (fault)	**deranjament** (n)	[deranʒa'ment]
repair (mending)	**reparație** (f)	[repa'ratsie]
to repair, to fix (vt)	**a repara**	[a repa'ra]
to adjust (machine, etc.)	**a regla**	[a re'gla]
to check (to examine)	**a verifica**	[a verifi'ka]
checking	**verificare** (f)	[verifi'kare]
readings	**indicație** (f)	[indi'katsie]
reliable, solid (machine)	**sigur**	['sigur]
complex (adj)	**complex**	[kom'pleks]

to rust (get rusted)	**a rugini**	[a rudʒi'ni]
rusty, rusted (adj)	**ruginit**	[rudʒi'nit]
rust	**rugină** (f)	[ru'dʒinə]

Transportation

169. Airplane

airplane	**avion** (n)	[a'vjon]
air ticket	**bilet** (n) **de avion**	[bi'let de a'vjon]
airline	**companie** (f) **aeriană**	[kompa'nie aeri'anə]
airport	**aeroport** (n)	[aero'port]
supersonic (adj)	**supersonic**	[super'sonik]
captain	**comandant** (m) **de navă**	[koman'dant de 'navə]
crew	**echipaj** (n)	[eki'paʒ]
pilot	**pilot** (m)	[pi'lot]
flight attendant (fem.)	**stewardesă** (f)	[stjuar'desə]
navigator	**navigator** (m)	[naviga'tor]
wings	**aripi** (f pl)	[a'ripʲ]
tail	**coadă** (f)	[ko'adə]
cockpit	**cabină** (f)	[ka'binə]
engine	**motor** (n)	[mo'tor]
undercarriage (landing gear)	**tren** (n) **de aterizare**	[tren de ateri'zare]
turbine	**turbină** (f)	[tur'binə]
propeller	**elice** (f)	[e'litʃe]
black box	**cutie** (f) **neagră**	[ku'tie 'nʲagrə]
yoke (control column)	**manşă** (f)	['manʃə]
fuel	**combustibil** (m)	[kombus'tibil]
safety card	**instrucțiune** (f)	[instruktsi'une]
oxygen mask	**mască** (f) **cu oxigen**	['maskə 'ku oksi'dʒen]
uniform	**uniformă** (f)	[uni'formə]
life vest	**vestă** (f) **de salvare**	['vestə de sal'vare]
parachute	**paraşută** (f)	[para'ʃutə]
takeoff	**decolare** (f)	[deko'lare]
to take off (vi)	**a decola**	[a deko'la]
runway	**pistă** (f) **de decolare**	['pistə de deko'lare]
visibility	**vizibilitate** (f)	[vizibili'tate]
flight (act of flying)	**zbor** (n)	[zbor]
altitude	**înălțime** (f)	[ɨnəl'tsime]
air pocket	**gol de aer** (n)	[gol de 'aer]
seat	**loc** (n)	[lok]
headphones	**căşti** (f pl)	[kəʃtʲ]

folding tray (tray table)	**măsuță** (f) **rabatabilă**	[mə'sutsə raba'tabilə]
airplane window	**hublou** (n)	[hu'blou]
aisle	**trecere** (f)	['tretʃere]

170. Train

train	**tren** (n)	[tren]
commuter train	**tren** (n) **electric**	['tren e'lektrik]
express train	**tren** (n) **accelerat**	['tren aktʃele'rat]
diesel locomotive	**locomotivă** (f) **cu motor diesel**	[lokomo'tivə ku mo'tor 'dizel]
steam locomotive	**locomotivă** (f)	[lokomo'tivə]
passenger car	**vagon** (n)	[va'gon]
dining car	**vagon-restaurant** (n)	[va'gon restau'rant]
rails	**şine** (f pl)	['ʃine]
railroad	**cale** (f) **ferată**	['kale fe'ratə]
railway tie	**traversă** (f)	[tra'versə]
platform (railway ~)	**peron** (n)	[pe'ron]
track (~ 1, 2, etc.)	**linie** (f)	['linie]
semaphore	**semafor** (n)	[sema'for]
station	**stație** (f)	['statsie]
engineer (train driver)	**maşinist** (m)	[maʃi'nist]
porter (of luggage)	**hamal** (m)	[ha'mal]
car attendant	**însoțitor** (m)	[ɨnsotsi'tor]
passenger	**pasager** (m)	[pasa'dʒer]
conductor (ticket inspector)	**controlor** (m)	[kontro'lor]
corridor (in train)	**coridor** (n)	[kori'dor]
emergency brake	**semnal** (n) **de alarmă**	[sem'nal de a'larmə]
compartment	**compartiment** (n)	[komparti'ment]
berth	**cuşetă** (f)	[ku'ʃetə]
upper berth	**patul** (n) **de sus**	['patul de sus]
lower berth	**patul** (n) **de jos**	['patul de ʒos]
bed linen, bedding	**lenjerie** (f) **de pat**	[lenʒe'rie de pat]
ticket	**bilet** (n)	[bi'let]
schedule	**orar** (n)	[o'rar]
information display	**panou** (n)	[pa'nou]
to leave, to depart	**a pleca**	[a ple'ka]
departure (of train)	**plecare** (f)	[ple'kare]
to arrive (ab. train)	**a sosi**	[a so'si]
arrival	**sosire** (f)	[so'sire]
to arrive by train	**a veni cu trenul**	[a ve'ni ku 'trenul]

to get on the train	**a se aşeza în tren**	[a se aʃə'za ɨn tren]
to get off the train	**a coborî din tren**	[a kobo'rɨ din tren]
train wreck	**accident** (n) **de tren**	[aktʃi'dent de tren]
to derail (vi)	**a deraia**	[dera'ja]
steam locomotive	**locomotivă** (f)	[lokomo'tivə]
stoker, fireman	**fochist** (m)	[fo'kist]
firebox	**focar** (n)	[fo'kar]
coal	**cărbune** (m)	[kər'bune]

171. Ship

ship	**corabie** (f)	[ko'rabie]
vessel	**navă** (f)	['navə]
steamship	**vapor** (n)	[va'por]
riverboat	**motonavă** (f)	[moto'navə]
cruise ship	**vas** (n) **de croazieră**	[vas de kroa'zjerə]
cruiser	**crucişător** (n)	[krutʃiʃə'tor]
yacht	**iaht** (n)	[jaht]
tugboat	**remorcher** (n)	[remor'ker]
barge	**şlep** (n)	[ʃlep]
ferry	**bac** (n)	[bak]
sailing ship	**velier** (n)	[ve'ljer]
brigantine	**brigantină** (f)	[brigan'tinə]
ice breaker	**spărgător** (n) **de gheaţă**	[spərgə'tor de 'gʲatsə]
submarine	**submarin** (n)	[subma'rin]
boat (flat-bottomed ~)	**barcă** (f)	['barkə]
dinghy	**şalupă** (f)	[ʃa'lupə]
lifeboat	**şalupă** (f) **de salvare**	[ʃa'lupə de sal'vare]
motorboat	**cuter** (n)	['kuter]
captain	**căpitan** (m)	[kəpi'tan]
seaman	**marinar** (m)	[mari'nar]
sailor	**marinar** (m)	[mari'nar]
crew	**echipaj** (n)	[eki'paʒ]
boatswain	**şef** (m) **de echipaj**	[ʃef de eki'paʒ]
ship's boy	**mus** (m)	[mus]
cook	**bucătar** (m)	[bukə'tar]
ship's doctor	**medic** (m) **pe navă**	['medik pe 'navə]
deck	**teugă** (f)	[te'ugə]
mast	**catarg** (n)	[ka'targ]
sail	**velă** (f)	['velə]
hold	**cală** (f)	['kalə]

bow (prow)	**proră** (f)	['prorə]
stern	**pupă** (f)	['pupə]
oar	**vâslă** (f)	['vislə]
screw propeller	**elice** (f)	[e'litʃe]
cabin	**cabină** (f)	[ka'binə]
wardroom	**salonul** (n) **ofițerilor**	[sa'lonul ofi'tserilor]
engine room	**sala** (f) **maşinilor**	['sala ma'ʃinilor]
bridge	**punte** (f) **de comandă**	['punte de ko'mandə]
radio room	**stație** (f) **de radio**	['statsie de 'radio]
wave (radio)	**undă** (f)	['undə]
logbook	**jurnal** (n) **de bord**	[ʒur'nal de bord]
spyglass	**lunetă** (f)	[lu'netə]
bell	**clopot** (n)	['klopot]
flag	**steag** (n)	['stʲag]
hawser (mooring ~)	**parâmă** (f)	[pa'rɨmə]
knot (bowline, etc.)	**nod** (n)	[nod]
deckrails	**bară** (f)	['barə]
gangway	**pasarelă** (f)	[pasa'relə]
anchor	**ancoră** (f)	['ankorə]
to weigh anchor	**a ridica ancora**	[a ridi'ka 'ankora]
to drop anchor	**a ancora**	[a anko'ra]
anchor chain	**lanț** (n) **de ancoră**	[lants de 'ankorə]
port (harbor)	**port** (n)	[port]
quay, wharf	**acostare** (f)	[akos'tare]
to berth (moor)	**a acosta**	[a akos'ta]
to cast off	**a demara**	[a dema'ra]
trip, voyage	**călătorie** (f)	[kələto'rie]
cruise (sea trip)	**croazieră** (f)	[kroa'zjerə]
course (route)	**direcție** (f)	[di'rektsie]
route (itinerary)	**rută** (f)	['rutə]
fairway (safe water channel)	**cale** (f) **navigabilă**	['kale navi'gabilə]
shallows	**banc** (n) **de nisip**	[bank de ni'sip]
to run aground	**a se împotmoli**	[a se ɨmpotmo'li]
storm	**furtună** (f)	[fur'tunə]
signal	**semnal** (n)	[sem'nal]
to sink (vi)	**a se scufunda**	[a se skufun'da]
Man overboard!	**Om la apă!**	[om la 'apə]
SOS (distress signal)	**SOS**	[sos]
ring buoy	**colac** (m) **de salvare**	[ko'lak de sal'vare]

172. Airport

airport	**aeroport** (n)	[aero'port]
airplane	**avion** (n)	[a'vjon]
airline	**companie** (f) **aeriană**	[kompa'nie aeri'anə]
air traffic controller	**dispecer** (n)	[dis'petʃer]
departure	**decolare** (f)	[deko'lare]
arrival	**aterizare** (f)	[ateri'zare]
to arrive (by plane)	**a ateriza**	[a ateri'za]
departure time	**ora** (f) **decolării**	['ora dekolərij]
arrival time	**ora** (f) **aterizării**	['ora aterizərij]
to be delayed	**a întârzia**	[a ɨntɨr'zija]
flight delay	**întârzierea** (f) **zborului**	[ɨntɨrzjer'a 'zboruluj]
information board	**panou** (n)	[pa'nou]
information	**informație** (f)	[infor'matsie]
to announce (vt)	**a anunța**	[a anun'tsa]
flight (e.g., next ~)	**cursă** (f)	['kursə]
customs	**vamă** (f)	['vamə]
customs officer	**vameş** (m)	['vameʃ]
customs declaration	**declarație** (f)	[dekla'ratsie]
to fill out (vt)	**a completa**	[a komple'ta]
to fill out the declaration	**a completa declarația**	[a komple'ta dekla'ratsija]
passport control	**controlul** (n) **paşapoartelor**	[kon'trolul paʃapo'artelor]
luggage	**bagaj** (n)	[ba'gaʒ]
hand luggage	**bagaj** (n) **de mână**	[ba'gaʒ de 'mɨnə]
luggage cart	**cărucior** (n) **pentru bagaj**	[kəru'tʃior 'pentru ba'gaʒ]
landing	**aterizare** (f)	[ateri'zare]
landing strip	**pistă** (f) **de aterizare**	['pistə de ateri'zare]
to land (vi)	**a ateriza**	[a ateri'za]
airstair (passenger stair)	**scară** (f)	['skarə]
check-in	**înregistrare** (f)	[ɨnredʒis'trare]
check-in counter	**birou** (n) **de înregistrare**	[bi'rou de ɨnredʒis'trare]
to check-in (vi)	**a se înregistra**	[a se ɨnredʒis'tra]
boarding pass	**număr** (n) **de bord**	['numər de bord]
departure gate	**debarcare** (f)	[debar'kare]
transit	**tranzit** (n)	['tranzit]
to wait (vt)	**a aştepta**	[a aʃtep'ta]
departure lounge	**sală** (f) **de aşteptare**	['salə de aʃtep'tare]
to see off	**a conduce**	[a kon'dutʃe]
to say goodbye	**a-şi lua rămas bun**	[aʃ lu'a rə'mas bun]

173. Bicycle. Motorcycle

bicycle	**bicicletă** (f)	[bitʃi'kletə]
scooter	**scuter** (n)	['skuter]
motorcycle, bike	**motocicletă** (f)	[mototʃi'kletə]
to go by bicycle	**a merge cu bicicleta**	[a 'merdʒe ku bitʃik'leta]
handlebars	**ghidon** (n)	[gi'don]
pedal	**pedală** (f)	[pe'dalə]
brakes	**frână** (f)	['frɨnə]
bicycle seat (saddle)	**şa** (f)	[ʃa]
pump	**pompă** (f)	['pompə]
luggage rack	**portbagaj** (n)	[portba'gaʒ]
front lamp	**felinar** (n)	[feli'nar]
helmet	**cască** (f)	['kaskə]
wheel	**roată** (f)	[ro'atə]
fender	**aripă** (f)	[a'ripə]
rim	**obada** (f) **roții**	[o'bada 'rotsij]
spoke	**spiță** (f)	['spitsə]

Cars

174. Types of cars

automobile, car	**automobil** (n)	[automo'bil]
sports car	**automobil** (n) **sport**	[automo'bil 'sport]
limousine	**limuzină** (f)	[limu'zinə]
off-road vehicle	**vehicul** (n) **de teren** (n)	[ve'hikul de te'ren]
convertible (n)	**cabrioletă** (f)	[kabrio'letə]
minibus	**microbuz** (n)	[mikro'buz]
ambulance	**ambulanță** (f)	[ambu'lantsə]
snowplow	**maşină** (f) **de deszăpezire**	[ma'ʃinə de deszəpe'zire]
truck	**autocamion** (n)	[autoka'mjon]
tanker truck	**autocisternă** (f) **pentru combustibil**	[autotʃis'ternə 'pentru kombus'tibil]
van (small truck)	**furgon** (n)	[fur'gon]
road tractor (trailer truck)	**remorcher** (n)	[remor'ker]
trailer	**remorcă** (f)	[re'morkə]
comfortable (adj)	**confortabil**	[konfor'tabil]
used (adj)	**uzat**	[u'zat]

175. Cars. Bodywork

hood	**capotă** (f)	[ka'potə]
fender	**aripă** (f)	[a'ripə]
roof	**acoperiş** (n)	[akope'riʃ]
windshield	**parbriz** (n)	[par'briz]
rear-view mirror	**oglindă** (f) **retrovizoare**	[og'lində retrovizo'are]
windshield washer	**ştergător** (n)	[ʃtergə'tor]
windshield wipers	**ştergător** (n) **de parbriz**	[ʃtergə'tor de par'briz]
side window	**fereastră** (f) **laterală**	[fe'rʲastrə late'ralə]
window lift (power window)	**macara** (f) **de geam**	[maka'ra de dʒʲam]
antenna	**antenă** (f)	[an'tenə]
sunroof	**trapă** (f)	['trapə]
bumper	**amortizor** (n)	[amorti'zor]
trunk	**portbagaj** (n)	[portba'gaʒ]

roof luggage rack	**portbagaj** (n)	[portba'gaʒ]
door	**portieră** (f)	[por'tjerə]
door handle	**mâner** (n)	[mɨ'ner]
door lock	**încuietoare** (f)	[ɨnkueto'are]
license plate	**număr** (n)	['numər]
muffler	**tobă** (f)	['tobə]
gas tank	**rezervor** (n) **de benzină**	[rezer'vor de ben'zinə]
tailpipe	**țeavă** (f) **de eşapament**	['tsʲavə de eʃapa'ment]
gas, accelerator	**gaz** (n)	[gaz]
pedal	**pedală** (f)	[pe'dalə]
gas pedal	**pedală** (f) **de accelerație**	[pe'dalə de aktʃele'ratsie]
brake	**frână** (f)	['frɨnə]
brake pedal	**pedală** (f) **de frână**	[pe'dalə de 'frɨnə]
to brake (use the brake)	**a frâna**	[a frɨ'na]
parking brake	**frână** (f) **de staționare**	['frɨnə de statsio'nare]
clutch	**ambreiaj** (n)	[ambre'jaʒ]
clutch pedal	**pedală** (f) **de ambreiaj**	[pe'dalə de ambre'jaʒ]
clutch disc	**disc** (n) **de ambreiaj**	['disk de ambre'jaʒ]
shock absorber	**amortizor** (n)	[amorti'zor]
wheel	**roată** (f)	[ro'atə]
spare tire	**roată** (f) **de rezervă**	[ro'atə de re'zervə]
tire	**cauciuc** (n)	[kau'tʃuk]
hubcap	**capac** (n)	[ka'pak]
driving wheels	**roți** (f pl) **de tracțiune**	['rotsʲ de traktsi'une]
front-wheel drive (as adj)	**tracțiune** (f) **frontală**	[traktsi'une fron'talə]
rear-wheel drive (as adj)	**tracțiune** (f) **spate**	[traktsi'une 'spate]
all-wheel drive (as adj)	**tracțiune** (f) **integrală**	[traktsi'une inte'gralə]
gearbox	**cutie** (f) **de viteză**	[ku'tie de vi'tezə]
automatic (adj)	**automat**	[auto'mat]
mechanical (adj)	**mecanic**	[me'kanik]
gear shift	**manetă** (f) **de viteze**	[ma'netə de vi'teze]
headlight	**far** (n)	[far]
headlights	**faruri** (n pl)	['farurʲ]
low beam	**fază** (f) **mică**	['fazə 'mikə]
high beam	**fază** (f) **mare**	['fazə 'mare]
brake light	**semnal** (n) **de oprire**	[sem'nal de o'prire]
parking lights	**semn** (n) **de gabarit**	[semn de gaba'rit]
hazard lights	**lumini** (f) **de avarie**	[lu'minʲ de a'varie]
fog lights	**faruri** (n pl) **anticeață**	['farurʲ anti'tʃatsə]
turn signal	**mecanism** (n) **de direcție**	[meka'nism de di'rektsie]
back-up light	**marşarier** (n)	[marʃari'er]

176. Cars. Passenger compartment

car inside (interior)	**interior** (n)	[inte'rjor]
leather (as adj)	**de piele**	[de 'pjele]
velour (as adj)	**de catifea**	[de kati'fʲa]
upholstery	**tapițare** (f)	[tapi'tsare]
instrument (gage)	**dispozitiv** (n)	[dispozi'tiv]
dashboard	**panou** (n) **de comandă**	[pa'nou de ko'mandə]
speedometer	**vitezometru** (n)	[vitezo'metru]
needle (pointer)	**ac** (n)	[ak]
odometer	**contor** (n)	[kon'tor]
indicator (sensor)	**indicator** (n)	[indika'tor]
level	**nivel** (n)	[ni'vel]
warning light	**bec** (n)	[bek]
steering wheel	**volan** (n)	[vo'lan]
horn	**claxon** (n)	[klak'son]
button	**buton** (n)	[bu'ton]
switch	**schimbător** (n) **de viteză**	[skimbə'tor de vi'tezə]
seat	**scaun** (n)	['skaun]
backrest	**spătar** (n)	[spə'tar]
headrest	**tetieră** (f)	[te'tjerə]
seat belt	**centură** (f) **de siguranță**	[tʃen'turə de sigu'rantsə]
to fasten the belt	**a pune centura de siguranță**	[a 'pune tʃen'tura de sigu'rantsə]
adjustment (of seats)	**reglare** (f)	[re'glare]
airbag	**airbag** (n)	['erbeg]
air-conditioner	**aer** (n) **condiționat**	['aer konditsio'nat]
radio	**radio** (n)	['radio]
CD player	**CD player** (n)	[si'di 'pleer]
to turn on	**a deschide**	[a des'kide]
antenna	**antenă** (f)	[an'tenə]
glove box	**torpedou** (m)	[torpe'dou]
ashtray	**scrumieră** (f)	[skru'mjerə]

177. Cars. Engine

engine, motor	**motor** (n)	[mo'tor]
diesel (as adj)	**diesel**	['dizel]
gasoline (as adj)	**pe benzină**	[pe ben'zinə]
engine volume	**capacitatea** (n) **motorului**	[kapatʃi'tatʲa mo'toruluj]
power	**putere** (f)	[pu'tere]
horsepower	**cal-putere** (m)	[kal pu'tere]

piston	**piston** (m)	[pis'ton]
cylinder	**cilindru** (m)	[tʃi'lindru]
valve	**supapă** (f)	[su'papə]
injector	**injector** (n)	[inʒek'tor]
generator (alternator)	**generator** (n)	[dʒenera'tor]
carburetor	**carburator** (n)	[karbura'tor]
motor oil	**ulei** (n) **pentru motor**	[u'lej 'pentru mo'tor]
radiator	**radiator** (n)	[radia'tor]
coolant	**antigel** (n)	[anti'dʒel]
cooling fan	**ventilator** (n)	[ventila'tor]
battery (accumulator)	**acumulator** (n)	[akumula'tor]
starter	**demaror** (n)	[dema'ror]
ignition	**aprindere** (f)	[a'prindere]
spark plug	**bujie** (f) **de aprindere**	[bu'ʒie de a'prindere]
terminal (of battery)	**bornă** (f)	['bornə]
positive terminal	**plus** (n)	[plus]
negative terminal	**minus** (m)	['minus]
fuse	**siguranță** (f)	[sigu'rantsə]
air filter	**filtru** (n) **de aer**	['filtru de 'aer]
oil filter	**filtru** (n) **pentru ulei**	['filtru 'pentru u'lej]
fuel filter	**filtru** (n) **pentru combustibil**	['filtru 'pentru kombus'tibil]

178. Cars. Crash. Repair

car crash	**accident** (n)	[aktʃi'dent]
traffic accident	**accident** (n) **rutier**	[aktʃi'dent ru'tjer]
to crash (into the wall, etc.)	**a se tampona**	[a se tampo'na]
to get smashed up	**a se sparge**	[a se 'spardʒe]
damage	**avariere** (f)	[ava'rjere]
intact (unscathed)	**întreg**	[in'treg]
breakdown	**pană** (f)	['panə]
to break down (vi)	**a se strica**	[a se stri'ka]
towrope	**cablu** (n) **de remorcaj**	['kablu de remor'kaʒ]
puncture	**găurire** (f)	[gəu'rire]
to be flat	**a se dezumfla**	[a se dezum'fla]
to pump up	**a pompa**	[a pom'pa]
pressure	**presiune** (f)	[presi'une]
to check (to examine)	**a verifica**	[a verifi'ka]
repair	**reparație** (f)	[repa'ratsie]
auto repair shop	**service** (n) **auto**	['servis 'auto]

spare part	**detalii** (f pl)	[de'talij]
part	**detaliu** (n)	[de'talju]
bolt (with nut)	**şurub** (n)	[ʃu'rub]
screw (fastener)	**şurub** (n)	[ʃu'rub]
nut	**piuliță** (f)	[pju'litsə]
washer	**şaibă** (f)	['ʃajbə]
bearing (e.g., ball ~)	**rulment** (m)	[rul'ment]
tube	**tub** (n)	[tub]
gasket (head ~)	**garnitură** (f)	[garni'turə]
cable, wire	**cablu** (n)	['kablu]
jack	**cric** (n)	[krik]
wrench	**cheie** (f) **fixă**	['kee 'fiksə]
hammer	**ciocan** (n)	[tʃio'kan]
pump	**pompă** (f)	['pompə]
screwdriver	**şurubelniță** (f)	[ʃuru'belnitsə]
fire extinguisher	**stingător** (n)	[stingə'tor]
warning triangle	**semn** (n) **de avarie**	[semn de a'varie]
to stall (vi)	**a se opri**	[a se o'pri]
stall (n)	**oprire** (f)	[o'prire]
to be broken	**a fi stricat**	[a fi stri'kat]
to overheat (vi)	**a se încălzi**	[a se ɨnkəl'zi]
to be clogged up	**a se înfunda**	[a se ɨnfun'da]
to freeze up (pipes, etc.)	**a îngheța**	[a ɨnge'tsa]
to burst (vi, ab. tube)	**a crăpa**	[a krə'pa]
pressure	**presiune** (f)	[presi'une]
level	**nivel** (n)	[ni'vel]
slack (~ belt)	**scăzut**	[skə'zut]
dent	**îndoitură** (f)	[ɨndoi'turə]
knocking noise (engine)	**lovitură** (f)	[lovi'turə]
crack	**crăpătură** (f)	[krəpə'turə]
scratch	**zgârietură** (f)	[zgɨrie'turə]

179. Cars. Road

road	**drum** (n)	[drum]
highway	**autostradă** (f)	[auto'stradə]
freeway	**şosea** (f)	[ʃo'sʲa]
direction (way)	**direcție** (f)	[di'rektsie]
distance	**distanță** (f)	[dis'tantsə]
bridge	**pod** (n)	[pod]
parking lot	**loc** (n) **de parcare**	[lok de par'kare]

square	**piață** (f)	['pjatsə]
interchange	**răscruce** (f)	[rəs'krutʃe]
tunnel	**tunel** (n)	[tu'nel]
gas station	**benzinărie** (f)	[benzinə'rie]
parking lot	**parcare** (f)	[par'kare]
gas pump (fuel dispenser)	**stație** (f) **de benzină**	['statsie de ben'zinə]
auto repair shop	**garaj** (n)	[ga'raʒ]
to get gas (to fill up)	**a alimenta**	[a alimen'ta]
fuel	**combustibil** (m)	[kombus'tibil]
jerrycan	**canistră** (f)	[ka'nistrə]
asphalt	**asfalt** (n)	[as'falt]
road markings	**marcare** (f)	[mar'kare]
curb	**bordură** (f)	[bor'durə]
guardrail	**îngrădire** (f)	[ɨngrə'dire]
ditch	**şanț** (n) **de scurgere**	[ʃants de 'skurdʒere]
roadside (shoulder)	**margine** (f)	['mardʒine]
lamppost	**stâlp** (m)	[stɨlp]
to drive (a car)	**a conduce**	[a kon'dutʃe]
to turn (e.g., ~ left)	**a întoarce**	[a ɨnto'artʃe]
to make a U-turn	**a vira**	[a vi'ra]
reverse (~ gear)	**mers** (n) **înapoi**	['mers ɨna'poj]
to honk (vi)	**a semnaliza**	[a semnali'za]
honk (sound)	**semnal** (n) **acustic**	[sem'nal a'kustik]
to get stuck (in the mud, etc.)	**a se împotmoli**	[a se ɨmpotmo'li]
to spin the wheels	**a remorca**	[a remor'ka]
to cut, to turn off (vt)	**a opri**	[a op'ri]
speed	**viteză** (f)	[vi'tezə]
to exceed the speed limit	**a depăşi viteza**	[a depə'ʃi vi'teza]
to give a ticket	**a amenda**	[a amen'da]
traffic lights	**semafor** (n)	[sema'for]
driver's license	**permis** (n) **de conducere**	[per'mis de kon'dutʃere]
grade crossing	**traversare** (f)	[traver'sare]
intersection	**intersecție** (f)	[inter'sektsie]
crosswalk	**trecere** (f) **de pietoni**	['tretʃere de pie'ton^j]
bend, curve	**curbă** (f)	['kurbə]
pedestrian zone	**zonă** (f) **pentru pietoni**	['zonə 'pentru pie'ton^j]

180. Traffic signs

rules of the road	**reguli** (f pl) **de circulație**	['regul^j de tʃirku'latsie]
road sign (traffic sign)	**semn** (n)	[semn]
passing (overtaking)	**întrecere** (f)	[ɨn'tretʃere]
curve	**viraj** (n)	[vi'raʒ]

U-turn	**întoarcere** (f)	[intu'artʃerə]
traffic circle	**mişcare** (f) **circulară**	[miʃ'kare tʃiru'larə]
No entry	**intrarea interzisă**	[in'trarʲa inter'zisə]
No vehicles allowed	**circulația interzisă**	[tʃirku'latsia inter'zisə]
No passing	**depăşirea interzisă**	[depə'ʃirʲa inter'zisə]
No parking	**parcarea interzisă**	[par'karʲa inter'zisə]
No stopping	**oprirea interzisă**	[o'prirʲa inter'zisə]
dangerous bend	**curbă** (f) **periculoasă**	['kurbə perikulo'asə]
steep descent	**pantă** (f) **abruptă**	['pantə a'bruptə]
one-way traffic	**într-o singură direcție** (f)	['intro 'singurə di'rektsie]
crosswalk	**trecere** (f) **de pietoni**	['tretʃere de pie'tonʲ]
slippery road	**drum** (n) **alunecos**	[drum alune'kos]
YIELD	**cedează trecerea**	[tʃe'dʲazə 'tretʃerʲa]

PEOPLE. LIFE EVENTS

Life events

181. Holidays. Event

celebration, holiday	**sărbătoare** (f)	[sərbəto'are]
national day	**sărbătoare** (f) **națională**	[sərbəto'are natsio'nalə]
public holiday	**zi** (f) **de sărbătoare**	[zi de sərbəto'are]
to commemorate (vt)	**a sărbători**	[a sərbəto'ri]
event (happening)	**eveniment** (n)	[eveni'ment]
event (organized activity)	**manifestare** (f)	[manifes'tare]
banquet (party)	**banchet** (n)	[ban'ket]
reception (formal party)	**recepție** (f)	[re'tʃeptsie]
feast	**ospăț** (n)	[os'pəts]
anniversary	**aniversare** (f)	[aniver'sare]
jubilee	**jubileu** (n)	[ʒubi'leu]
to celebrate (vt)	**a sărbători**	[a sərbəto'ri]
New Year	**Anul** (m) **Nou**	['anul 'nou]
Happy New Year!	**La Mulți Ani!**	[la 'multsʲ anʲ]
Christmas	**Crăciun** (n)	[krə'tʃiun]
Merry Christmas!	**Crăciun Fericit!**	[krə'tʃiun feri'tʃit]
Christmas tree	**pom** (m) **de Crăciun**	[pom de krə'tʃiun]
fireworks (fireworks show)	**artificii** (n)	[arti'fitʃij]
wedding	**nuntă** (f)	['nuntə]
groom	**mire** (m)	['mire]
bride	**mireasă** (f)	[mi'rʲasə]
to invite (vt)	**a invita**	[a invi'ta]
invitation card	**invitație** (f)	[invi'tatsie]
guest	**oaspete** (m)	[o'aspete]
to visit (~ your parents, etc.)	**a merge în ospeție**	[a 'merdʒe ɨn ospe'tsie]
to meet the guests	**a întâmpina oaspeții**	[a ɨntɨmpi'na o'aspetsij]
gift, present	**cadou** (n)	[ka'dou]
to give (sth as present)	**a dărui**	[a dəru'i]
to receive gifts	**a primi cadouri**	[a pri'mi ka'dourʲ]
bouquet (of flowers)	**buchet** (n)	[bu'ket]

congratulations	**urare** (f)	[u'rare]
to congratulate (vt)	**a felicita**	[a felitʃi'ta]
greeting card	**felicitare** (f)	[felitʃi'tare]
to send a postcard	**a expedia o felicitare**	[a ekspedi'ja o felitʃi'tare]
to get a postcard	**a primi o felicitare**	[a pri'mi o felitʃi'tare]
toast	**toast** (n)	[tost]
to offer (a drink, etc.)	**a servi**	[a ser'vi]
champagne	**şampanie** (f)	[ʃam'panie]
to enjoy oneself	**a se veseli**	[a se vese'li]
merriment (gaiety)	**veselie** (f)	[vese'lie]
joy (emotion)	**bucurie** (f)	[buku'rie]
dance	**dans** (n)	[dans]
to dance (vi, vt)	**a dansa**	[a dan'sa]
waltz	**vals** (n)	[vals]
tango	**tangou** (n)	[tan'gou]

182. Funerals. Burial

cemetery	**cimitir** (n)	[tʃimi'tir]
grave, tomb	**mormânt** (n)	[mor'mɨnt]
cross	**cruce** (f)	['krutʃe]
gravestone	**piatră funerară** (n)	['pjatrə fune'rarə]
fence	**gard** (n)	[gard]
chapel	**capelă** (f)	[ka'pelə]
death	**moarte** (f)	[mo'arte]
to die (vi)	**a muri**	[a mu'ri]
the deceased	**mort** (m)	[mort]
mourning	**doliu** (n)	['dolju]
to bury (vt)	**a îngropa**	[a ɨngro'pa]
funeral home	**pompe** (f pl) **funebre**	['pompe fu'nebre]
funeral	**înmormântare** (f)	[ɨnmormɨn'tare]
wreath	**cunună** (f)	[ku'nunə]
casket, coffin	**sicriu** (n)	[si'kriu]
hearse	**dric** (n)	[drik]
shroud	**giulgiu** (n)	['dʒiuldʒiu]
funeral procession	**cortegiu** (n) **funerar**	[kor'tedʒiu fune'rar]
funerary urn	**urnă** (f) **funerară**	['urnə fune'rarə]
crematory	**crematoriu** (n)	[krema'torju]
obituary	**necrolog** (m)	[nekro'log]
to cry (weep)	**a plânge**	[a 'plɨndʒe]
to sob (vi)	**a plânge în hohote**	[a 'plɨndʒe ɨn 'hohote]

183. War. Soldiers

platoon	**pluton** (n)	[plu'ton]
company	**companie** (f)	[kompa'nie]
regiment	**regiment** (n)	[redʒi'ment]
army	**armată** (f)	[ar'matə]
division	**divizie** (f)	[di'vizie]
section, squad	**detaşament** (n)	[detaʃa'ment]
host (army)	**armată** (f)	[ar'matə]
soldier	**soldat** (m)	[sol'dat]
officer	**ofiţer** (m)	[ofi'ʦer]
private	**soldat** (m)	[sol'dat]
sergeant	**sergent** (m)	[ser'dʒent]
lieutenant	**locotenent** (m)	[lokote'nent]
captain	**căpitan** (m)	[kəpi'tan]
major	**maior** (m)	[ma'jor]
colonel	**colonel** (m)	[kolo'nel]
general	**general** (m)	[dʒene'ral]
sailor	**marinar** (m)	[mari'nar]
captain	**căpitan** (m)	[kəpi'tan]
boatswain	**şef** (m) **de echipaj**	[ʃef de eki'paʒ]
artilleryman	**artilerist** (m)	[artile'rist]
paratrooper	**paraşutist** (m)	[paraʃu'tist]
pilot	**pilot** (m)	[pi'lot]
navigator	**navigator** (m)	[naviga'tor]
mechanic	**mecanic** (m)	[me'kanik]
pioneer (sapper)	**genist** (m)	[dʒe'nist]
parachutist	**paraşutist** (m)	[paraʃu'tist]
reconnaissance scout	**cercetaş** (m)	[ʧerʧe'taʃ]
sniper	**lunetist** (m)	[lune'tist]
patrol (group)	**patrulă** (f)	[pa'trulə]
to patrol (vt)	**a patrula**	[a patru'la]
sentry, guard	**santinelă** (f)	[santi'nelə]
warrior	**ostaş** (m)	[os'taʃ]
patriot	**patriot** (m)	[patri'ot]
hero	**erou** (m)	[e'rou]
heroine	**eroină** (f)	[ero'inə]
traitor	**trădător** (m)	[trədə'tor]
to betray (vt)	**a trăda**	[a trə'da]
deserter	**dezertor** (m)	[dezer'tor]
to desert (vi)	**a dezerta**	[a dezer'ta]
mercenary	**mercenar** (m)	[merʧe'nar]

recruit	**recrut** (m)	[re'krut]
volunteer	**voluntar** (m)	[volun'tar]
dead (n)	**ucis** (m)	[u'ʧis]
wounded (n)	**rănit** (m)	[rə'nit]
prisoner of war	**prizonier** (m)	[prizo'njer]

184. War. Military actions. Part 1

war	**război** (n)	[rəz'boj]
to be at war	**a lupta**	[a lup'ta]
civil war	**război** (n) **civil**	[rəz'boj ʧi'vil]
treacherously (adv)	**în mod perfid**	[in mod per'fid]
declaration of war	**declarare** (f)	[dekla'rare]
to declare (~ war)	**a declara**	[a dekla'ra]
aggression	**agresiune** (f)	[agresi'une]
to attack (invade)	**a ataca**	[a ata'ka]
to invade (vt)	**a captura**	[a kaptu'ra]
invader	**cotropitor** (m)	[kotropi'tor]
conqueror	**cuceritor** (m)	[kuʧeri'tor]
defense	**apărare** (f)	[apə'rare]
to defend (a country, etc.)	**a apăra**	[a apə'ra]
to defend (against ...)	**a se apăra**	[a se apə'ra]
enemy	**duşman** (m)	[duʃ'man]
foe, adversary	**adversar** (m)	[adver'sar]
enemy (as adj)	**duşmănos**	[duʃmə'nos]
strategy	**strategie** (f)	[strate'dʒie]
tactics	**tactică** (f)	['taktikə]
order	**ordin** (n)	['ordin]
command (order)	**comandă** (f)	[ko'mandə]
to order (vt)	**a ordona**	[a ordo'na]
mission	**misiune** (f)	[misi'une]
secret (adj)	**secret**	[se'kret]
battle	**bătălie** (f)	[bətə'lie]
combat	**luptă** (f)	['luptə]
attack	**atac** (n)	[a'tak]
charge (assault)	**asalt** (n)	[a'salt]
to storm (vt)	**a asalta**	[a asal'ta]
siege (to be under ~)	**asediu** (n)	[a'sedju]
offensive (n)	**atac** (n)	[a'tak]
to go on the offensive	**a ataca**	[a ata'ka]

retreat	**retragere** (f)	[re'tradʒere]
to retreat (vi)	**a se retrage**	[a se re'tradʒe]
encirclement	**încercuire** (f)	[ɨntʃerku'ire]
to encircle (vt)	**a încercui**	[a ɨntʃerku'i]
bombing (by aircraft)	**bombardament** (n)	[bombarda'ment]
to drop a bomb	**a arunca o bombă**	[a arun'ka o 'bombə]
to bomb (vt)	**a bombarda**	[a bombar'da]
explosion	**explozie** (f)	[eks'plozie]
shot	**împuşcătură** (f)	[ɨmpuʃkə'turə]
to fire (~ a shot)	**a împuşca**	[a ɨmpuʃ'ka]
firing (burst of ~)	**foc** (n)	[fok]
to aim (to point a weapon)	**a ținti**	[a tsin'ti]
to point (a gun)	**a îndrepta**	[a ɨndrep'ta]
to hit (the target)	**a nimeri**	[a nime'ri]
to sink (~ a ship)	**a scufunda**	[a skufun'da]
hole (in a ship)	**gaură** (f)	['gaurə]
to founder, to sink (vi)	**a se scufunda**	[a se skufun'da]
front (war ~)	**front** (n)	[front]
evacuation	**evacuare** (f)	[evaku'are]
to evacuate (vt)	**a evacua**	[a evaku'a]
trench	**tranşee** (f)	[tran'ʃee]
barbwire	**sârmă** (f) **ghimpată**	['sɨrmə gim'patə]
barrier (anti tank ~)	**îngrădire** (f)	[ɨngrə'dire]
watchtower	**turlă** (f)	['turlə]
military hospital	**spital** (n)	[spi'tal]
to wound (vt)	**a răni**	[a rə'ni]
wound	**rană** (f)	['ranə]
wounded (n)	**rănit** (m)	[rə'nit]
to be wounded	**a fi rănit**	[a fi rə'nit]
serious (wound)	**serios**	[se'rjos]

185. War. Military actions. Part 2

captivity	**prizonierat** (n)	[prizonie'rat]
to take captive	**a lua prizonier**	[a lu'a prizo'njer]
to be held captive	**a fi prizonier**	[a fi prizo'njer]
to be taken captive	**a cădea prizonier**	[a kə'dʲa prizo'njer]
concentration camp	**lagăr** (n) **de concentrare**	['lagər de kontʃen'trare]
prisoner of war	**prizonier** (m)	[prizo'njer]
to escape (vi)	**a evada**	[a eva'da]
to betray (vt)	**a trăda**	[a trə'da]

betrayer	**trădător** (m)	[trədə'tor]
betrayal	**trădare** (f)	[trə'dare]
to execute (by firing squad)	**a împuşca**	[a ɨmpuʃ'ka]
execution (by firing squad)	**împuşcare** (f)	[ɨmpuʃ'kare]
equipment (military gear)	**echipare** (f)	[eki'pare]
shoulder board	**epolet** (m)	[epo'let]
gas mask	**mască** (f) **de gaze**	['maskə de 'gaze]
field radio	**stație** (f) **de radio**	['statsie de 'radio]
cipher, code	**cifru** (n)	['tʃifru]
secrecy	**conspirație** (f)	[konspi'ratsie]
password	**parolă** (f)	[pa'rolə]
land mine	**mină** (f)	['minə]
to mine (road, etc.)	**a mina**	[a mi'na]
minefield	**câmp** (n) **minat**	[kɨmp mi'nat]
air-raid warning	**alarmă** (f) **aeriană**	[a'larmə aeri'anə]
alarm (alert signal)	**alarmă** (f)	[a'larmə]
signal	**semnal** (n)	[sem'nal]
signal flare	**rachetă** (f) **de semnalizare**	[ra'ketə de semnali'zare]
headquarters	**stat-major** (n)	[stat ma'ʒor]
reconnaissance	**cercetare** (f)	[tʃertʃe'tare]
situation	**condiții** (f pl)	[kon'ditsij]
report	**raport** (n)	[ra'port]
ambush	**ambuscadă** (f)	[ambus'kadə]
reinforcement (of army)	**întărire** (f)	[ɨntə'rire]
target	**țintă** (f)	['tsintə]
proving ground	**poligon** (n)	[poli'gon]
military exercise	**manevre** (f pl)	[ma'nevre]
panic	**panică** (f)	['panikə]
devastation	**ruină** (f)	[ru'inə]
destruction, ruins	**distrugere** (f)	[dis'trudʒere]
to destroy (vt)	**a distruge**	[a dis'trudʒe]
to survive (vi, vt)	**a scăpa cu viață**	[a skə'pa ku 'vjatsə]
to disarm (vt)	**a dezarma**	[a dezar'ma]
to handle (~ a gun)	**a mânui**	[a mɨnu'i]
Attention!	**Drepți!**	[drepts]
At ease!	**Pe loc repaus!**	[pe lok re'paus]
feat, act of courage	**faptă** (f) **eroică**	['faptə ero'ikə]
oath (vow)	**jurământ** (n)	[ʒurə'mɨnt]
to swear (an oath)	**a jura**	[a ʒu'ra]

decoration (medal, etc.)	**premiu** (n)	['premju]
to award (give medal to)	**a premia**	[a premi'ja]
medal	**medalie** (f)	[me'dalie]
order (e.g., ~ of Merit)	**ordin** (n)	['ordin]
victory	**victorie** (f)	[vik'torie]
defeat	**înfrângere** (f)	[ɨn'frɨndʒere]
armistice	**armistițiu** (n)	[armis'titsju]
standard (battle flag)	**drapel** (n)	[dra'pel]
glory (honor, fame)	**glorie** (f)	['glorie]
parade	**paradă** (f)	[pa'radə]
to march (on parade)	**a mărşălui**	[a mərʃəlu'i]

186. Weapons

weapons	**armă** (f)	['armə]
firearms	**armă** (f) **de foc**	['armə de fok]
cold weapons (knives, etc.)	**armă** (f) **albă**	['armə 'albə]
chemical weapons	**armă** (f) **chimică**	['armə 'kimikə]
nuclear (adj)	**nuclear**	[nukle'ar]
nuclear weapons	**armă** (f) **nucleară**	['armə nukle'arə]
bomb	**bombă** (f)	['bombə]
atomic bomb	**bombă** (f) **atomică**	['bombə a'tomikə]
pistol (gun)	**pistol** (n)	[pis'tol]
rifle	**armă** (f)	['armə]
submachine gun	**automat** (n)	[auto'mat]
machine gun	**mitralieră** (f)	[mitra'ljerə]
muzzle	**gură** (f)	['gurə]
barrel	**țeavă** (f)	['tsʲavə]
caliber	**calibru** (n)	[ka'libru]
trigger	**cocoş** (m)	[ko'koʃ]
sight (aiming device)	**înălțător** (n)	[ɨnəltsə'tor]
magazine	**magazie** (f)	[maga'zie]
butt (shoulder stock)	**patul** (n) **de puşcă**	['patul de 'puʃka]
hand grenade	**grenadă** (f)	[gre'nadə]
explosive	**exploziv** (n)	[eksplo'ziv]
bullet	**glonț** (n)	[glonts]
cartridge	**cartuş** (n)	[kar'tuʃ]
charge	**încărcătură** (f)	[ɨnkərkə'turə]
ammunition	**muniții** (f pl)	[mu'nitsij]
bomber (aircraft)	**bombardier** (n)	[bombar'djer]

fighter	**distrugător** (n)	[distrugə'tor]
helicopter	**elicopter** (n)	[elikop'ter]
anti-aircraft gun	**tun** (n) **antiaerian**	[tun antiaeri'an]
tank	**tanc** (n)	[tank]
tank gun	**tun** (n)	[tun]
artillery	**artilerie** (f)	[artile'rie]
gun (cannon, howitzer)	**tun** (n)	[tun]
to lay (a gun)	**a îndrepta**	[a ɨndrep'ta]
shell (projectile)	**proiectil** (n)	[proek'til]
mortar bomb	**mină** (f)	['minə]
mortar	**aruncător** (n) **de mine**	[arunkə'tor de 'mine]
splinter (shell fragment)	**schijă** (f)	['skiʒə]
submarine	**submarin** (n)	[subma'rin]
torpedo	**torpilă** (f)	[tor'pilə]
missile	**rachetă** (f)	[ra'ketə]
to load (gun)	**a încărca**	[a ɨnkər'ka]
to shoot (vi)	**a trage**	[a 'tradʒə]
to point at (the cannon)	**a ținti**	[a tsin'ti]
bayonet	**baionetă** (f)	[bajo'netə]
rapier	**spadă** (f)	['spadə]
saber (e.g., cavalry ~)	**sabie** (f)	['sabie]
spear (weapon)	**suliță** (f)	['sulitsə]
bow	**arc** (n)	[ark]
arrow	**săgeată** (f)	[sə'dʒʲatə]
musket	**flintă** (f)	['flintə]
crossbow	**arbaletă** (f)	[arba'letə]

187. Ancient people

primitive (prehistoric)	**primitiv**	[primi'tiv]
prehistoric (adj)	**preistoric**	[preis'torik]
ancient (~ civilization)	**străvechi**	[strə'veki]
Stone Age	**Epoca** (f) **de piatră**	['epoka de 'pjatrə]
Bronze Age	**Epoca** (f) **de bronz**	['epoka de 'bronz]
Ice Age	**Epoca** (f) **glaciară**	['epoka glatʃi'arə]
tribe	**trib** (n)	[trib]
cannibal	**canibal** (m)	[kani'bal]
hunter	**vânător** (m)	[vɨnə'tor]
to hunt (vi, vt)	**a vâna**	[a vɨ'na]
mammoth	**mamut** (m)	[ma'mut]
cave	**peşteră** (f)	['peʃterə]
fire	**foc** (n)	[fok]

campfire	**foc** (n) **de tabără**	[fok də ta'bərə]
cave painting	**desen** (n) **pe piatră**	[de'sen pe 'pjatrə]
tool (e.g., stone ax)	**unealtă** (f)	[u'nʲaltə]
spear	**suliță** (f)	['sulitsə]
stone ax	**topor** (n) **de piatră**	[to'por din 'pjatrə]
to be at war	**a lupta**	[a lup'ta]
to domesticate (vt)	**a domestici**	[a domesti'tʃi]
idol	**idol** (m)	['idol]
to worship (vt)	**a se închina**	[a se ɨnki'na]
superstition	**superstiție** (f)	[supers'titsie]
evolution	**evoluție** (f)	[evo'lutsie]
development	**dezvoltare** (f)	[dezvol'tare]
disappearance (extinction)	**dispariție** (f)	[dispa'ritsie]
to adapt oneself	**a se acomoda**	[a se akomo'da]
archeology	**arheologie** (f)	[arheolo'dʒie]
archeologist	**arheolog** (m)	[arheo'log]
archeological (adj)	**arheologic**	[arheo'lodʒik]
excavation site	**săpături** (f pl)	[səpə'turʲ]
excavations	**săpături** (f pl)	[səpə'turʲ]
find (object)	**descoperire** (f)	[deskope'rire]
fragment	**fragment** (n)	[frag'ment]

188. Middle Ages

people (ethnic group)	**popor** (n)	[po'por]
peoples	**popoare** (n pl)	[popo'are]
tribe	**trib** (n)	[trib]
tribes	**triburi** (n pl)	['triburʲ]
barbarians	**barbari** (m pl)	[bar'barʲ]
Gauls	**gali** (m pl)	[galʲ]
Goths	**goți** (m pl)	[gotsʲ]
Slavs	**slavi** (m pl)	[slavʲ]
Vikings	**vikingi** (m pl)	['vikindʒʲ]
Romans	**romani** (m pl)	[ro'manʲ]
Roman (adj)	**roman**	[ro'man]
Byzantines	**bizantinieni** (m pl)	[bizantini'enʲ]
Byzantium	**Imperiul** (n) **Bizantin**	[im'perjul bizan'tin]
Byzantine (adj)	**bizantin**	[bizan'tin]
emperor	**împărat** (m)	[ɨmpə'rat]
leader, chief (tribal ~)	**căpetenie** (f)	[kəpe'tenie]
powerful (~ king)	**puternic**	[pu'ternik]

king	**rege** (m)	['redʒe]
ruler (sovereign)	**conducător** (m)	[kondukə'tor]
knight	**cavaler** (m)	[kava'ler]
feudal lord	**feudal** (m)	[feu'dal]
feudal (adj)	**feudal**	[feu'dal]
vassal	**vasal** (m)	[va'sal]
duke	**duce** (m)	['dutʃe]
earl	**conte** (m)	['konte]
baron	**baron** (m)	[ba'ron]
bishop	**episcop** (m)	[e'piskop]
armor	**armură** (f)	[ar'murə]
shield	**scut** (n)	[skut]
sword	**sabie** (f)	['sabie]
visor	**vizieră** (f)	[vi'zjerə]
chainmail	**zale** (f pl)	['zale]
Crusade	**cruciadă** (f)	[krutʃi'adə]
crusader	**cruciat** (m)	[krutʃi'at]
territory	**teritoriu** (n)	[teri'torju]
to attack (invade)	**a ataca**	[a ata'ka]
to conquer (vt)	**a cuceri**	[a kutʃe'ri]
to occupy (invade)	**a cotropi**	[a kotro'pi]
siege (to be under ~)	**asediu** (n)	[a'sedju]
besieged (adj)	**asediat** (m)	[asedi'at]
to besiege (vt)	**a asedia**	[a asedi'a]
inquisition	**inchiziție** (f)	[inki'zitsie]
inquisitor	**inchizitor** (m)	[inkizi'tor]
torture	**tortură** (f)	[tor'turə]
cruel (adj)	**crud**	[krud]
heretic	**eretic** (m)	[e'retik]
heresy	**erezie** (f)	[ere'zie]
seafaring	**navigație** (f) **maritimă**	[navi'gatsie ma'ritime]
pirate	**pirat** (m)	[pi'rat]
piracy	**piraterie** (f)	[pirate'rie]
boarding (attack)	**abordaj** (n)	[abor'daʒ]
loot, booty	**captură** (f)	[kap'turə]
treasures	**comoară** (f)	[komo'arə]
discovery	**descoperire** (f)	[deskope'rire]
to discover (new land, etc.)	**a descoperi**	[a deskope'ri]
expedition	**expediție** (f)	[ekspe'ditsie]
musketeer	**mușchetar** (m)	[muʃke'tar]
cardinal	**cardinal** (m)	[kardi'nal]
heraldry	**heraldică** (f)	[he'raldikə]
heraldic (adj)	**heraldic**	[he'raldik]

189. Leader. Chief. Authorities

king	**rege** (m)	['redʒe]
queen	**regină** (f)	[re'dʒinə]
royal (adj)	**regal**	[re'gal]
kingdom	**regat** (n)	[re'gat]
prince	**prinț** (m)	[prints]
princess	**prințesă** (f)	[prin'tsesə]
president	**preşedinte** (m)	[preʃə'dinte]
vice-president	**vice-preşedinte** (m)	['vitʃe preʃə'dinte]
senator	**senator** (m)	[sena'tor]
monarch	**monarh** (m)	[mo'narh]
ruler (sovereign)	**conducător** (m)	[kondukə'tor]
dictator	**dictator** (m)	[dikta'tor]
tyrant	**tiran** (m)	[ti'ran]
magnate	**magnat** (m)	[mag'nat]
director	**director** (m)	[di'rektor]
chief	**şef** (m)	[ʃef]
manager (director)	**manager** (m)	['menedʒə]
boss	**boss** (m)	[bos]
owner	**patron** (m)	[pa'tron]
head (~ of delegation)	**şef** (m)	[ʃef]
authorities	**autorități** (f pl)	[autoritətsʲ]
superiors	**conducere** (f)	[kon'dutʃere]
governor	**guvernator** (m)	[guverna'tor]
consul	**consul** (m)	['konsul]
diplomat	**diplomat** (m)	[diplo'mat]
mayor	**primar** (m)	[pri'mar]
sheriff	**şerif** (m)	[ʃə'rif]
emperor	**împărat** (m)	[impə'rat]
tsar, czar	**țar** (m)	[tsar]
pharaoh	**faraon** (m)	[fara'on]
khan	**han** (m)	[han]

190. Road. Way. Directions

road	**drum** (n)	[drum]
way (direction)	**cale** (f)	['kale]
freeway	**şosea** (f)	[ʃo'sʲa]
highway	**autostradă** (f)	[auto'stradə]
interstate	**drum** (n) **național**	['drum natsio'nal]

main road	**drumul** (n) **principal**	['drumul printʃi'pal]
dirt road	**drum** (n) **vicinal**	['drum vitʃi'nal]
pathway	**potecă** (f)	[po'təkə]
footpath (troddenpath)	**cărare** (f)	[kə'rare]
Where?	**Unde?**	['unde]
Where (to)?	**Unde?**	['unde]
From where?	**De unde?**	[de 'unde]
direction (way)	**direcție** (f)	[di'rektsie]
to point (~ the way)	**a arăta**	[a arə'ta]
to the left	**la stânga**	[la 'stɨnga]
to the right	**la dreapta**	[la 'drʲapta]
straight ahead (adv)	**înainte**	[ɨna'inte]
back (e.g., to turn ~)	**înapoi**	[ɨna'poj]
bend, curve	**curbă** (f)	['kurbə]
to turn (e.g., ~ left)	**a vira**	[a vi'ra]
to make a U-turn	**a întoarce**	[a ɨnto'artʃe]
to be visible (mountains, castle, etc.)	**a se zări**	[a se zə'ri]
to appear (come into view)	**a se arăta**	[a se arə'ta]
stop, halt (e.g., during a trip)	**oprire** (f)	[o'prire]
to rest, to pause (vi)	**a se odihni**	[a se odih'ni]
rest (pause)	**odihnă** (f)	[o'dihnə]
to lose one's way	**a se rătăci**	[a se rətə'tʃi]
to lead to ... (ab. road)	**a duce spre ...**	[a 'dutʃe spre]
to come out (e.g., on the highway)	**a ieşi la ...**	[a e'ʃi la]
stretch (of road)	**porțiune** (f)	[portsi'une]
asphalt	**asfalt** (n)	[as'falt]
curb	**bordură** (f)	[bor'durə]
ditch	**şanț** (n)	[ʃants]
manhole	**capac** (n) **de canalizare**	[ka'pak de kanali'zare]
roadside (shoulder)	**margine** (f)	['mardʒine]
pit, pothole	**groapă** (f)	[gro'apə]
to go (on foot)	**a merge**	[a 'merdʒe]
to pass (overtake)	**a depăşi**	[a depə'ʃi]
step (footstep)	**pas** (m)	[pas]
on foot (adv)	**pe jos**	[pe ʒos]
to block (road)	**a despărți**	[a despər'tsi]
boom gate	**barieră** (f)	[ba'rjerə]
dead end	**fundătură** (f)	[fundə'turə]

191. Breaking the law. Criminals. Part 1

bandit	**bandit** (m)	[ban'dit]
crime	**crimă** (f)	['krimə]
criminal (person)	**criminal** (m)	[krimi'nal]
thief	**hoț** (m)	[hots]
to steal (vi, vt)	**a fura**	[a fu'ra]
stealing (larceny)	**hoție** (f)	[ho'tsie]
theft	**furt** (n)	[furt]
to kidnap (vt)	**a răpi**	[a rə'pi]
kidnapping	**răpire** (f)	[rə'pire]
kidnapper	**răpitor** (m)	[rəpi'tor]
ransom	**răscumpărare** (f)	[rəskumpə'rare]
to demand ransom	**a cere răscumpărare**	[a 'tʃere rəskumpə'rare]
to rob (vt)	**a jefui**	[a ʒefu'i]
robbery	**jaf** (n)	[ʒaf]
robber	**jefuitor** (m)	[ʒefui'tor]
to extort (vt)	**a escroca**	[a eskro'ka]
extortionist	**escroc** (m)	[es'krok]
extortion	**escrocherie** (f)	[eskroke'rie]
to murder, to kill	**a ucide**	[a u'tʃide]
murder	**asasinat** (n)	[asasi'nat]
murderer	**asasin** (m)	[asa'sin]
gunshot	**împuşcătură** (f)	[ɨmpuʃkə'turə]
to fire (~ a shot)	**a împuşca**	[a ɨmpuʃ'ka]
to shoot to death	**a împuşca**	[a ɨmpuʃ'ka]
to shoot (vi)	**a trage**	[a 'tradʒə]
shooting	**focuri** (n) **de armă**	['fokur^j de 'armə]
incident (fight, etc.)	**întâmplare** (f)	[ɨntɨm'plare]
fight, brawl	**bătaie** (f)	[bə'tae]
Help!	**Ajutor!**	[aʒu'tor]
victim	**jertfă** (f)	['ʒertfə]
to damage (vt)	**a prejudicia**	[a preʒuditʃi'a]
damage	**daună** (f)	['daunə]
dead body, corpse	**cadavru** (n)	[ka'davru]
grave (~ crime)	**grav**	[grav]
to attack (vt)	**a ataca**	[a ata'ka]
to beat (to hit)	**a bate**	[a 'bate]
to beat up	**a snopi în bătăi**	[a sno'pi ɨn bətəj]
to take (rob of sth)	**a lua**	[a lu'a]
to stab to death	**a înjunghia**	[a ɨnʒungi'ja]

to maim (vt)	**a schilodi**	[a skilo'di]
to wound (vt)	**a răni**	[a rə'ni]
blackmail	**şantaj** (n)	[ʃan'taʒ]
to blackmail (vt)	**a şantaja**	[a ʃanta'ʒa]
blackmailer	**şantajist** (m)	[ʃanta'ʒist]
protection racket	**banditism** (n)	[bandi'tizm]
racketeer	**bandit** (m)	[ban'dit]
gangster	**gangster** (m)	['gangster]
mafia, Mob	**mafie** (f)	['mafie]
pickpocket	**hoţ** (m) **de buzunare**	[hots de buzu'nare]
burglar	**spărgător** (m)	[spərgə'tor]
smuggling	**contrabandă** (f)	[kontra'bandə]
smuggler	**contrabandist** (m)	[kontraban'dist]
forgery	**falsificare** (f)	[falsifi'kare]
to forge (counterfeit)	**a falsifica**	[a falsifi'ka]
fake (forged)	**fals**	[fals]

192. Breaking the law. Criminals. Part 2

rape	**viol** (n)	[vi'ol]
to rape (vt)	**a viola**	[a vio'la]
rapist	**violator** (m)	[viola'tor]
maniac	**maniac** (m)	[mani'ak]
prostitute (fem.)	**prostituată** (f)	[prostitu'atə]
prostitution	**prostituţie** (f)	[prosti'tutsie]
pimp	**proxenet** (m)	[prokse'net]
drug addict	**narcoman** (m)	[narko'man]
drug dealer	**vânzător** (m) **de droguri**	[vɨnzə'tor de 'drogurʲ]
to blow up (bomb)	**a arunca în aer**	[a arun'ka ɨn 'aer]
explosion	**explozie** (f)	[eks'plozie]
to set fire	**a incendia**	[a intʃendi'a]
arsonist	**incendiator** (m)	[intʃendia'tor]
terrorism	**terorism** (n)	[tero'rism]
terrorist	**terorist** (m)	[tero'rist]
hostage	**ostatic** (m)	[os'tatik]
to swindle (deceive)	**a înşela**	[a ɨnʃə'la]
swindle, deception	**înşelăciune** (f)	[ɨnʃələ'tʃiune]
swindler	**şarlatan** (m)	[ʃarla'tan]
to bribe (vt)	**a mitui**	[a mitu'i]
bribery	**mituire** (f)	[mitu'ire]

bribe	**mită** (f)	['mitə]
poison	**otravă** (f)	[o'travə]
to poison (vt)	**a otrăvi**	[a otrə'vi]
to poison oneself	**a se otrăvi**	[a se otrə'vi]
suicide (act)	**sinucidere** (f)	[sinu'ʧidere]
suicide (person)	**sinucigaş** (m)	[sinuʧi'gaʃ]
to threaten (vt)	**a amenința**	[a amenin'tsa]
threat	**amenințare** (f)	[amenin'tsare]
to make an attempt	**a atenta la**	[a aten'ta la]
attempt (attack)	**atentat** (n)	[aten'tat]
to steal (a car)	**a goni**	[a go'ni]
to hijack (a plane)	**a goni**	[a go'ni]
revenge	**răzbunare** (f)	[rəzbu'nare]
to avenge (get revenge)	**a răzbuna**	[a rəzbu'na]
to torture (vt)	**a tortura**	[a tortu'ra]
torture	**tortură** (f)	[tor'turə]
to torment (vt)	**a chinui**	[a kinu'i]
pirate	**pirat** (m)	[pi'rat]
hooligan	**huligan** (m)	[huli'gan]
armed (adj)	**înarmat**	[ɨnar'mat]
violence	**violență** (f)	[vio'lentsə]
illegal (unlawful)	**ilegal**	[ile'gal]
spying (espionage)	**spionaj** (n)	[spio'naʒ]
to spy (vi)	**a spiona**	[a spio'na]

193. Police. Law. Part 1

justice	**justiție** (f)	[ʒus'titsie]
court (see you in ~)	**curte** (f)	['kurte]
judge	**judecător** (m)	[ʒudekə'tor]
jurors	**jurați** (m pl)	[ʒu'ratsʲ]
jury trial	**curte** (f) **de jurați**	['kurte de ʒu'ratsʲ]
to judge, to try (vt)	**a judeca**	[a ʒude'ka]
lawyer, attorney	**avocat** (m)	[avo'kat]
defendant	**acuzat** (m)	[aku'zat]
dock	**banca** (f) **acuzaților**	['banka aku'zatsilor]
charge	**învinuire** (f)	[ɨnvinu'ire]
accused	**învinuit** (m)	[ɨnvinu'it]
sentence	**verdict** (n)	[ver'dikt]
to sentence (vt)	**a condamna**	[a kondam'na]

guilty (culprit)	**vinovat** (m)	[vino'vat]
to punish (vt)	**a pedepsi**	[a pedep'si]
punishment	**pedeapsă** (f)	[pe'd^japsə]
fine (penalty)	**amendă** (f)	[a'mendə]
life imprisonment	**închisoare** (f) **pe viață**	[ɨnkiso'are pe 'vjatsə]
death penalty	**pedeapsă** (f) **capitală**	[pe'd^japsə kapi'talə]
electric chair	**scaun** (n) **electric**	['skaun e'lektrik]
gallows	**spânzurătoare** (f)	[spɨnzurəto'are]
to execute (vt)	**a executa**	[a egzeku'ta]
execution	**execuție** (f)	[egze'kutsie]
prison, jail	**închisoare** (f)	[ɨnkiso'are]
cell	**cameră** (f)	['kamerə]
escort (convoy)	**convoi** (n)	[kon'voj]
prison guard	**paznic** (m)	['paznik]
prisoner	**arestat** (m)	[ares'tat]
handcuffs	**cătușe** (f pl)	[kə'tuʃə]
to handcuff (vt)	**a pune cătușele**	[a 'pune kə'tuʃəle]
prison break	**evadare** (f)	[eva'dare]
to break out (vi)	**a evada**	[a eva'da]
to disappear (vi)	**a dispărea**	[a dispə'r^ja]
to release (from prison)	**a elibera**	[a elibe'ra]
amnesty	**amnistie** (f)	[am'nistie]
police	**poliție** (f)	[po'litsie]
police officer	**polițist** (m)	[poli'tsist]
police station	**secție** (f) **de poliție**	['sektsie de po'litsie]
billy club	**baston** (n) **de cauciuc**	[bas'ton de kau'tʃiuk]
bullhorn	**portavoce** (f)	[porta'votʃe]
patrol car	**mașină** (f) **de patrulă**	[ma'ʃine de pa'trulə]
siren	**sirenă** (f)	[si'renə]
to turn on the siren	**a conecta sirena**	[a konek'ta si'rena]
siren call	**alarma** (f) **sirenei**	[a'larma si'renej]
crime scene	**locul** (n) **faptei**	['lokul 'faptej]
witness	**martor** (m)	['martor]
freedom	**libertate** (f)	[liber'tate]
accomplice	**complice** (m)	[kom'plitʃe]
to flee (vi)	**a se ascunde**	[a se as'kunde]
trace (to leave a ~)	**urmă** (f)	['urmə]

194. Police. Law. Part 2

search (investigation)	**investigație** (f)	[investi'gatsie]
to look for ...	**a căuta**	[a kəu'ta]

suspicion	**suspiciune** (f)	[suspitʃi'une]
suspicious (e.g., ~ vehicle)	**suspect**	[sus'pekt]
to stop (cause to halt)	**a opri**	[a op'ri]
to detain (keep in custody)	**a reține**	[a re'tsine]
case (lawsuit)	**dosar** (n)	[do'sar]
investigation	**anchetă** (f)	[an'ketə]
detective	**detectiv** (m)	[detek'tiv]
investigator	**anchetator** (m)	[anketa'tor]
hypothesis	**versiune** (f)	[versi'une]
motive	**motiv** (n)	[mo'tiv]
interrogation	**interogatoriu** (n)	[interoga'torju]
to interrogate (vt)	**a interoga**	[a intero'ga]
to question (~ neighbors, etc.)	**a audia**	[a audi'a]
check (identity ~)	**verificare** (f)	[verifi'kare]
round-up (raid)	**razie** (f)	['razie]
search (~ warrant)	**percheziție** (f)	[perke'zitsie]
chase (pursuit)	**urmărire** (f)	[urmə'rire]
to pursue, to chase	**a urmări**	[a urmə'ri]
to track (a criminal)	**a urmări**	[a urmə'ri]
arrest	**arestare** (f)	[ares'tare]
to arrest (sb)	**a aresta**	[a ares'ta]
to catch (thief, etc.)	**a prinde**	[a 'prinde]
capture	**prindere** (f)	['prindere]
document	**act** (n)	[akt]
proof (evidence)	**dovadă** (f)	[do'vadə]
to prove (vt)	**a dovedi**	[a dove'di]
footprint	**amprentă** (f)	[am'prentə]
fingerprints	**amprente** (f pl) **digitale**	[am'prente didʒi'tale]
piece of evidence	**probă** (f)	['probə]
alibi	**alibi** (n)	['alibi]
innocent (not guilty)	**nevinovat** (m)	[nevino'vat]
injustice	**nedreptate** (f)	[nedrep'tate]
unjust, unfair (adj)	**nedrept**	[ne'drept]
criminal (adj)	**criminal** (m)	[krimi'nal]
to confiscate (vt)	**a confisca**	[a konfis'ka]
drug (illegal substance)	**narcotic** (n)	[nar'kotik]
weapon, gun	**armă** (f)	['armə]
to disarm (vt)	**a dezarma**	[a dezar'ma]
to order (command)	**a ordona**	[a ordo'na]
to disappear (vi)	**a dispărea**	[a dispə'rʲa]
law	**lege** (f)	['ledʒe]
legal, lawful (adj)	**legal**	[le'gal]
illegal, illicit (adj)	**ilegal**	[ile'gal]

responsibility (blame)	**responsabilitate** (f)	[responsabili'tate]
responsible (adj)	**responsabil**	[respon'sabil]

NATURE

The Earth. Part 1

195. Outer space

space	**cosmos** (n)	['kosmos]
space (as adj)	**cosmic**	['kosmik]
outer space	**spațiu** (n) **cosmic**	['spatsju 'kosmik]
world	**lume** (f)	['lume]
universe	**univers** (n)	[uni'vers]
galaxy	**galaxie** (f)	[galak'sie]
star	**stea** (f)	[stʲa]
constellation	**constelație** (f)	[konste'latsie]
planet	**planetă** (f)	[pla'netə]
satellite	**satelit** (m)	[sate'lit]
meteorite	**meteorit** (m)	[meteo'rit]
comet	**cometă** (f)	[ko'metə]
asteroid	**asteroid** (m)	[astero'id]
orbit	**orbită** (f)	[or'bitə]
to revolve (~ around the Earth)	**a se roti**	[a se ro'ti]
atmosphere	**atmosferă** (f)	[atmos'ferə]
the Sun	**soare** (n)	[so'are]
solar system	**sistem** (n) **solar**	[sis'tem so'lar]
solar eclipse	**eclipsă** (f) **de soare**	[ek'lipsə de so'are]
the Earth	**Pământ** (n)	[pə'mɨnt]
the Moon	**Lună** (f)	['lunə]
Mars	**Marte** (m)	['marte]
Venus	**Venus** (f)	['venus]
Jupiter	**Jupiter** (m)	['ʒupiter]
Saturn	**Saturn** (m)	[sa'turn]
Mercury	**Mercur** (m)	[mer'kur]
Uranus	**Uranus** (m)	[u'ranus]
Neptune	**Neptun** (m)	[nep'tun]
Pluto	**Pluto** (m)	['pluto]
Milky Way	**Calea** (f) **Lactee**	['kalʲa lak'tee]
Great Bear (Ursa Major)	**Ursa** (f) **mare**	['ursa 'mare]

North Star	**Steaua** (f) **polară**	['stʲawa po'larə]
Martian	**marțian** (m)	[martsi'an]
extraterrestrial (n)	**extraterestru** (m)	[ekstrate'restru]
alien	**extraterestru** (m)	[ekstrate'restru]
flying saucer	**farfurie** (f) **zburătoare**	[farfu'rie zburəto'are]
spaceship	**navă** (f) **spațială**	['navə spatsi'alə]
space station	**stație** (f) **orbitală**	['statsie orbi'talə]
blast-off	**start** (n)	[start]
engine	**motor** (n)	[mo'tor]
nozzle	**ajutaj** (n)	[aʒu'taʒ]
fuel	**combustibil** (m)	[kombus'tibil]
cockpit, flight deck	**cabină** (f)	[ka'binə]
antenna	**antenă** (f)	[an'tenə]
porthole	**hublou** (n)	[hu'blou]
solar panel	**baterie** (f) **solară**	[bate'rie so'larə]
spacesuit	**scafandru** (m)	[ska'fandru]
weightlessness	**imponderabilitate** (f)	[imponderabili'tate]
oxygen	**oxigen** (n)	[oksi'dʒen]
docking (in space)	**unire** (f)	[u'nire]
to dock (vi, vt)	**a uni**	[a u'ni]
observatory	**observator** (n) **astronomic**	[observa'tor astro'nomik]
telescope	**telescop** (n)	[tele'skop]
to observe (vt)	**a observa**	[a obser'va]
to explore (vt)	**a cerceta**	[a tʃertʃe'ta]

196. The Earth

the Earth	**Pământ** (n)	[pə'mɨnt]
the globe (the Earth)	**globul** (n) **pământesc**	['globul pəmɨn'tesk]
planet	**planetă** (f)	[pla'netə]
atmosphere	**atmosferă** (f)	[atmos'ferə]
geography	**geografie** (f)	[dʒeogra'fie]
nature	**natură** (f)	[na'turə]
globe (table ~)	**glob** (n)	[glob]
map	**hartă** (f)	['hartə]
atlas	**atlas** (n)	[at'las]
Europe	**Europa** (f)	[eu'ropa]
Asia	**Asia** (f)	['asia]
Africa	**Africa** (f)	['afrika]
Australia	**Australia** (f)	[au'stralia]

America	**America** (f)	[a'merika]
North America	**America** (f) **de Nord**	[a'merika de nord]
South America	**America** (f) **de Sud**	[a'merika de sud]
Antarctica	**Antarctida** (f)	[antark'tida]
the Arctic	**Arctica** (f)	['arktika]

197. Cardinal directions

north	**nord** (n)	[nord]
to the north	**la nord**	[la nord]
in the north	**la nord**	[la nord]
northern (adj)	**de nord**	[de nord]
south	**sud** (n)	[sud]
to the south	**la sud**	[la sud]
in the south	**la sud**	[la sud]
southern (adj)	**de sud**	[de sud]
west	**vest** (n)	[vest]
to the west	**la vest**	[la vest]
in the west	**la vest**	[la vest]
western (adj)	**de vest**	[de vest]
east	**est** (n)	[est]
to the east	**la est**	[la est]
in the east	**la est**	[la est]
eastern (adj)	**de est**	[de est]

198. Sea. Ocean

sea	**mare** (f)	['mare]
ocean	**ocean** (n)	[otʃə'an]
gulf (bay)	**golf** (n)	[golf]
straits	**strâmtoare** (f)	[strɨmto'are]
land (solid ground)	**pământ** (n)	[pə'mɨnt]
continent (mainland)	**continent** (n)	[konti'nent]
island	**insulă** (f)	['insulə]
peninsula	**peninsulă** (f)	[pe'ninsulə]
archipelago	**arhipelag** (n)	[arhipe'lag]
bay, cove	**golf** (n)	[golf]
harbor	**port** (n)	[port]
lagoon	**lagună** (f)	[la'gunə]
cape	**cap** (n)	[kap]
atoll	**atol** (m)	[a'tol]
reef	**recif** (m)	[re'tʃif]

coral	**coral** (m)	[ko'ral]
coral reef	**recif** (m) **de corali**	[re'ʧif de ko'ralʲ]
deep (adj)	**adânc**	[a'dɨnk]
depth (deep water)	**adâncime** (f)	[adɨn'ʧime]
abyss	**abis** (n)	[a'bis]
trench (e.g., Mariana ~)	**groapă** (f)	[gro'apə]
current (Ocean ~)	**curent** (n)	[ku'rent]
to surround (bathe)	**a spăla**	[a spə'la]
shore	**mal** (n)	[mal]
coast	**litoral** (n)	[lito'ral]
flow (flood tide)	**flux** (n)	[fluks]
ebb (ebb tide)	**reflux** (n)	[re'fluks]
shoal	**banc** (n) **de nisip**	[bank de ni'sip]
bottom (~ of the sea)	**fund** (n)	[fund]
wave	**val** (n)	[val]
crest (~ of a wave)	**creasta** (f) **valului**	['krʲasta 'valuluj]
spume (sea foam)	**spumă** (f)	['spumə]
storm (sea storm)	**furtună** (f)	[fur'tunə]
hurricane	**uragan** (m)	[ura'gan]
tsunami	**tsunami** (n)	[ʦu'nami]
calm (dead ~)	**timp** (n) **calm**	[timp kalm]
quiet, calm (adj)	**liniştit**	[liniʃ'tit]
pole	**pol** (n)	[pol]
polar (adj)	**polar**	[po'lar]
latitude	**longitudine** (f)	[londʒi'tudine]
longitude	**latitudine** (f)	[lati'tudine]
parallel	**paralelă** (f)	[para'lelə]
equator	**ecuator** (n)	[ekua'tor]
sky	**cer** (n)	[ʧer]
horizon	**orizont** (n)	[ori'zont]
air	**aer** (n)	['aer]
lighthouse	**far** (n)	[far]
to dive (vi)	**a se scufunda**	[a se skufun'da]
to sink (ab. boat)	**a se duce la fund**	[a se duʧə lʲa fund]
treasures	**comoară** (f)	[komo'arə]

199. Seas' and Oceans' names

Atlantic Ocean	**Oceanul** (n) **Atlantic**	[oʧə'anul at'lantik]
Indian Ocean	**Oceanul** (n) **Indian**	[oʧə'anul indi'an]

Pacific Ocean	**Oceanul** (n) **Pacific**	[otʃə'anul pa'tʃifik]
Arctic Ocean	**Oceanul** (n) **Înghețat de Nord**	[otʃə'anul inge'tsat de nord]
Black Sea	**Marea** (f) **Neagră**	['marʲa 'nʲagrə]
Red Sea	**Marea** (f) **Roşie**	['marʲa 'roʃie]
Yellow Sea	**Marea** (f) **Galbenă**	['marʲa 'galbenə]
White Sea	**Marea** (f) **Albă**	['marʲa 'albə]
Caspian Sea	**Marea** (f) **Caspică**	['marʲa 'kaspikə]
Dead Sea	**Marea** (f) **Moartă**	['marʲa mo'artə]
Mediterranean Sea	**Marea** (f) **Mediterană**	['marʲa medite'ranə]
Aegean Sea	**Marea** (f) **Egee**	['marʲa e'dʒee]
Adriatic Sea	**Marea** (f) **Adriatică**	['marʲa adri'atikə]
Arabian Sea	**Marea** (f) **Arabiei**	['marʲa a'rabiej]
Sea of Japan	**Marea** (f) **Japoneză**	['marʲa ʒapo'nezə]
Bering Sea	**Marea** (f) **Bering**	['marʲa 'bering]
South China Sea	**Marea** (f) **Chinei de Sud**	['marʲa 'kinej de sud]
Coral Sea	**Marea** (f) **Coral**	['marʲa ko'ral]
Tasman Sea	**Marea** (f) **Tasmaniei**	['marʲa tas'maniej]
Caribbean Sea	**Marea** (f) **Caraibelor**	['marʲa kara'ibelor]
Barents Sea	**Marea** (f) **Barents**	['marʲa ba'rents]
Kara Sea	**Marea** (f) **Kara**	['marʲa 'kara]
North Sea	**Marea** (f) **Nordului**	['marʲa 'norduluj]
Baltic Sea	**Marea** (f) **Baltică**	['marʲa 'baltikə]
Norwegian Sea	**Marea** (f) **Norvegiei**	['marʲa nor'vedʒiej]

200. Mountains

mountain	**munte** (m)	['munte]
mountain range	**lanț** (n) **muntos**	[lants mun'tos]
mountain ridge	**lanț** (n) **de munți**	[lants de munts]
summit, top	**vârf** (n)	[vɨrf]
peak	**culme** (f)	['kulmə]
foot (~ of the mountain)	**poale** (f pl)	[po'ale]
slope (mountainside)	**pantă** (f)	['pantə]
volcano	**vulcan** (n)	[vul'kan]
active volcano	**vulcan** (n) **activ**	[vul'kan ak'tiv]
dormant volcano	**vulcan** (n) **stins**	[vul'kan stins]
eruption	**erupție** (f)	[e'ruptsie]
crater	**crater** (n)	['krater]
magma	**magmă** (f)	['magmə]

lava	**lavă** (f)	['lavə]
molten (~ lava)	**încins**	[ɨn'ʧins]
canyon	**canion** (n)	[kani'on]
gorge	**defileu** (n)	[defi'leu]
crevice	**pas** (n)	[pas]
abyss (chasm)	**prăpastie** (f)	[prə'pastie]
pass, col	**trecătoare** (f)	[trekəto'are]
plateau	**podiş** (n)	[po'diʃ]
cliff	**stâncă** (f)	['stɨnkə]
hill	**deal** (n)	['dʲal]
glacier	**gheţar** (m)	[ge'ʦar]
waterfall	**cascadă** (f)	[kas'kadə]
geyser	**gheizer** (m)	['gejzer]
lake	**lac** (n)	[lak]
plain	**şes** (n)	[ʃəs]
landscape	**peisaj** (n)	[pej'saʒ]
echo	**ecou** (n)	[e'kou]
alpinist	**alpinist** (m)	[alpi'nist]
rock climber	**căţărător** (m)	[kəʦərə'tor]
to conquer (in climbing)	**a cuceri**	[a kuʧe'ri]
climb (an easy ~)	**ascensiune** (f)	[asʧensi'une]

201. Mountains names

The Alps	**Alpi** (m pl)	['alpʲ]
Mont Blanc	**Mont Blanc** (m)	[mon 'blan]
The Pyrenees	**Pirinei** (m)	[piri'nej]
The Carpathians	**Carpaţi** (m pl)	[kar'paʦʲ]
The Ural Mountains	**Munţii** (m pl) **Ural**	['munʦij u'ral]
The Caucasus Mountains	**Caucaz** (m)	[kau'kaz]
Mount Elbrus	**Elbrus** (m)	['elbrus]
The Altai Mountains	**Altai** (m)	[al'taj]
The Tian Shan	**Tian-Şan** (m)	['tjan 'ʃan]
The Pamir Mountains	**Pamir** (m)	[pa'mir]
The Himalayas	**Himalaya**	[hima'laja]
Mount Everest	**Everest** (m)	[eve'rest]
The Andes	**Anzi**	['anzʲ]
Mount Kilimanjaro	**Kilimanjaro** (m)	[kiliman'ʒaro]

202. Rivers

river	**râu** (n)	['rɨu]
spring (natural source)	**izvor** (n)	[iz'vor]
riverbed (river channel)	**matcă** (f)	['matkə]
basin (river valley)	**bazin** (n)	[ba'zin]
to flow into ...	**a se vărsa**	[a se vər'sa]
tributary	**afluent** (m)	[aflu'ent]
bank (of river)	**mal** (n)	[mal]
current (stream)	**curs** (n)	[kurs]
downstream (adv)	**în josul apei**	[ɨn 'ʒosul 'apej]
upstream (adv)	**în susul apei**	[ɨn 'susul 'apej]
inundation	**inundație** (f)	[inun'datsie]
flooding	**revărsare** (f) **a apelor**	[revər'sare a 'apelor]
to overflow (vi)	**a se revărsa**	[a se revər'sa]
to flood (vt)	**a inunda**	[a inun'da]
shallow (shoal)	**banc** (n) **de nisip**	[bank de ni'sip]
rapids	**prag** (n)	[prag]
dam	**baraj** (n)	[ba'raʒ]
canal	**canal** (n)	[ka'nal]
reservoir (artificial lake)	**bazin** (n)	[ba'zin]
sluice, lock	**ecluză** (f)	[e'kluzə]
water body (pond, etc.)	**bazin** (n)	[ba'zin]
swamp (marshland)	**mlaştină** (f)	['mlaʃtinə]
bog, marsh	**mlaştină** (f), **smârc** (n)	['mlaʃtinə], [smɨrk]
whirlpool	**vârtej** (n) **de apă**	[vɨr'teʒ de 'apə]
stream (brook)	**pârâu** (n)	[pɨ'rɨu]
drinking (ab. water)	**potabil**	[po'tabil]
fresh (~ water)	**nesărat**	[nesə'rat]
ice	**gheață** (f)	['gʲatsə]
to freeze over (ab. river, etc.)	**a îngheța**	[a ɨnge'tsa]

203. Rivers' names

Seine	**Sena** (f)	['sena]
Loire	**Loara** (f)	[lo'ara]
Thames	**Tamisa** (f)	[ta'misa]
Rhine	**Rin** (m)	[rin]
Danube	**Dunăre** (f)	['dunəre]

Volga	**Volga** (f)	['volga]
Don	**Don** (m)	[don]
Lena	**Lena** (f)	['lena]
Yellow River	**Huang He** (m)	[huan 'he]
Yangtze	**Yangtze** (m)	[jants'zi]
Mekong	**Mekong** (m)	[me'kong]
Ganges	**Gang** (m)	[gang]
Nile River	**Nil** (m)	[nil]
Congo River	**Congo** (m)	['kongo]
Okavango River	**Okavango** (m)	[oka'vango]
Zambezi River	**Zambezi** (m)	[zam'bezi]
Limpopo River	**Limpopo** (m)	[limpo'po]
Mississippi River	**Mississippi** (m)	[misi'sipi]

204. Forest

forest, wood	**pădure** (f)	[pə'dure]
forest (as adj)	**de pădure**	[de pə'dure]
thick forest	**desiş** (n)	[de'siʃ]
grove	**pădurice** (f)	[pədu'ritʃe]
forest clearing	**poiană** (f)	[po'janə]
thicket	**tufiş** (n)	[tu'fiʃ]
scrubland	**arbust** (m)	[ar'bust]
footpath (troddenpath)	**cărare** (f)	[kə'rare]
gully	**râpă** (f)	['rɨpə]
tree	**copac** (m)	[ko'pak]
leaf	**frunză** (f)	['frunzə]
leaves (foliage)	**frunziş** (n)	[frun'ziʃ]
fall of leaves	**cădere** (f) **a frunzelor**	[kə'dere a 'frunzelor]
to fall (ab. leaves)	**a cădea**	[a kə'dʲa]
top (of the tree)	**vârf** (n)	[vɨrf]
branch	**ramură** (f)	['ramurə]
bough	**creangă** (f)	['krʲangə]
bud (on shrub, tree)	**mugur** (m)	['mugur]
needle (of pine tree)	**ac** (n)	[ak]
pine cone	**con** (n)	[kon]
tree hollow	**scorbură** (f)	['skorburə]
nest	**cuib** (n)	[kujb]
burrow (animal hole)	**vizuină** (f)	[vizu'inə]
trunk	**trunchi** (n)	[trunkʲ]
root	**rădăcină** (f)	[rədə'tʃinə]

bark	**scoarță** (f)	[sko'artsə]
moss	**muşchi** (m)	[muʃkʲ]
to uproot (remove trees or tree stumps)	**a defrişa**	[a defri'ʃa]
to chop down	**a tăia**	[a tə'ja]
to deforest (vt)	**a doborî**	[a dobo'rɨ]
tree stump	**buturugă** (f)	[butu'rugə]
campfire	**foc** (n)	[fok]
forest fire	**incendiu** (n)	[in'tʃendju]
to extinguish (vt)	**a stinge**	[a 'stindʒe]
forest ranger	**pădurar** (m)	[pədu'rar]
protection	**protecție** (f)	[pro'tektsie]
to protect (~ nature)	**a ocroti**	[a okro'ti]
poacher	**braconier** (m)	[brako'njer]
steel trap	**capcană** (f)	[kap'kanə]
to gather, to pick (vt)	**a strânge**	[a 'strɨndʒe]
to lose one's way	**a se rătăci**	[a se rətə'tʃi]

205. Natural resources

natural resources	**resurse** (f pl) **naturale**	[re'surse natu'rale]
minerals	**bogății** (f pl) **minerale**	[bogə'tsij mine'rale]
deposits	**depozite** (n pl)	[de'pozite]
field (e.g., oilfield)	**zăcământ** (n)	[zəkə'mɨnt]
to mine (extract)	**a extrage**	[a eks'tradʒe]
mining (extraction)	**obținere** (f)	[ob'tsinere]
ore	**minereu** (n)	[mine'reu]
mine (e.g., for coal)	**mină** (f)	['minə]
shaft (mine ~)	**puț** (n)	['puts]
miner	**miner** (m)	[mi'ner]
gas (natural ~)	**gaz** (n)	[gaz]
gas pipeline	**conductă** (f) **de gaze**	[kon'duktə de 'gaze]
oil (petroleum)	**petrol** (n)	[pe'trol]
oil pipeline	**conductă** (f) **de petrol**	[kon'duktə de pe'trol]
oil well	**sondă** (f) **de țiței** (n)	['sondə de tsi'tsej]
derrick (tower)	**turlă** (f) **de foraj**	['turlə de fo'raʒ]
tanker	**tanc** (n) **petrolier**	['tank petro'ljer]
sand	**nisip** (n)	[ni'sip]
limestone	**calcar** (n)	[kal'kar]
gravel	**pietriş** (n)	[pe'triʃ]
peat	**turbă** (f)	['turbə]
clay	**argilă** (f)	[ar'dʒilə]

coal	**cărbune** (m)	[kər'bune]
iron (ore)	**fier** (m)	[fier]
gold	**aur** (n)	['aur]
silver	**argint** (n)	[ar'dʒint]
nickel	**nichel** (n)	['nikel]
copper	**cupru** (n)	['kupru]
zinc	**zinc** (n)	[zink]
manganese	**mangan** (n)	[man'gan]
mercury	**mercur** (n)	[mer'kur]
lead	**plumb** (n)	[plumb]
mineral	**mineral** (n)	[mine'ral]
crystal	**cristal** (n)	[kris'tal]
marble	**marmură** (f)	['marmurə]
uranium	**uraniu** (n)	[u'ranju]

The Earth. Part 2

206. Weather

weather	**timp** (n)	[timp]
weather forecast	**prognoză** (f) **meteo**	[prog'nozə 'meteo]
temperature	**temperatură** (f)	[tempera'turə]
thermometer	**termometru** (n)	[termo'metru]
barometer	**barometru** (n)	[baro'metru]
humid (adj)	**umed**	['umed]
humidity	**umiditate** (f)	[umidi'tate]
heat (extreme ~)	**caniculă** (f)	[ka'nikulə]
hot (torrid)	**fierbinte**	[fier'binte]
it's hot	**e foarte cald**	[e fo'arte kald]
it's warm	**e cald**	[e kald]
warm (moderately hot)	**cald**	[kald]
it's cold	**e frig**	[e frig]
cold (adj)	**rece**	['retʃe]
sun	**soare** (n)	[so'are]
to shine (vi)	**a străluci**	[a strəlu'tʃi]
sunny (day)	**însorit**	[ɨnso'rit]
to come up (vi)	**a răsări**	[a rəsə'ri]
to set (vi)	**a apune**	[a a'pune]
cloud	**nor** (m)	[nor]
cloudy (adj)	**înnorat**	[ɨnno'rat]
rain cloud	**nor** (m)	[nor]
somber (gloomy)	**mohorât**	[moho'rɨt]
rain	**ploaie** (f)	[plo'ae]
it's raining	**plouă**	['plowə]
rainy (~ day, weather)	**ploios**	[plo'jos]
to drizzle (vi)	**a bura**	[a bu'ra]
pouring rain	**ploaie** (f) **torențială**	[plo'ae toren'tsjalə]
downpour	**rupere** (f) **de nori**	['rupere de 'nor^j]
heavy (e.g., ~ rain)	**puternic**	[pu'ternik]
puddle	**băltoacă** (f)	[bəlto'akə]
to get wet (in rain)	**a se uda**	[a se u'da]
fog (mist)	**ceață** (f)	['tʃatsə]
foggy	**cețos**	[tʃe'tsos]

snow	**zăpadă** (f)	[zə'padə]
it's snowing	**ninge**	['nindʒe]

207. Severe weather. Natural disasters

thunderstorm	**furtună** (f)	[fur'tunə]
lightning (~ strike)	**fulger** (n)	['fuldʒer]
to flash (vi)	**a fulgera**	[a fuldʒe'ra]
thunder	**tunet** (n)	['tunet]
to thunder (vi)	**a tuna**	[a tu'na]
it's thundering	**tună**	['tunə]
hail	**grindină** (f)	[grin'dinə]
it's hailing	**plouă cu gheață**	['plowə ku 'gʲatsə]
to flood (vt)	**a inunda**	[a inun'da]
flood, inundation	**inundație** (f)	[inun'datsie]
earthquake	**cutremur** (n)	[ku'tremur]
tremor, shoke	**zguduire** (f)	[zgudu'ire]
epicenter	**epicentru** (m)	[epi'tʃentru]
eruption	**erupție** (f)	[e'ruptsie]
lava	**lavă** (f)	['lavə]
twister	**vârtej** (n)	[vɨr'teʒ]
tornado	**tornadă** (f)	[tor'nadə]
typhoon	**taifun** (n)	[taj'fun]
hurricane	**uragan** (m)	[ura'gan]
storm	**furtună** (f)	[fur'tunə]
tsunami	**tsunami** (n)	[tsu'nami]
cyclone	**ciclon** (m)	[tʃi'klon]
bad weather	**vreme** (f) **rea**	['vreme rʲa]
fire (accident)	**incendiu** (n)	[in'tʃendju]
disaster	**catastrofă** (f)	[katas'trofə]
meteorite	**meteorit** (m)	[meteo'rit]
avalanche	**avalanșă** (f)	[ava'lanʃə]
snowslide	**prăbușire** (f)	[prəbu'ʃire]
blizzard	**viscol** (n)	['viskol]
snowstorm	**viscol** (n)	['viskol]

208. Noises. Sounds

silence (quiet)	**tăcere** (f)	[tə'tʃere]
sound	**sunet** (n)	['sunet]

noise	**zgomot** (n)	['zgomot]
to make noise	**a face zgomot**	[a 'fatʃe 'zgomot]
noisy (adj)	**zgomotos**	[zgomo'tos]
loudly (to speak, etc.)	**tare**	['tare]
loud (voice, etc.)	**tare**	['tare]
constant (e.g., ~ noise)	**permanent**	[perma'nent]
cry, shout (n)	**strigăt** (n)	['strigət]
to cry, to shout (vi)	**a striga**	[a stri'ga]
whisper	**şoaptă** (f)	[ʃo'aptə]
to whisper (vi, vt)	**a şopti**	[a ʃop'ti]
barking (dog's ~)	**lătrat** (n)	[lə'trat]
to bark (vi)	**a lătra**	[a lə'tra]
groan (of pain, etc.)	**geamăt** (n)	['dʒamət]
to groan (vi)	**a geme**	[a 'dʒeme]
cough	**tuse** (f)	['tuse]
to cough (vi)	**a tuşi**	[a tu'ʃi]
whistle	**fluierat** (n)	[flue'rat]
to whistle (vi)	**a fluiera**	[a flue'ra]
knock (at the door)	**lovitură** (f)	[lovi'turə]
to knock (on the door)	**a bate**	[a 'bate]
to crack (vi)	**a trosni**	[a tros'ni]
crack (cracking sound)	**trosnitură** (f)	[trosni'ture]
siren	**sirenă** (f)	[si'renə]
whistle (factory ~, etc.)	**fluier** (n)	['flujer]
to whistle (ab. train)	**a vui**	[a vu'i]
honk (car horn sound)	**claxon** (n)	[klak'son]
to honk (vi)	**a semnaliza**	[a semnali'za]

209. Winter

winter (n)	**iarnă** (f)	['jarnə]
winter (as adj)	**de iarnă**	[de 'jarnə]
in winter	**iarna**	['jarna]
snow	**zăpadă** (f)	[zə'padə]
it's snowing	**ninge**	['nindʒe]
snowfall	**ninsoare** (f)	[ninso'are]
snowdrift	**troian** (n)	[tro'jan]
snowflake	**fulg** (m) **de zăpadă**	[fulg de zə'padə]
snowball	**bulgăre** (m) **de zăpadă**	['bulgəre de zə'padə]
snowman	**om** (m) **de zăpadă**	[om de zə'padə]
icicle	**ţurţur** (m)	['tsurtsur]

December	**decembrie** (m)	[de'tʃembrie]
January	**ianuarie** (m)	[janu'arie]
February	**februarie** (m)	[febru'arie]
frost (severe ~, freezing cold)	**ger** (n)	[dʒer]
frosty (weather, air)	**geros**	[dʒe'ros]
below zero (adv)	**sub zero grade**	[sub 'zero 'grade]
first frost	**îngheț** (n) **uşor**	[ɨ'ngets u'ʃor]
hoarfrost	**brumă** (f)	['brumə]
cold (cold weather)	**frig** (n)	[frig]
it's cold	**frig**	[frig]
fur coat	**şubă** (f)	['ʃubə]
mittens	**mănuşi** (f pl) **cu un singur deget**	[mə'nuʃ ku un 'singur 'dedʒet]
to get sick	**a se îmbolnăvi**	[a se ɨmbolnə'vi]
cold (illness)	**răceală** (f)	[rə'tʃalə]
to catch a cold	**a răci**	[a rə'tʃi]
ice	**gheață** (f)	['gʲatsə]
black ice	**polei** (n)	[po'lej]
to freeze over (ab. river, etc.)	**a îngheța**	[a ɨnge'tsa]
ice floe	**sloi** (n)	[sloj]
skis	**schiuri** (n pl)	['skjurʲ]
skier	**schior** (m)	['skjor]
to ski (vi)	**a schia**	[a ski'a]
to skate (vi)	**a patina**	[a pati'na]

Fauna

210. Mammals. Predators

predator	**prădător** (n)	[prədə'tor]
tiger	**tigru** (m)	['tigru]
lion	**leu** (m)	['leu]
wolf	**lup** (m)	[lup]
fox	**vulpe** (f)	['vulpe]
jaguar	**jaguar** (m)	[ʒagu'ar]
leopard	**leopard** (m)	[leo'pard]
cheetah	**ghepard** (m)	[ge'pard]
black panther	**panteră** (f)	[pan'terə]
puma	**pumă** (f)	['pumə]
snow leopard	**ghepard** (m)	[ge'pard]
lynx	**râs** (m)	[ris]
coyote	**coiot** (m)	[ko'jot]
jackal	**şacal** (m)	[ʃa'kal]
hyena	**hienă** (f)	[hi'enə]

211. Wild animals

animal	**animal** (n)	[ani'mal]
beast (animal)	**animal** (n) **sălbatic**	[ani'mal səl'batik]
squirrel	**veveriță** (f)	[veve'ritsə]
hedgehog	**arici** (m)	[a'ritʃi]
hare	**iepure** (m)	['jepure]
rabbit	**iepure** (m) **de casă**	['jepure de 'kasə]
badger	**bursuc** (m)	[bur'suk]
raccoon	**enot** (m)	[e'not]
hamster	**hârciog** (m)	[hir'tʃiog]
marmot	**marmotă** (f)	[mar'motə]
mole	**cârtiță** (f)	['kirtitsə]
mouse	**şoarece** (m)	[ʃo'aretʃe]
rat	**şobolan** (m)	[ʃobo'lan]
bat	**liliac** (m)	[lili'ak]
ermine	**hermină** (f)	[her'minə]
sable	**samur** (m)	[sa'mur]

marten	**jder** (m)	[ʒder]
weasel	**nevăstuică** (f)	[nevəs'tujkə]
mink	**nurcă** (f)	['nurkə]
beaver	**castor** (m)	['kastor]
otter	**vidră** (f)	['vidrə]
horse	**cal** (m)	[kal]
moose	**elan** (m)	[e'lan]
deer	**cerb** (m)	[ʧerb]
camel	**cămilă** (f)	[kə'milə]
bison	**bizon** (m)	[bi'zon]
wisent	**zimbru** (m)	['zimbru]
buffalo	**bivol** (m)	['bivol]
zebra	**zebră** (f)	['zebrə]
antelope	**antilopă** (f)	[anti'lopə]
roe deer	**căprioară** (f)	[kəprio'arə]
fallow deer	**ciută** (f)	['ʧiutə]
chamois	**capră** (f) **neagră**	['kaprə 'nʲagrə]
wild boar	**mistreț** (m)	[mis'treʦ]
whale	**balenă** (f)	[ba'lenə]
seal	**focă** (f)	['fokə]
walrus	**morsă** (f)	['morsə]
fur seal	**urs** (m) **de mare**	[urs de 'mare]
dolphin	**delfin** (m)	[del'fin]
bear	**urs** (m)	[urs]
polar bear	**urs** (m) **polar**	[urs po'lar]
panda	**panda** (m)	['panda]
monkey	**maimuță** (f)	[maj'muʦə]
chimpanzee	**cimpanzeu** (m)	[ʧimpan'zeu]
orangutan	**urangutan** (m)	[urangu'tan]
gorilla	**gorilă** (f)	[go'rilə]
macaque	**macac** (m)	[ma'kak]
gibbon	**gibon** (m)	[ʤi'bon]
elephant	**elefant** (m)	[ele'fant]
rhinoceros	**rinocer** (m)	[rino'ʧer]
giraffe	**girafă** (f)	[ʤi'rafə]
hippopotamus	**hipopotam** (m)	[hipopo'tam]
kangaroo	**cangur** (m)	['kangur]
koala (bear)	**koala** (f)	[ko'ala]
mongoose	**mangustă** (f)	[man'gustə]
chinchilla	**şinşilă** (f)	[ʃin'ʃilə]
skunk	**sconcs** (m)	[skonks]
porcupine	**porc** (m) **spinos**	[pork spi'nos]

212. Domestic animals

cat	**pisică** (f)	[pi'sikə]
tomcat	**motan** (m)	[mo'tan]
dog	**câine** (m)	['kɨjne]
horse	**cal** (m)	[kal]
stallion (male horse)	**armăsar** (m)	[armə'sar]
mare	**iapă** (f)	['japə]
cow	**vacă** (f)	['vakə]
bull	**taur** (m)	['taur]
ox	**bou** (m)	['bou]
sheep (ewe)	**oaie** (f)	[o'ae]
ram	**berbec** (m)	[ber'bek]
goat	**capră** (f)	['kaprə]
billy goat, he-goat	**țap** (m)	[ʦap]
donkey	**măgar** (m)	[mə'gar]
mule	**catâr** (m)	[ka'tɨr]
pig, hog	**porc** (m)	[pork]
piglet	**purcel** (m)	[pur'ʧel]
rabbit	**iepure** (m) **de casă**	['jepure de 'kasə]
hen (chicken)	**găină** (f)	[gə'inə]
rooster	**cocoş** (m)	[ko'koʃ]
duck	**rață** (f)	['raʦə]
drake	**rățoi** (m)	[rə'ʦoj]
goose	**gâscă** (f)	['gɨskə]
tom turkey, gobbler	**curcan** (m)	[kur'kan]
turkey (hen)	**curcă** (f)	['kurkə]
domestic animals	**animale** (n pl) **domestice**	[ani'male do'mestiʧe]
tame (e.g., ~ hamster)	**domestic**	[do'mestik]
to tame (vt)	**a domestici**	[a domesti'ʧi]
to breed (vt)	**a creşte**	[a 'kreʃte]
farm	**fermă** (f)	['fermə]
poultry	**păsări** (f pl) **de curte**	[pəsər^j de 'kurte]
cattle	**vite** (f pl)	['vite]
herd (cattle)	**turmă** (f)	['turmə]
stable	**grajd** (n)	[graʒd]
pigpen	**cocină** (f) **de porci**	[ko'ʧinə de 'porʧi]
cowshed	**grajd** (n) **pentru vaci**	['graʒd 'pentru 'vaʧi]
rabbit hutch	**cuşcă** (f) **pentru iepuri**	['kuʃkə 'pentru 'epur^j]
hen house	**coteț** (n) **de găini**	[ko'teʦ de gə'in^j]

213. Dogs. Dog breeds

dog	**câine** (m)	['kɨjne]
sheepdog	**câine** (m) **ciobănesc**	['kɨjne ʧiobə'nesk]
German shepherd	**ciobănesc german** (m)	[ʧiobə'nesk ʤer'man]
poodle	**pudel** (m)	[pu'del]
dachshund	**teckel** (m)	['tekel]
bulldog	**buldog** (m)	[bul'dog]
boxer	**boxer** (m)	[bok'ser]
mastiff	**mastif** (m)	[mas'tif]
Rottweiler	**rottweiler** (m)	[rot'wejler]
Doberman	**doberman** (m)	[dober'man]
basset	**basset** (m)	[ba'set]
bobtail	**bobtail** (m)	[bob'tejl]
Dalmatian	**dalmațian** (m)	[dalmaʦi'an]
cocker spaniel	**cocker spaniel** (m)	['koker spani'el]
Newfoundland	**newfoundland** (m)	[nju'faundlend]
Saint Bernard	**sentbernar** (m)	[senber'nar]
husky	**huski** (m)	['haski]
Chow Chow	**chow chow** (m)	['ʧau 'ʧau]
spitz	**spitz** (m)	[ʃpiʦ]
pug	**mops** (m)	[mops]

214. Sounds made by animals

barking (n)	**lătrat** (n)	[lə'trat]
to bark (vi)	**a lătra**	[a lə'tra]
to meow (vi)	**a mieuna**	[a meu'na]
to purr (vi)	**a toarce**	[a to'arʧe]
to moo (vi)	**a mugi**	[a mu'ʤi]
to bellow (bull)	**a rage**	[a 'raʤe]
to growl (vi)	**a mârâi**	[a mɨrɨ'i]
howl (n)	**urlet** (n)	['urlet]
to howl (vi)	**a urla**	[a ur'la]
to whine (vi)	**a scheuna**	[a skeu'na]
to bleat (sheep)	**a behăi**	[a behə'i]
to oink, to grunt (pig)	**a grohăi**	[a grohə'i]
to squeal (vi)	**a țipa**	[a ʦi'pa]
to croak (vi)	**a orăcăi**	[a orəkə'i]
to buzz (insect)	**a bâzâi**	[a bɨzɨ'i]
to chirp (crickets, grasshopper)	**a țârâi**	[a ʦɨrɨ'i]

215. Young animals

cub	**pui** (m) **de animal**	[puj de ani'mal]
kitten	**motănaş** (m)	[motə'naʃ]
baby mouse	**şoricel** (m)	[ʃori'tʃel]
puppy	**căţeluş** (m)	[kətse'luʃ]
leveret	**iepuraş** (m)	[jepu'raʃ]
baby rabbit	**iepuraş** (m)	[jepu'raʃ]
wolf cub	**pui** (m) **de lup**	[puj de lup]
fox cub	**pui** (m) **de vulpe**	[puj de 'vulpe]
bear cub	**ursuleţ** (m)	[ursu'lets]
lion cub	**pui** (m) **de leu**	[puj de 'leu]
tiger cub	**pui** (m) **de tigru**	[puj de 'tigru]
elephant calf	**pui** (m) **de elefant**	[puj de ele'fant]
piglet	**purcel** (m)	[pur'tʃel]
calf (young cow, bull)	**viţel** (m)	[vi'tsel]
kid (young goat)	**ied** (m)	[jed]
lamb	**miel** (m)	[mjel]
fawn (young deer)	**pui** (m) **de cerb**	[puj de tʃerb]
young camel	**pui** (m) **de cămilă**	[puj de kə'milə]
snakelet (baby snake)	**pui** (m) **de şarpe**	[puj de 'ʃarpe]
froglet (baby frog)	**broscuţă** (f)	[bros'kutsə]
baby bird	**pui** (m) **de pasăre**	[puj de 'pasəre]
chick (of chicken)	**pui** (m)	[puj]
duckling	**răţuşcă** (f)	[rə'tsuʃkə]

216. Birds

bird	**pasăre** (f)	['pasəre]
pigeon	**porumbel** (m)	[porum'bel]
sparrow	**vrabie** (f)	['vrabie]
tit (great tit)	**piţigoi** (m)	[pitsi'goj]
magpie	**coţofană** (f)	[kotso'fanə]
raven	**corb** (m)	[korb]
crow	**cioară** (f)	[tʃio'arə]
jackdaw	**stancă** (f)	['stankə]
rook	**cioară** (f) **de câmp**	[tʃio'arə de 'kɨmp]
duck	**raţă** (f)	['ratsə]
goose	**gâscă** (f)	['gɨskə]
pheasant	**fazan** (m)	[fa'zan]
eagle	**acvilă** (f)	['akvilə]
hawk	**uliu** (m)	['ulju]

falcon	**şoim** (m)	[ʃojm]
vulture	**vultur** (m)	['vultur]
condor (Andean ~)	**condor** (m)	[kon'dor]
swan	**lebădă** (f)	['lebədə]
crane	**cocor** (m)	[ko'kor]
stork	**cocostârc** (m)	[kokos'tɨrk]
parrot	**papagal** (m)	[papa'gal]
hummingbird	**pasărea** (f) **colibri**	['pasərʲa ko'libri]
peacock	**păun** (m)	[pə'un]
ostrich	**struț** (m)	[struʦ]
heron	**stârc** (m)	[stɨrk]
flamingo	**flamingo** (m)	[fla'mingo]
pelican	**pelican** (m)	[peli'kan]
nightingale	**privighetoare** (f)	[privigeto'are]
swallow	**rândunică** (f)	[rɨndu'nikə]
thrush	**mierlă** (f)	['merlə]
song thrush	**sturz-cântător** (m)	[sturz kɨntə'tor]
blackbird	**mierlă** (f) **sură**	['merlə 'surə]
swift	**lăstun** (m)	[ləs'tun]
lark	**ciocârlie** (f)	[ʧiokɨr'lie]
quail	**prepeliță** (f)	[prepe'liʦə]
woodpecker	**ciocănitoare** (f)	[ʧiokənito'are]
cuckoo	**cuc** (m)	[kuk]
owl	**bufniță** (f)	['bufniʦə]
eagle owl	**buha mare** (f)	['buhə 'mare]
wood grouse	**cocoş** (m) **de munte**	[ko'koʃ de 'munte]
black grouse	**cocoş** (m) **sălbatic**	[ko'koʃ səlba'tik]
partridge	**potârniche** (f)	[potɨr'nike]
starling	**graur** (m)	['graur]
canary	**canar** (m)	[ka'nar]
hazel grouse	**găinuşă de alun** (f)	[gəi'nuʃə de a'lun]
chaffinch	**cinteză** (f)	[ʧin'tezə]
bullfinch	**botgros** (m)	[bot'gros]
seagull	**pescăruş** (m)	[peskə'ruʃ]
albatross	**albatros** (m)	[alba'tros]
penguin	**pinguin** (m)	[pigu'in]

217. Birds. Singing and sounds

to sing (vi)	**a cânta**	[a kɨn'ta]
to call (animal, bird)	**a striga**	[a stri'ga]

to crow (rooster)	**a cânta cucurigu**	[a kɨn'ta kuku'rigu]
cock-a-doodle-doo	**cucurigu** (m)	[kuku'rigu]
to cluck (hen)	**a cotcodăci**	[a kotkodə'ʧi]
to caw (crow call)	**a croncăni**	[a kronkə'ni]
to quack (duck call)	**a măcăi**	[a məkə'i]
to cheep (vi)	**a piui**	[a pju'i]
to chirp, to twitter	**a ciripi**	[a ʧiri'pi]

218. Fish. Marine animals

bream	**plătică** (f)	[plə'tikə]
carp	**crap** (m)	[krap]
perch	**biban** (m)	[bi'ban]
catfish	**somn** (m)	[somn]
pike	**ştiucă** (f)	['ʃtjukə]
salmon	**somon** (m)	[so'mon]
sturgeon	**nisetru** (m)	[ni'setru]
herring	**scrumbie** (f)	[skrum'bie]
Atlantic salmon	**somon** (m)	[so'mon]
mackerel	**macrou** (n)	[ma'krou]
flatfish	**cambulă** (f)	[kam'bulə]
zander, pike perch	**şalău** (m)	[ʃa'ləu]
cod	**batog** (m)	[ba'tog]
tuna	**ton** (m)	[ton]
trout	**păstrăv** (m)	[pəs'trəv]
eel	**ţipar** (m)	[ʦi'par]
electric ray	**peşte-torpilă** (m)	['peʃte tor'pilə]
moray eel	**murenă** (f)	[mu'renə]
piranha	**piranha** (f)	[pi'ranija]
shark	**rechin** (m)	[re'kin]
dolphin	**delfin** (m)	[del'fin]
whale	**balenă** (f)	[ba'lenə]
crab	**crab** (m)	[krab]
jellyfish	**meduză** (f)	[me'duzə]
octopus	**caracatiţă** (f)	[kara'katiʦə]
starfish	**stea de mare** (f)	[stʲa de 'mare]
sea urchin	**arici de mare** (m)	[a'riʧi de 'mare]
seahorse	**căluţ** (m) **de mare** (f)	[ka'luʦ de 'mare]
oyster	**stridie** (f)	['stridie]
shrimp	**crevetă** (f)	[kre'vetə]
lobster	**stacoj** (m)	[sta'koʒ]
spiny lobster	**langustă** (f)	[lan'gustə]

219. Amphibians. Reptiles

snake	**şarpe** (m)	['ʃarpe]
venomous (snake)	**veninos**	[veni'nos]
viper	**viperă** (f)	['vipərə]
cobra	**cobră** (f)	['kobrə]
python	**piton** (m)	[pi'ton]
boa	**şarpe** (m) **boa**	['ʃarpe bo'a]
grass snake	**şarpe** (m) **de casă**	['ʃarpe de 'kasə]
rattle snake	**şarpe** (m) **cu clopoţei**	['ʃarpe ku klopo'ʦej]
anaconda	**anacondă** (f)	[ana'kondə]
lizard	**şopârlă** (f)	[ʃo'pɨrlə]
iguana	**iguană** (f)	[igu'anə]
monitor lizard	**şopârlă** (f)	[ʃo'pɨrlə]
salamander	**salamandră** (f)	[sala'mandrə]
chameleon	**cameleon** (m)	[kamele'on]
scorpion	**scorpion** (m)	[skorpi'on]
turtle	**broască** (f) **ţestoasă**	[bro'askə ʦesto'asə]
frog	**broască** (f)	[bro'askə]
toad	**broască** (f) **râioasă**	[bro'askə rɨjo'asə]
crocodile	**crocodil** (m)	[kroko'dil]

220. Insects

insect, bug	**insectă** (f)	[in'sektə]
butterfly	**fluture** (m)	['fluture]
ant	**furnică** (f)	[fur'nikə]
fly	**muscă** (f)	['muskə]
mosquito	**ţânţar** (m)	[ʦɨn'ʦar]
beetle	**gândac** (m)	[gɨn'dak]
wasp	**viespe** (f)	['vespe]
bee	**albină** (f)	[al'binə]
bumblebee	**bondar** (m)	[bon'dar]
gadfly (botfly)	**tăun** (m)	[tə'un]
spider	**păianjen** (m)	[pə'janʒen]
spiderweb	**pânză** (f) **de păianjen**	['pɨnzə de pə'janʒen]
dragonfly	**libelulă** (f)	[libe'lulə]
grasshopper	**greier** (m)	['greer]
moth (night butterfly)	**fluture** (m)	['fluture]
cockroach	**gândac** (m)	[gɨn'dak]
tick	**căpuşă** (f)	[kə'puʃə]

flea	**purice** (m)	['puritʃe]
midge	**musculiță** (f)	[musku'litsə]
locust	**lăcustă** (f)	[lə'kustə]
snail	**melc** (m)	[melk]
cricket	**greier** (m)	['greer]
lightning bug	**licurici** (m)	[liku'ritʃi]
ladybug	**buburuză** (f)	[bubu'ruzə]
cockchafer	**cărăbuş** (m)	[kərə'buʃ]
leech	**lipitoare** (f)	[lipito'are]
caterpillar	**omidă** (f)	[o'midə]
earthworm	**vierme** (m)	['verme]
larva	**larvă** (f)	['larvə]

221. Animals. Body parts

beak	**cioc** (n)	[tʃiok]
wings	**aripi** (f pl)	[a'ripʲ]
foot (of bird)	**labă** (f)	['labə]
feathers (plumage)	**penaj** (n)	[pe'naʒ]
feather	**pană** (f)	['panə]
crest	**moț** (n)	[mots]
gills	**branhii** (f pl)	[bran'hij]
spawn	**icre** (f pl)	['ikre]
larva	**larvă** (f)	['larvə]
fin	**aripioară** (f)	[ari'pjoarə]
scales (of fish, reptile)	**solzi** (m pl)	[solzʲ]
fang (canine)	**dinte** (m) **canin**	['dinte ka'nin]
paw (e.g., cat's ~)	**labă** (f)	['labə]
muzzle (snout)	**bot** (n)	[bot]
maw (mouth)	**bot** (n)	[bot]
tail	**coadă** (f)	[ko'adə]
whiskers	**mustăți** (f pl)	[mus'tətsʲ]
hoof	**copită** (f)	[ko'pitə]
horn	**corn** (n)	[korn]
carapace	**carapace** (f)	[kara'patʃe]
shell (of mollusk)	**schelet** (n)	[ske'let]
eggshell	**găoace** (f)	[gəo'atʃe]
animal's hair (pelage)	**blană** (f)	['blanə]
pelt (hide)	**piele** (f)	['pjele]

222. Actions of animals

to fly (vi)	**a zbura**	[a zbu'ra]
to fly in circles	**a se roti**	[a se ro'ti]
to fly away	**a-şi lua zborul**	[aʃ lu'a 'zborul]
to flap (~ the wings)	**a bate din aripi**	[a 'bate din 'aripʲ]
to peck (vi)	**a ciuguli**	[a ʧiugu'li]
to sit on eggs	**a cloci**	[a klo'ʧi]
to hatch out (vi)	**a ieşi din ou**	[a e'ʃi din ow]
to build a nest	**a face cuib**	[a 'faʧe kujb]
to slither, to crawl	**a se târî**	[a se tɨ'rɨ]
to sting, to bite (insect)	**a înțepa**	[a ɨnʦe'pa]
to bite (ab. animal)	**a muşca**	[a muʃ'ka]
to sniff (vt)	**a mirosi**	[a miro'si]
to bark (vi)	**a lătra**	[a lə'tra]
to hiss (snake)	**a sâsâi**	[a sisɨ'i]
to scare (vt)	**a speria**	[a speri'ja]
to attack (vt)	**a ataca**	[a ata'ka]
to gnaw (bone, etc.)	**a roade**	[a ro'ade]
to scratch (with claws)	**a zgâria**	[a zgɨri'ja]
to hide (vi)	**a se ascunde**	[a se as'kunde]
to play (kittens, etc.)	**a juca**	[a ʒu'ka]
to hunt (vi, vt)	**a vâna**	[a vɨ'na]
to hibernate (vi)	**a hiberna**	[a hiber'na]
to go extinct	**a dispărea**	[a dispə'rʲa]

223. Animals. Habitats

habitat	**mediu** (n) **ambiant**	['medju am'bjant]
migration	**migrație** (f)	[mi'graʦie]
mountain	**munte** (m)	['munte]
reef	**recif** (m)	[re'ʧif]
cliff	**stâncă** (f)	['stɨnkə]
forest	**pădure** (f)	[pə'dure]
jungle	**junglă** (f)	['ʒunglə]
savanna	**savană** (f)	[sa'vanə]
tundra	**tundră** (f)	['tundrə]
steppe	**stepă** (f)	['stepə]
desert	**deşert** (n)	[de'ʃərt]
oasis	**oază** (f)	[o'azə]
sea	**mare** (f)	['mare]

lake	**lac** (n)	[lak]
ocean	**ocean** (n)	[otʃə'an]
swamp (marshland)	**mlaştină** (f)	['mlaʃtinə]
freshwater (adj)	**de apă dulce**	[de 'apə 'dultʃe]
pond	**iaz** (n)	[jaz]
river	**râu** (n)	['riu]
den (bear's ~)	**bârlog** (n)	[bɨr'log]
nest	**cuib** (n)	[kujb]
tree hollow	**scorbură** (f)	['skorburə]
burrow (animal hole)	**vizuină** (f)	[vizu'inə]
anthill	**furnicar** (n)	[furni'kar]

224. Animal care

zoo	**grădină** (f) **zoologică**	[grə'dinə zoo'lodʒikə]
nature preserve	**rezervaţie** (f) **naturală**	[rezer'vatsie natu'ralə]
breeder (cattery, kennel, etc.)	**pepinieră** (f)	[pepi'njerə]
open-air cage	**volieră** (f)	[voli'erə]
cage	**cuşcă** (f)	['kuʃkə]
doghouse (kennel)	**coteţ** (n) **de câine**	[ko'tets de 'kɨnə]
dovecot	**porumbărie** (f)	[porumbə'rie]
aquarium (fish tank)	**acvariu** (n)	[ak'varju]
dolphinarium	**delfinariu** (n)	[delfi'narju]
to breed (animals)	**a creşte**	[a 'kreʃte]
brood, litter	**pui** (m pl)	[puj]
to tame (vt)	**a domestici**	[a domesti'tʃi]
to train (animals)	**a dresa**	[a dre'sa]
feed (fodder, etc.)	**hrană** (f)	['hranə]
to feed (vt)	**a hrăni**	[a hrə'ni]
pet store	**magazin** (n) **zoo**	[maga'zin 'zoo]
muzzle (for dog)	**botniţă** (f)	['botnitsə]
collar (e.g., dog ~)	**zgardă** (f)	['zgardə]
name (of animal)	**porecla** (f)	[po'reklə]
pedigree (of dog)	**genealogie** (f)	[dʒenealo'dʒie]

225. Animals. Miscellaneous

pack (wolves)	**haită** (f)	['hajtə]
flock (birds)	**stol** (n)	[stol]
shoal, school (fish)	**banc** (n)	[bank]
herd (horses)	**herghelie** (f)	[herge'lie]

male (n)	**mascul** (m)	[mas'kul]
female (n)	**femelă** (f)	[fe'melə]
hungry (adj)	**flămând**	[flə'mɨnd]
wild (adj)	**sălbatic**	[səl'batik]
dangerous (adj)	**periculos**	[periku'los]

226. Horses

horse	**cal** (m)	[kal]
breed (race)	**rasă** (f)	['rasə]
foal	**mânz** (m)	[mɨnz]
mare	**iapă** (f)	['japə]
mustang	**mustang** (m)	[mus'tang]
pony	**ponei** (m)	['ponej]
draft horse	**cal** (m) **de tracțiune**	[kal de traktsi'une]
mane	**coamă** (f)	[ko'amə]
tail	**coadă** (f)	[ko'adə]
hoof	**copită** (f)	[ko'pitə]
horseshoe	**potcoavă** (f)	[potko'avə]
to shoe (vt)	**a potcovi**	[a potko'vi]
blacksmith	**fierar** (m)	[fe'rar]
saddle	**şa** (f)	[ʃa]
stirrup	**scară** (f)	['skarə]
bridle	**frâu** (n)	['frɨu]
reins	**hățuri** (n pl)	[hətsurʲ]
whip (for riding)	**bici** (n)	[bitʃi]
rider	**călăreț** (m)	[kələ'rets]
to saddle up (vt)	**a înşeua**	[a ɨnʃəu'a]
to mount a horse	**a se aşeza în şa**	[a se aʃə'za 'ɨn 'ʃa]
gallop	**galop** (n)	[ga'lop]
to gallop (vi)	**a galopa**	[a galo'pa]
trot (n)	**trap** (n)	[trap]
at a trot (adv)	**la trap**	[la trap]
racehorse	**cal** (m) **de curse**	[kal de 'kurse]
horse racing	**cursă** (f) **de cai**	['kursə de kaj]
stable	**grajd** (n)	[graʒd]
to feed (vt)	**a hrăni**	[a hrə'ni]
hay	**fân** (n)	[fɨn]
to water (animals)	**a adăpa**	[a adə'pa]
to wash (horse)	**a țesăla**	[a tsesə'la]

horse-drawn cart	**car** (n)	[kar]
to graze (vi)	**a paşte**	[a 'paʃte]
to neigh (vi)	**a necheza**	[a neke'za]
to kick (to buck)	**a zvârli cu copita**	[a zvɨr'li ku ko'pita]

Flora

227. Trees

tree	**copac** (m)	[ko'pak]
deciduous (adj)	**foios**	[fo'jos]
coniferous (adj)	**conifer**	[koni'fere]
evergreen (adj)	**veşnic verde**	['veʃnik 'verde]
apple tree	**măr** (m)	[mər]
pear tree	**păr** (m)	[pər]
sweet cherry tree	**cireş** (m)	[ʧi'reʃ]
sour cherry tree	**vişin** (m)	['viʃin]
plum tree	**prun** (m)	[prun]
birch	**mesteacăn** (m)	[mes'tʲakən]
oak	**stejar** (m)	[ste'ʒar]
linden tree	**tei** (m)	[tej]
aspen	**plop tremurător** (m)	['plop tremurə'tor]
maple	**arţar** (m)	[ar'ʦar]
spruce	**brad** (m)	[brad]
pine	**pin** (m)	[pin]
larch	**zadă** (f)	['zadə]
fir tree	**brad** (m) **alb**	['brad 'alb]
cedar	**cedru** (m)	['ʧedru]
poplar	**plop** (m)	[plop]
rowan	**sorb** (m)	[sorb]
willow	**salcie** (f)	['salʧie]
alder	**arin** (m)	[a'rin]
beech	**fag** (m)	[fag]
elm	**ulm** (m)	[ulm]
ash (tree)	**frasin** (m)	['frasin]
chestnut	**castan** (m)	[kas'tan]
magnolia	**magnolie** (f)	[mag'nolie]
palm tree	**palmier** (m)	[palmi'er]
cypress	**chiparos** (m)	[kipa'ros]
mangrove	**manglier** (m)	[mangli'jer]
baobab	**baobab** (m)	[bao'bab]
eucalyptus	**eucalipt** (m)	[euka'lipt]
sequoia	**secvoia** (m)	[sek'voja]

228. Shrubs

bush	**tufă** (f)	['tufə]
shrub	**arbust** (m)	[ar'bust]
grapevine	**viță** (f) **de vie**	['vitsə de 'vie]
vineyard	**vie** (f)	['vie]
raspberry bush	**zmeură** (f)	['zmeurə]
blackcurrant bush	**coacăz** (m) **negru**	[ko'akəz 'negru]
redcurrant bush	**coacăz** (m) **roşu**	[ko'akəz 'roʃu]
gooseberry bush	**agriş** (m)	[a'griʃ]
acacia	**salcâm** (m)	[sal'kɨm]
barberry	**lemn** (m) **galben**	['lemn 'galben]
jasmine	**iasomie** (f)	[jaso'mie]
juniper	**ienupăr** (m)	[je'nupər]
rosebush	**tufă** (f) **de trandafir**	['tufə de tranda'fir]
dog rose	**măceş** (m)	[mə'tʃeʃ]

229. Mushrooms

mushroom	**ciupercă** (f)	[tʃiu'perkə]
edible mushroom	**ciupercă** (f) **comestibilă**	[tʃiu'perkə komes'tibilə]
poisonous mushroom	**ciupercă** (f) **otrăvitoare**	[tʃiu'perkə otrəvito'are]
cap (of mushroom)	**pălărie** (f)	[pələ'rie]
stipe (of mushroom)	**picior** (n)	[pi'tʃior]
cep (Boletus edulis)	**hrib** (m)	[hrib]
orange-cap boletus	**pitărcuță** (f)	[pitər'kutsə]
birch bolete	**pitarcă** (f)	[pi'tarkə]
chanterelle	**gălbior** (m)	[gəlbi'or]
russula	**vinețică** (f)	[vine'tsikə]
morel	**zbârciog** (m)	[zbɨr'tʃiog]
fly agaric	**burete** (m) **pestriț**	[bu'rete pes'trits]
death cap	**ciupercă** (f) **otrăvitoare**	[tʃiu'perkə otrəvito'are]

230. Fruits. Berries

fruit	**fruct** (n)	[frukt]
fruits	**fructe** (n pl)	[frukte]
apple	**măr** (n)	[mər]
pear	**pară** (f)	['parə]
plum	**prună** (f)	['prunə]
strawberry (garden ~)	**căpşună** (f)	[kəp'ʃunə]

sour cherry	**vişină** (f)	['viʃinə]
sweet cherry	**cireaşă** (f)	[tʃi'rʲaʃə]
grape	**struguri** (m pl)	['strugurʲ]
raspberry	**zmeură** (f)	['zmeurə]
blackcurrant	**coacăză** (f) **neagră**	[ko'akəzə 'nʲagrə]
redcurrant	**coacăză** (f) **roşie**	[ko'akəzə 'roʃie]
gooseberry	**agrişă** (f)	[a'griʃə]
cranberry	**răchițele** (f pl)	[rəki'tsele]
orange	**portocală** (f)	[porto'kalə]
mandarin	**mandarină** (f)	[manda'rinə]
pineapple	**ananas** (m)	[ana'nas]
banana	**banană** (f)	[ba'nanə]
date	**curmală** (f)	[kur'malə]
lemon	**lămâie** (f)	[lə'mɨe]
apricot	**caisă** (f)	[ka'isə]
peach	**piersică** (f)	['pjersikə]
kiwi	**kiwi** (n)	['kivi]
grapefruit	**grepfrut** (n)	['grepfrut]
berry	**boabă** (f)	[bo'abə]
berries	**fructe** (n pl) **de pădure**	['frukte de pə'dure]
cowberry	**merişor** (m)	[meri'ʃor]
wild strawberry	**frag** (m)	[frag]
bilberry	**afină** (f)	[a'finə]

231. Flowers. Plants

flower	**floare** (f)	[flo'are]
bouquet (of flowers)	**buchet** (n)	[bu'ket]
rose (flower)	**trandafir** (m)	[tranda'fir]
tulip	**lalea** (f)	[la'lʲa]
carnation	**garoafă** (f)	[garo'afə]
gladiolus	**gladiolă** (f)	[gladi'olə]
cornflower	**albăstrea** (f)	[albəs'trʲa]
harebell	**clopoțel** (m)	[klopo'tsel]
dandelion	**păpădie** (f)	[pəpə'die]
camomile	**romaniță** (f)	[roma'nitsə]
aloe	**aloe** (f)	[a'loe]
cactus	**cactus** (m)	['kaktus]
rubber plant, ficus	**ficus** (m)	['fikus]
lily	**crin** (m)	[krin]
geranium	**muşcată** (f)	[muʃ'katə]
hyacinth	**zambilă** (f)	[zam'bilə]

mimosa	**mimoză** (f)	[mi'mozə]
narcissus	**narcisă** (f)	[nar'ʧisə]
nasturtium	**condurul-doamnei** (m)	[kon'durul do'amnej]
orchid	**orhidee** (f)	[orhi'dee]
peony	**bujor** (m)	[bu'ʒor]
violet	**toporaş** (m)	[topo'raʃ]
pansy	**pansele** (f)	[pan'sele]
forget-me-not	**nu-mă-uita** (f)	[nu mə uj'ta]
daisy	**margaretă** (f)	[marga'retə]
poppy	**mac** (m)	[mak]
hemp	**cânepă** (f)	['kɨnepə]
mint	**mentă** (f)	['mentə]
lily of the valley	**lăcrămioară** (f)	[ləkrəmjo'arə]
snowdrop	**ghiocel** (m)	[gio'ʧel]
nettle	**urzică** (f)	[ur'zikə]
sorrel	**măcriş** (m)	[mə'kriʃ]
water lily	**nufăr** (m)	['nufər]
fern	**ferigă** (f)	['ferigə]
lichen	**lichen** (m)	[li'ken]
conservatory (greenhouse)	**seră** (f)	['serə]
lawn	**gazon** (n)	[ga'zon]
flowerbed	**strat** (n) **de flori**	[strat de 'florʲ]
plant	**plantă** (f)	['plantə]
grass	**iarbă** (f)	['jarbə]
blade of grass	**fir** (n) **de iarbă**	[fir de 'jarbə]
leaf	**frunză** (f)	['frunzə]
petal	**petală** (f)	[pe'talə]
stem	**tulpină** (f)	[tul'pinə]
tuber	**tubercul** (m)	[tu'berkul]
young plant (shoot)	**mugur** (m)	['mugur]
thorn	**ghimpe** (m)	['gimpe]
to blossom (vi)	**a înflori**	[a ɨnflo'ri]
to fade, to wither	**a se ofili**	[a se ofe'li]
smell (odor)	**miros** (n)	[mi'ros]
to cut (flowers)	**a tăia**	[a tə'ja]
to pick (a flower)	**a rupe**	[a 'rupe]

232. Cereals, grains

grain	**grăunțe** (n pl)	[grə'unʦe]
cereal crops	**cereale** (f pl)	[ʧere'ale]

ear (of barley, etc.)	**spic** (n)	[spik]
wheat	**grâu** (n)	['grɨu]
rye	**secară** (f)	[se'karə]
oats	**ovăz** (n)	[ovəz]
millet	**mei** (m)	[mej]
barley	**orz** (n)	[orz]
corn	**porumb** (m)	[po'rumb]
rice	**orez** (n)	[o'rez]
buckwheat	**hrişcă** (f)	['hriʃkə]
pea plant	**mazăre** (f)	['mazəre]
kidney bean	**fasole** (f)	[fa'sole]
soy	**soia** (f)	['soja]
lentil	**linte** (n)	['linte]
beans (pulse crops)	**boabe** (f pl)	[bo'abe]

233. Vegetables. Greens

vegetables	**legume** (f pl)	[le'gume]
greens	**verdeață** (f)	[ver'dʲatsə]
tomato	**roşie** (f)	['roʃie]
cucumber	**castravete** (m)	[kastra'vete]
carrot	**morcov** (m)	['morkov]
potato	**cartof** (m)	[kar'tof]
onion	**ceapă** (f)	['ʧapə]
garlic	**usturoi** (m)	[ustu'roj]
cabbage	**varză** (f)	['varzə]
cauliflower	**conopidă** (f)	[kono'pidə]
Brussels sprouts	**varză** (f) **de Bruxelles**	['varzə de bruk'sel]
broccoli	**broccoli** (m)	['brokoli]
beet	**sfeclă** (f)	['sfeklə]
eggplant	**vânătă** (f)	['vɨnətə]
zucchini	**dovlecel** (m)	[dovle'ʧel]
pumpkin	**dovleac** (m)	[dov'lʲak]
turnip	**nap** (m)	[nap]
parsley	**pătrunjel** (m)	[pətrun'ʒel]
dill	**mărar** (m)	[mə'rar]
lettuce	**salată** (f)	[sa'latə]
celery	**țelină** (f)	['ʦelinə]
asparagus	**sparanghel** (m)	[sparan'gel]
spinach	**spanac** (m)	[spa'nak]
pea	**mazăre** (f)	['mazəre]
beans	**boabe** (f pl)	[bo'abe]
corn (maize)	**porumb** (m)	[po'rumb]

kidney bean	**fasole** (f)	[fa'sole]
pepper	**piper** (m)	[pi'per]
radish	**ridiche** (f)	[ri'dike]
artichoke	**anghinare** (f)	[angi'nare]

REGIONAL GEOGRAPHY

Countries. Nationalities

234. Western Europe

Europe	**Europa** (f)	[eu'ropa]
European Union	**Uniunea** (f) **Europeană**	[uni'unʲa euro'pʲanə]
European (n)	**european** (m)	[euro'pʲan]
European (adj)	**european**	[euro'pʲan]
Austria	**Austria** (f)	[a'ustrija]
Austrian (masc.)	**austriac** (m)	[austri'ak]
Austrian (fem.)	**austriacă** (f)	[austri'akə]
Austrian (adj)	**austriac**	[austri'ak]
Great Britain	**Marea Britanie** (f)	['marʲa bri'tanie]
England	**Anglia** (f)	['anglija]
British (masc.)	**englez** (m)	[en'glez]
British (fem.)	**englezoaică** (f)	[englezo'ajkə]
English, British (adj)	**englez**	[en'glez]
Belgium	**Belgia** (f)	['belʤia]
Belgian (masc.)	**belgian** (m)	[belʤi'an]
Belgian (fem.)	**belgiană** (f)	[belʤi'anə]
Belgian (adj)	**belgian**	[belʤi'an]
Germany	**Germania** (f)	[ʤer'manija]
German (masc.)	**neamț** (m)	['nʲamʦ]
German (fem.)	**nemțoaică** (f)	[nemʦo'ajkə]
German (adj)	**nemțesc**	[nem'ʦesk]
Netherlands	**Țările de Jos** (f pl)	['ʦərile de ʒos]
Holland	**Olanda** (f)	[o'landa]
Dutch (masc.)	**olandez** (m)	[olan'dez]
Dutch (fem.)	**olandeză** (f)	[olan'dezə]
Dutch (adj)	**olandez**	[olan'dez]
Greece	**Grecia** (f)	['greʧia]
Greek (masc.)	**grec** (m)	[grek]
Greek (fem.)	**grecoaică** (f)	[greko'ajkə]
Greek (adj)	**grecesc**	[gre'ʧesk]
Denmark	**Danemarca** (f)	[dane'marka]
Dane (masc.)	**danez** (m)	[da'nez]

Dane (fem.)	**daneză** (f)	[da'nezə]
Danish (adj)	**danez**	[da'nez]
Ireland	**Irlanda** (f)	[ir'landa]
Irish (masc.)	**irlandez** (m)	[irlan'dez]
Irish (fem.)	**irlandeză** (f)	[irlan'dezə]
Irish (adj)	**irlandez**	[irlan'dez]
Iceland	**Islanda** (f)	[is'landa]
Icelander (masc.)	**islandez** (m)	[islan'dez]
Icelander (fem.)	**islandeză** (f)	[islan'dezə]
Icelandic (adj)	**islandez**	[islan'dez]
Spain	**Spania** (f)	['spania]
Spaniard (masc.)	**spaniol** (m)	[spa'njol]
Spaniard (fem.)	**spanioloaică** (f)	[spanjolo'ajkə]
Spanish (adj)	**spaniol**	[spa'njol]
Italy	**Italia** (f)	[i'talia]
Italian (masc.)	**italian** (m)	[itali'an]
Italian (fem.)	**italiancă** (f)	[itali'ankə]
Italian (adj)	**italian**	[itali'an]
Cyprus	**Cipru** (n)	['ʧipru]
Cypriot (masc.)	**cipriot** (m)	[ʧipri'ot]
Cypriot (fem.)	**cipriotă** (f)	[ʧipri'otə]
Cypriot (adj)	**cipriot**	[ʧipri'ot]
Malta	**Malta** (f)	['malta]
Maltese (masc.)	**maltez** (m)	[mal'tez]
Maltese (fem.)	**malteză** (f)	[mal'tezə]
Maltese (adj)	**maltez**	[mal'tez]
Norway	**Norvegia** (f)	[nor'veʤia]
Norwegian (masc.)	**norvegian** (m)	[norveʤi'an]
Norwegian (fem.)	**norvegiancă** (f)	[norveʤi'ankə]
Norwegian (adj)	**norvegian**	[norveʤi'an]
Portugal	**Portugalia** (f)	[portu'galia]
Portuguese (masc.)	**portughez** (m)	[portu'gez]
Portuguese (fem.)	**portugheză** (f)	[portu'gezə]
Portuguese (adj)	**portughez**	[portu'gez]
Finland	**Finlanda** (f)	[fin'landa]
Finn (masc.)	**finlandez** (m)	[finlan'dez]
Finn (fem.)	**finlandeză** (f)	[finlan'dezə]
Finnish (adj)	**finlandez**	[finlan'dez]
France	**Franța** (f)	['frantsa]
French (masc.)	**francez** (m)	[fran'ʧez]
French (fem.)	**franțuzoaică** (f)	[frantsuzo'ajkə]
French (adj)	**francez**	[fran'ʧez]

Sweden	**Suedia** (f)	[su'edia]
Swede (masc.)	**suedez** (m)	[sue'dez]
Swede (fem.)	**suedeză** (f)	[sue'dezə]
Swedish (adj)	**suedez**	[sue'dez]
Switzerland	**Elveția** (f)	[el'vetsia]
Swiss (masc.)	**elvețian** (m)	[elvetsi'an]
Swiss (fem.)	**elvețiancă** (f)	[elvetsi'ankə]
Swiss (adj)	**elvețian**	[elvetsi'an]
Scotland	**Scoția** (f)	['skotsia]
Scottish (masc.)	**scoțian** (m)	[skotsi'an]
Scottish (fem.)	**scoțiancă** (f)	[skotsi'ankə]
Scottish (adj)	**scoțian**	[skotsi'an]
Vatican	**Vatican** (m)	[vati'kan]
Liechtenstein	**Liechtenstein** (m)	[lihten'ʃtajn]
Luxembourg	**Luxemburg** (m)	[luksem'burg]
Monaco	**Monaco** (m)	[mo'nako]

235. Central and Eastern Europe

Albania	**Albania** (f)	[al'banija]
Albanian (masc.)	**albanez** (m)	[alba'nez]
Albanian (fem.)	**albaneză** (f)	[alba'nezə]
Albanian (adj)	**albanez**	[alba'nez]
Bulgaria	**Bulgaria** (f)	[bul'garia]
Bulgarian (masc.)	**bulgar** (m)	[bul'gar]
Bulgarian (fem.)	**bulgăroaică** (f)	[bulgəro'ajkə]
Bulgarian (adj)	**bulgăresc**	[bulgə'resk]
Hungary	**Ungaria** (f)	[un'garia]
Hungarian (masc.)	**ungur** (m)	['ungur]
Hungarian (fem.)	**unguroaică** (f)	[unguro'ajkə]
Hungarian (adj)	**unguresc**	[ungu'resk]
Latvia	**Letonia** (f)	[le'tonia]
Latvian (masc.)	**leton** (m)	[le'ton]
Latvian (fem.)	**letonă** (f)	[le'tonə]
Latvian (adj)	**leton**	[le'ton]
Lithuania	**Lituania** (f)	[litu'ania]
Lithuanian (masc.)	**lituanian** (m)	[lituani'an]
Lithuanian (fem.)	**lituaniană** (f)	[lituani'anə]
Lithuanian (adj)	**lituanian**	[lituani'an]
Poland	**Polonia** (f)	[po'lonia]
Pole (masc.)	**polonez** (m)	[polo'nez]
Pole (fem.)	**poloneză** (f)	[polo'nezə]

Polish (adj)	**polonez**	[polo'nez]
Romania	**România** (f)	[rominia]
Romanian (masc.)	**român** (m)	[ro'min]
Romanian (fem.)	**româncă** (f)	[ro'minkə]
Romanian (adj)	**român**	[ro'min]
Serbia	**Serbia** (f)	['serbija]
Serbian (masc.)	**sârb** (m)	[sirb]
Serbian (fem.)	**serbă** (f)	['serbə]
Serbian (adj)	**sârb**	[sirb]
Slovakia	**Slovacia** (f)	[slo'vatʃia]
Slovak (masc.)	**slovac** (m)	[slo'vak]
Slovak (fem.)	**slovacă** (f)	[slo'vakə]
Slovak (adj)	**slovac**	[slo'vak]
Croatia	**Croația** (f)	[kro'atsia]
Croatian (masc.)	**croat** (m)	[kro'at]
Croatian (fem.)	**croată** (f)	[kro'atə]
Croatian (adj)	**croat**	[kro'at]
Czech Republic	**Cehia** (f)	['tʃehija]
Czech (masc.)	**ceh** (m)	[tʃeh]
Czech (fem.)	**cehă** (f)	['tʃehə]
Czech (adj)	**ceh**	[tʃeh]
Estonia	**Estonia** (f)	[es'tonia]
Estonian (masc.)	**estonian** (m)	[estoni'an]
Estonian (fem.)	**estoniană** (f)	[estoni'anə]
Estonian (adj)	**estonian**	[estoni'an]
Bosnia and Herzegovina	**Bosnia şi Herțegovina** (f)	['bosnia ʃi hertsego'vina]
Macedonia (Republic of ~)	**Macedonia** (f)	[matʃe'donia]
Slovenia	**Slovenia** (f)	[slo'venia]
Montenegro	**Muntenegru** (m)	[munte'negru]

236. Former USSR countries

Azerbaijan	**Azerbaidjan** (m)	[azerbaj'dʒan]
Azerbaijani (masc.)	**azerbaidjan** (m)	[azerbaj'dʒan]
Azerbaijani (fem.)	**azerbaidjană** (f)	[azerbaj'dʒanə]
Azerbaijani, Azeri (adj)	**azerbaidjan**	[azerbaj'dʒan]
Armenia	**Armenia** (f)	[ar'menia]
Armenian (masc.)	**armean** (m)	[ar'mʲan]
Armenian (fem.)	**armeancă** (f)	[ar'mʲankə]
Armenian (adj)	**armenesc**	[arme'nesk]
Belarus	**Belarus** (f)	[bela'rus]
Belarusian (masc.)	**bielorus** (m)	[belo'rus]

Belarusian (fem.)	**bielorusă** (f)	[belo'rusə]
Belarusian (adj)	**bielorus**	[belo'rus]
Georgia	**Georgia** (f)	['dʒordʒia]
Georgian (masc.)	**gruzin** (m)	[gru'zin]
Georgian (fem.)	**georgiană** (f)	[dʒordʒi'anə]
Georgian (adj)	**gruzin**	[gru'zin]
Kazakhstan	**Kazahstan** (n)	[kazah'stan]
Kazakh (masc.)	**kazah** (m)	[ka'zah]
Kazakh (fem.)	**kazahă** (f)	[ka'zahə]
Kazakh (adj)	**kazah**	[ka'zah]
Kirghizia	**Kîrgîzstan** (m)	[kɨrgɨz'stan]
Kirghiz (masc.)	**kirghiz** (m)	[kir'giz]
Kirghiz (fem.)	**kirghiză** (f)	[kir'gize]
Kirghiz (adj)	**kirghiz**	[kir'giz]
Moldova, Moldavia	**Moldova** (f)	[mol'dova]
Moldavian (masc.)	**moldovean** (m)	[moldo'vʲan]
Moldavian (fem.)	**moldoveancă** (f)	[moldo'vʲankə]
Moldavian (adj)	**moldovenesc**	[moldove'nesk]
Russia	**Rusia** (f)	['rusia]
Russian (masc.)	**rus** (m)	[rus]
Russian (fem.)	**rusoaică** (f)	[ruso'ajkə]
Russian (adj)	**rusesc**	[ru'sesk]
Tajikistan	**Tadjikistan** (m)	[tadʒiki'stan]
Tajik (masc.)	**tadjic** (m)	[ta'dʒik]
Tajik (fem.)	**tadjică** (f)	[ta'dʒikə]
Tajik (adj)	**tadjic**	[ta'dʒik]
Turkmenistan	**Turkmenistan** (n)	[turkmeni'stan]
Turkmen (masc.)	**turkmen** (m)	[turk'men]
Turkmen (fem.)	**turkmenă** (f)	[turk'menə]
Turkmenian (adj)	**turkmen**	[turk'men]
Uzbekistan	**Uzbekistan** (n)	[uzbeki'stan]
Uzbek (masc.)	**uzbec** (m)	[uz'bek]
Uzbek (fem.)	**uzbecă** (f)	[uz'bekə]
Uzbek (adj)	**uzbec**	[uz'bek]
Ukraine	**Ucraina** (f)	[ukra'ina]
Ukrainian (masc.)	**ucrainean** (m)	[ukrai'nʲan]
Ukrainian (fem.)	**ucraineancă** (f)	[ukrai'nʲankə]
Ukrainian (adj)	**ucrainean**	[ukrai'nʲan]

237. Asia

Asia	**Asia** (f)	['asia]
Asian (adj)	**asiatic**	[asi'atik]

Vietnam	**Vietnam** (n)	[viet'nam]
Vietnamese (masc.)	**vietnamez** (m)	[vetna'mez]
Vietnamese (fem.)	**vietnameză** (f)	[vetna'mezə]
Vietnamese (adj)	**vietnamez**	[vetna'mezə]
India	**India** (f)	['india]
Indian (masc.)	**indian** (m)	[indi'an]
Indian (fem.)	**indiancă** (f)	[indi'ankə]
Indian (adj)	**indian**	[indi'an]
Israel	**Israel** (n)	[isra'el]
Israeli (masc.)	**israelian** (m)	[israeli'an]
Israeli (fem.)	**israeliană** (f)	[israeli'anə]
Israeli (adj)	**israelit**	[israe'lit]
Jew (n)	**evreu** (m)	[e'vreu]
Jewess (n)	**evreică** (f)	[e'vrejkə]
Jewish (adj)	**evreiesc**	[evre'esk]
China	**China** (f)	['kina]
Chinese (masc.)	**chinez** (m)	[ki'nez]
Chinese (fem.)	**chineză** (f)	[ki'neze]
Chinese (adj)	**chinezesc**	[kine'zesk]
Korean (masc.)	**coreean** (m)	[kore'an]
Korean (fem.)	**coreeancă** (f)	[kore'ankə]
Korean (adj)	**coreean**	[kore'an]
Lebanon	**Liban** (n)	[li'ban]
Lebanese (masc.)	**libanez** (m)	[liba'nez]
Lebanese (fem.)	**libaneză** (f)	[liba'nezə]
Lebanese (adj)	**libanez**	[liba'nez]
Mongolia	**Mongolia** (f)	[mon'golia]
Mongolian (masc.)	**mongol** (m)	[mon'gol]
Mongolian (fem.)	**mongolă** (f)	[mon'golə]
Mongolian (adj)	**mongol**	[mon'gol]
Malaysia	**Malaezia** (f)	[mala'ezia]
Malaysian (masc.)	**malaezian** (f)	[malaezi'an]
Malaysian (fem.)	**malaeziană** (f)	[malaezi'anə]
Malaysian (adj)	**malaez**	[mala'ez]
Pakistan	**Pakistan** (n)	[paki'stan]
Pakistani (masc.)	**pakistanez** (m)	[pakista'nez]
Pakistani (fem.)	**pakistaneză** (f)	[pakista'nezə]
Pakistani (adj)	**pakistanez**	[pakista'nez]
Saudi Arabia	**Arabia** (f) **Saudită**	[a'rabia sau'ditə]
Arab (masc.)	**arab** (m)	[a'rab]
Arab (fem.)	**arăboaică** (f)	[arəbo'ajkə]
Arab, Arabic (adj)	**arab**	[a'rab]

Thailand	**Thailanda** (f)	[taj'landa]
Thai (masc.)	**thailandez** (m)	[tajlan'dez]
Thai (fem.)	**thailandeză** (f)	[tajlan'dezə]
Thai (adj)	**thailandez**	[tajlan'dez]
Taiwan	**Taiwan** (m)	[taj'van]
Taiwanese (masc.)	**taiwanez** (m)	[tajva'nez]
Taiwanese (fem.)	**taiwaneză** (f)	[tajva'nezə]
Taiwanese (adj)	**taiwanez**	[tajva'nez]
Turkey	**Turcia** (f)	['turʧia]
Turk (masc.)	**turc** (m)	[turk]
Turk (fem.)	**turcoaică** (f)	[turko'ajkə]
Turkish (adj)	**turcesc**	[tur'ʧesk]
Japan	**Japonia** (f)	[ʒa'ponia]
Japanese (masc.)	**japonez** (m)	[ʒapo'nez]
Japanese (fem.)	**japoneză** (f)	[ʒapo'nezə]
Japanese (adj)	**japonez**	[ʒapo'nez]
Afghanistan	**Afganistan** (n)	[afganis'tan]
Bangladesh	**Bangladeş** (m)	[bangla'deʃ]
Indonesia	**Indonezia** (f)	[indo'nezia]
Jordan	**Iordania** (f)	[jor'dania]
Iraq	**Irak** (n)	[i'rak]
Iran	**Iran** (n)	[i'ran]
Cambodia	**Cambodgia** (f)	[kam'bodʒia]
Kuwait	**Kuweit** (n)	[kuve'it]
Laos	**Laos** (n)	['laos]
Myanmar	**Myanmar** (m)	[mjan'mar]
Nepal	**Nepal** (n)	[ne'pal]
United Arab Emirates	**Emiratele** (n pl) **Arabe Unite**	[emi'ratele a'rabe u'nite]
Syria	**Siria** (f)	['sirija]
Palestine	**Palestina** (f)	[pales'tina]
South Korea	**Coreea** (f) **de Sud**	[ko'rea de 'sud]
North Korea	**Coreea** (f) **de Nord**	[ko'rea de 'nord]

238. North America

United States of America	**Statele** (n pl) **Unite ale Americii**	['statele u'nite 'ale a'meriʧij]
American (masc.)	**american** (m)	[ameri'kan]
American (fem.)	**americancă** (f)	[ameri'kankə]
American (adj)	**american**	[ameri'kan]
Canada	**Canada** (f)	[ka'nada]
Canadian (masc.)	**canadian** (m)	[kanadi'an]

Canadian (fem.)	**canadiancă** (f)	[kanadi'ankə]
Canadian (adj)	**canadian**	[kanadi'an]
Mexico	**Mexic** (n)	['meksik]
Mexican (masc.)	**mexican** (m)	[meksi'kan]
Mexican (fem.)	**mexicancă** (f)	[meksi'kankə]
Mexican (adj)	**mexican**	[meksi'kan]

239. Central and South America

Argentina	**Argentina** (f)	[arʒen'tina]
Argentinian (masc.)	**argentinian** (m)	[arʒentini'an]
Argentinian (fem.)	**argentiniană** (f)	[ardʒentini'anə]
Argentinian (adj)	**argentinian**	[arʒentini'an]
Brazil	**Brazilia** (f)	[bra'zilia]
Brazilian (masc.)	**brazilian** (m)	[brazili'an]
Brazilian (fem.)	**braziliancă** (f)	[brazili'ankə]
Brazilian (adj)	**brazilian**	[brazili'an]
Colombia	**Columbia** (f)	[ko'lumbia]
Colombian (masc.)	**columbian** (m)	[kolumbi'an]
Colombian (fem.)	**columbiană** (f)	[kolumbi'anə]
Colombian (adj)	**columbian**	[kolumbi'an]
Cuba	**Cuba** (f)	['kuba]
Cuban (masc.)	**cubanez** (m)	[kuba'nez]
Cuban (fem.)	**cubaneză** (f)	[kuba'nezə]
Cuban (adj)	**cubanez**	[kuba'nez]
Chile	**Chile** (n)	['ʧile]
Chilean (masc.)	**chilian** (m)	[ʧili'an]
Chilean (fem.)	**chiliană** (f)	[ʧili'anə]
Chilean (adj)	**chilian**	[ʧili'an]
Bolivia	**Bolivia** (f)	[bo'livia]
Venezuela	**Venezuela** (f)	[venezu'ela]
Paraguay	**Paraguay** (n)	[paragu'aj]
Peru	**Peru** (n)	['peru]
Suriname	**Surinam** (n)	[suri'nam]
Uruguay	**Uruguay** (n)	[urugu'aj]
Ecuador	**Ecuador** (m)	[ekua'dor]
The Bahamas	**Insulele** (f pl) **Bahamas**	['insulele ba'hamas]
Haiti	**Haiti** (n)	[ha'iti]
Dominican Republic	**Republica** (f) **Dominicană**	[re'publika domini'kanə]
Panama	**Panama** (f)	[pana'ma]
Jamaica	**Jamaica** (f)	[ʒa'majka]

240. Africa

Egypt	**Egipt** (n)	[e'ʤipt]
Egyptian (masc.)	**egiptean** (m)	[eʤip'tʲan]
Egyptian (fem.)	**egipteancă** (f)	[eʤip'tʲankə]
Egyptian (adj)	**egiptean**	[eʤip'tʲan]
Morocco	**Maroc** (n)	[ma'rok]
Moroccan (masc.)	**marocan** (m)	[maro'kan]
Moroccan (fem.)	**marocană** (f)	[maro'kanə]
Moroccan (adj)	**marocan**	[maro'kan]
Tunisia	**Tunisia** (f)	[tu'nisia]
Tunisian (masc.)	**tunisian** (m)	[tunisi'an]
Tunisian (fem.)	**tunisiancă** (f)	[tunisi'ankə]
Tunisian (adj)	**tunisian**	[tunisi'an]
Ghana	**Ghana** (f)	['gana]
Zanzibar	**Zanzibar** (n)	[zanzi'bar]
Kenya	**Kenia** (f)	['kenia]
Libya	**Libia** (f)	['libia]
Madagascar	**Madagascar** (n)	[madagas'kar]
Namibia	**Namibia** (f)	[na'mibia]
Senegal	**Senegal** (n)	[sene'gal]
Tanzania	**Tanzania** (f)	[tan'zania]
South Africa	**Africa de Sud** (f)	['afrika de sud]
African (masc.)	**african** (m)	[afri'kan]
African (fem.)	**africană** (f)	[afri'kanə]
African (adj)	**african**	[afri'kan]

241. Australia. Oceania

Australia	**Australia** (f)	[au'stralia]
Australian (masc.)	**australian** (m)	[australi'an]
Australian (fem.)	**australiană** (f)	[australi'anə]
Australian (adj)	**australian**	[australi'an]
New Zealand	**Noua Zeelandă** (f)	['nowa zee'landə]
New Zealander (masc.)	**neozeelandez** (m)	[neozeelan'dez]
New Zealander (fem.)	**neozeelandeză** (f)	[neozeelan'dezə]
New Zealand (as adj)	**neozeelandez**	[neozeelan'dez]
Tasmania	**Tasmania** (f)	[tas'mania]
French Polynesia	**Polinezia** (f)	[poli'nezia]

242. Cities

Amsterdam	**Amsterdam** (n)	['amsterdam]
Ankara	**Ankara** (f)	[an'kara]
Athens	**Atena** (f)	[a'tena]
Baghdad	**Bagdad** (n)	[bag'dad]
Bangkok	**Bangkok** (m)	[ba'nkok]
Barcelona	**Barcelona** (f)	[barse'lona]
Beijing	**Beijing** (n)	[bej'ʒing]
Beirut	**Beirut** (n)	[bej'rut]
Berlin	**Berlin** (n)	[ber'lin]
Mumbai (Bombay)	**Bombay** (n)	[bom'bej]
Bonn	**Bonn** (n)	[bon]
Bordeaux	**Bordeaux** (n)	[bor'do]
Bratislava	**Bratislava** (f)	[bratislava]
Brussels	**Bruxelles** (n)	[bruk'sel]
Bucharest	**Bucure ti** (n)	[buku'reʃtʲ]
Budapest	**Budapesta** (f)	[buda'pesta]
Cairo	**Cairo** (n)	[ka'iro]
Kolkata (Calcutta)	**Calcutta** (f)	[kal'kuta]
Chicago	**Chicago** (n)	[ʧi'kago]
Copenhagen	**Copenhaga** (f)	[kopen'haga]
Dar-es-Salaam	**Dar es Salaam** (n)	[dar es sala'am]
Delhi	**Delhi, New Delhi** (m)	['deli], [nju 'deli]
Dubai	**Dubai** (n)	[du'baj]
Dublin	**Dublin** (n)	[dub'lin]
Düsseldorf	**Düsseldorf** (m)	[djusel'dorf]
Florence	**Florența** (f)	[flo'rentsa]
Frankfurt	**Frankfurt** (m)	['frankfurt]
Geneva	**Geneva** (f)	[ʤe'neva]
The Hague	**Haga** (f)	['haga]
Hamburg	**Hamburg** (n)	['hamburg]
Hanoi	**Hanoi** (n)	[ha'noj]
Havana	**Havana** (f)	[ha'vana]
Helsinki	**Helsinki** (n)	['helsinki]
Hiroshima	**Hiroşima** (f)	[hiro'ʃima]
Hong Kong	**Hong-Kong** (n)	['hong 'kong]
Istanbul	**Istanbul** (n)	[istan'bul]
Jerusalem	**Ierusalim** (n)	[jerusa'lim]
Kyiv	**Kiev** (n)	[ki'ev]
Kuala Lumpur	**Kuala Lumpur** (m)	[ku'ala lum'pur]
Lisbon	**Lisabona** (f)	[lisa'bona]
London	**Londra** (f)	['londra]
Los Angeles	**Los Angeles** (n)	['los 'anʤeles]

Lyons	**Lyon** (m)	[li'on]
Madrid	**Madrid** (n)	[ma'drid]
Marseille	**Marsilia** (f)	[mar'silia]
Mexico City	**Mexico City** (n)	['meksiko 'siti]
Miami	**Miami** (n)	[ma'jami]
Montreal	**Montreal** (m)	[monre'al]
Moscow	**Moscova** (f)	['moskova]
Munich	**Munchen** (m)	['mʲunhen]
Nairobi	**Nairobi** (n)	[naj'robi]
Naples	**Napoli** (m)	['napoli]
New York	**New York** (n)	[nju 'jork]
Nice	**Nisa** (f)	['nisa]
Oslo	**Oslo** (n)	['oslo]
Ottawa	**Ottawa** (f)	[ot'tava]
Paris	**Paris** (n)	[pa'ris]
Prague	**Praga** (f)	['praga]
Rio de Janeiro	**Rio de Janeiro** (n)	['rio de ʒa'nejro]
Rome	**Roma** (f)	['roma]
Saint Petersburg	**Sankt Petersburg** (n)	['sankt peters'burg]
Seoul	**Seul** (n)	[se'ul]
Shanghai	**Shanghai** (m)	[ʃan'haj]
Singapore	**Singapore** (n)	[singa'pore]
Stockholm	**Stockholm** (m)	['stokholm]
Sydney	**Sydney** (m)	['sidnej]
Taipei	**Taipei** (m)	[taj'pej]
Tokyo	**Tokio** (n)	['tokio]
Toronto	**Toronto** (n)	[to'ronto]
Venice	**Veneția** (f)	[ve'netsia]
Vienna	**Viena** (f)	[vi'ena]
Warsaw	**Varşovia** (f)	[var'ʃovia]
Washington	**Washington** (n)	['waʃington]

243. Politics. Government. Part 1

politics	**politică** (f)	[po'litikə]
political (adj)	**politic**	[po'litik]
politician	**politician** (m)	[politiʧi'an]
state (country)	**stat** (n)	[stat]
citizen	**cetățean** (m)	[ʧetə'tsʲan]
citizenship	**cetățenie** (f)	[ʧetətse'nie]
national emblem	**stemă** (f) **națională**	['stemə natsio'nalə]
national anthem	**imn** (n) **de stat**	[imn de stat]
government	**guvern** (n)	[gu'vern]

head of state	**conducătorul** (m) **țării**	[kondukə'torul tsərij]
parliament	**parlament** (n)	[parla'ment]
party	**partid** (n)	[par'tid]
capitalism	**capitalism** (n)	[kapita'lism]
capitalist (adj)	**capitalist**	[kapita'list]
socialism	**socialism** (n)	[sotʃia'lizm]
socialist (adj)	**socialist**	[sotʃia'list]
communism	**comunism** (n)	[komu'nizm]
communist (adj)	**comunist**	[komu'nist]
communist (n)	**comunist** (m)	[komu'nist]
democracy	**democrație** (f)	[demokra'tsie]
democrat	**democrat** (m)	[demo'krat]
democratic (adj)	**democrat**	[demo'krat]
Democratic party	**partid** (n) **democrat**	[par'tid demo'krat]
liberal (n)	**liberal** (m)	[libe'ral]
liberal (adj)	**liberal**	[libe'ral]
conservative (n)	**conservator** (m)	[konserva'tor]
conservative (adj)	**conservator**	[konserva'tor]
republic (n)	**republică** (f)	[re'publikə]
republican (n)	**republican** (m)	[republi'kan]
Republican party	**partid** (n) **republican**	[par'tid republi'kan]
elections	**alegeri** (f pl)	[a'ledʒerʲ]
to elect (vt)	**a alege**	[a a'ledʒe]
elector, voter	**alegător** (m)	[alegə'tor]
election campaign	**campanie** (f) **electorală**	[kam'panie elekto'ralə]
voting (n)	**votare** (f)	[vo'tare]
to vote (vi)	**a vota**	[a vo'ta]
suffrage, right to vote	**drept** (n) **de vot**	[drept de vot]
candidate	**candidat** (m)	[kandi'dat]
to be a candidate	**a candida**	[a kandi'da]
campaign	**campanie** (f)	[kam'panie]
opposition (as adj)	**de opoziție**	[de opo'zitsie]
opposition (n)	**opoziție** (f)	[opo'zitsie]
visit	**vizită** (f)	['vizitə]
official visit	**vizită** (f) **oficială**	['vizitə ofitʃi'alə]
international (adj)	**internațional**	[internatsio'nal]
negotiations	**tratative** (n pl)	[trata'tive]
to negotiate (vi)	**a purta tratative**	[a pur'ta trata'tive]

244. Politics. Government. Part 2

society	**societate** (f)	[sotʃie'tate]
constitution	**constituție** (f)	[konsti'tutsie]
power (political control)	**autoritate** (f)	[autori'tate]
corruption	**corupție** (f)	[ko'ruptsie]
law (justice)	**lege** (f)	['ledʒe]
legal (legitimate)	**legal**	[le'gal]
justice (fairness)	**dreptate** (f)	[drep'tate]
just (fair)	**echitabil**	[eki'tabil]
committee	**comitet** (n)	[komi'tet]
bill (draft law)	**proiect** (n) **de lege**	[pro'ekt de 'ledʒe]
budget	**buget** (n)	[bu'dʒet]
policy	**politică** (f)	[po'litikə]
reform	**reformă** (f)	[re'formə]
radical (adj)	**radical**	[radi'kal]
power (strength, force)	**putere** (f)	[pu'tere]
powerful (adj)	**puternic**	[pu'ternik]
supporter	**adept** (m)	[a'dept]
influence	**influență** (f)	[influ'entsə]
regime (e.g., military ~)	**regim** (n)	[re'dʒim]
conflict	**conflict** (n)	[kon'flikt]
conspiracy (plot)	**conspirație** (f)	[konspi'ratsie]
provocation	**provocare** (f)	[provo'kare]
to overthrow (regime, etc.)	**a răsturna**	[a rəstur'na]
overthrow (of government)	**răsturnare** (f)	[rəstur'nare]
revolution	**revoluție** (f)	[revo'lutsie]
coup d'état	**lovitură** (f) **de stat**	[lovi'tura də stat]
military coup	**lovitură** (f) **de stat militară**	[lovi'tura də stat mili'tarə]
crisis	**criză** (f)	['krizə]
economic recession	**scădere** (f) **economică**	[skə'dere eko'nomikə]
demonstrator (protester)	**manifestant** (m)	[manifes'tant]
demonstration	**manifestație** (f)	[manifes'tatsie]
martial law	**stare** (f) **de război**	['stare de rəz'boj]
military base	**bază** (f) **militară**	['bazə mili'tarə]
stability	**stabilitate** (f)	[stabili'tatə]
stable (adj)	**stabil**	[sta'bil]
exploitation	**exploatare** (f)	[ekploa'tare]
to exploit (workers)	**a exploata**	[a eksploa'ta]
racism	**rasism** (n)	[ra'sism]
racist	**rasist** (m)	[ra'sist]

fascism	**fascism** (n)	[fas'ʧism]
fascist	**fascist** (m)	[fas'ʧist]

245. Countries. Miscellaneous

foreigner	**cetățean** (m) **străin**	[ʧetə'tsʲan strə'in]
foreign (adj)	**străin**	[strə'in]
abroad (in a foreign country)	**peste hotare**	['peste ho'tare]
emigrant	**emigrant** (m)	[emi'grant]
emigration	**emigrare** (f)	[emi'grare]
to emigrate (vi)	**a emigra**	[a emi'gra]
the West	**Vest** (n)	[vest]
the East	**Est** (n)	[est]
the Far East	**Extremul Orient** (n)	[eks'tremul o'rjent]
civilization	**civilizație** (f)	[ʧivili'zatsie]
humanity (mankind)	**umanitate** (f)	[umani'tate]
the world (earth)	**lume** (f)	['lume]
peace	**pace** (f)	['paʧe]
worldwide (adj)	**mondial**	[mon'djal]
homeland	**patrie** (f)	['patrie]
people (population)	**popor** (n)	[po'por]
population	**populație** (f)	[popu'latsie]
people (a lot of ~)	**oameni** (m pl)	[o'amenʲ]
nation (people)	**națiune** (f)	[natsi'une]
generation	**generație** (f)	[dʒene'ratsie]
territory (area)	**teritoriu** (n)	[teri'torju]
region	**regiune** (f)	[redʒi'une]
state (part of a country)	**stat** (n)	[stat]
tradition	**tradiție** (f)	[tra'ditsie]
custom (tradition)	**obicei** (n)	[obi'ʧej]
ecology	**ecologie** (f)	[ekolo'dʒie]
Indian (Native American)	**indian** (m)	[indi'an]
Gypsy (masc.)	**țigan** (m)	[tsi'gan]
Gypsy (fem.)	**țigancă** (f)	[tsi'gankə]
Gypsy (adj)	**țigănesc**	[tsigə'nesk]
empire	**imperiu** (n)	[im'perju]
colony	**colonie** (f)	[kolo'nie]
slavery	**sclavie** (f)	[skla'vie]
invasion	**invazie** (f)	[in'vazie]
famine	**foamete** (f)	[fo'amete]

246. Major religious groups. Confessions

religion	**religie** (f)	[re'lidʒie]
religious (adj)	**religios**	[relidʒi'os]
faith, belief	**credință** (f)	[kre'dintsə]
to believe (in God)	**a crede**	[a 'krede]
believer	**credincios** (m)	[kredin'tʃios]
atheism	**ateism** (n)	[ate'izm]
atheist	**ateu** (m)	[a'teu]
Christianity	**creştinism** (n)	[kreʃti'nism]
Christian (n)	**creştin** (m)	[kreʃ'tin]
Christian (adj)	**creştin**	[kreʃ'tin]
Catholicism	**Catolicism** (n)	[katoli'tʃism]
Catholic (n)	**catolic** (m)	[ka'tolik]
Catholic (adj)	**catolic**	[ka'tolik]
Protestantism	**Protestantism** (n)	[protestan'tizm]
Protestant Church	**Biserica** (f) **Protestantă**	[bi'serika protes'tantə]
Protestant (n)	**protestant** (m)	[protes'tant]
Orthodoxy	**Ortodoxie** (f)	[ortodok'sie]
Orthodox Church	**Biserica** (f) **Ortodoxă**	[bi'serika orto'doksə]
Orthodox (n)	**ortodox** (m)	[orto'doks]
Presbyterianism	**calvinism** (n)	[kalvi'nism]
Presbyterian Church	**Biserica** (f) **Calvinistă**	[bi'serika kalvi'nistə]
Presbyterian (n)	**calvinist** (m)	[kalvi'nist]
Lutheranism	**Biserica** (f) **Luterană**	[bi'serika lute'ranə]
Lutheran (n)	**luteran** (m)	[lute'ran]
Baptist Church	**Baptism** (n)	[bap'tism]
Baptist (n)	**baptist** (m)	[bap'tist]
Anglican Church	**Biserica** (f) **Anglicană**	[bi'serika angli'kanə]
Anglican (n)	**anglican** (m)	[angli'kan]
Mormonism	**Mormonism** (n)	[mormo'nism]
Mormon (n)	**mormon** (m)	[mor'mon]
Judaism	**Iudaism** (n)	[juda'izm]
Jew (n)	**iudeu** (m)	[ju'deu]
Buddhism	**Budism** (n)	[bu'dizm]
Buddhist (n)	**budist** (m)	[bu'dist]
Hinduism	**Hinduism** (n)	[hindu'izm]
Hindu (n)	**hindus** (m)	[hin'dus]

Islam	**Islamism** (n)	[isla'mizm]
Muslim (n)	**musulman** (m)	[musul'man]
Muslim (adj)	**musulman**	[musul'man]
Shiah Islam	**Şiism** (n)	[ʃi'ism]
Shiite (n)	**şiit** (m)	[ʃi'it]
Sunni Islam	**Sunnism** (n)	[su'nism]
Sunnite (n)	**sunnit** (m)	[su'nit]

247. Religions. Priests

priest	**preot** (m)	['preot]
the Pope	**Papa Romei** (m)	['papa 'romej]
monk, friar	**călugăr** (m)	[kə'lugər]
nun	**călugăriță** (f)	[kə'lugəritsə]
pastor	**pastor** (m)	['pastor]
abbot	**abate** (m)	[a'bate]
vicar (parish priest)	**vicar** (m)	[vi'kar]
bishop	**episcop** (m)	[e'piskop]
cardinal	**cardinal** (m)	[kardi'nal]
preacher	**propovăduitor** (m)	[propovədui'tor]
preaching	**predică** (f)	['predikə]
parishioners	**enoriaşi** (m pl)	[enori'aʃ]
believer	**credincios** (m)	[kredin'tʃios]
atheist	**ateu** (m)	[a'teu]

248. Faith. Christianity. Islam

Adam	**Adam** (m)	[a'dam]
Eve	**Eva** (f)	['eva]
God	**Dumnezeu** (m)	[dumne'zeu]
the Lord	**Domnul** (m)	['domnulʲ]
the Almighty	**Atotputernic** (m)	[atotpu'ternik]
sin	**păcat** (n)	[pə'kat]
to sin (vi)	**a păcătui**	[a pəkətu'i]
sinner (masc.)	**păcătos** (m)	[pəkə'tos]
sinner (fem.)	**păcătoasă** (f)	[pəkəto'asə]
hell	**iad** (n)	[jad]
paradise	**rai** (f)	[raj]
Jesus	**Isus** (m)	[i'sus]

Jesus Christ	**Isus Hristos** (m)	[i'sus hris'tos]
the Holy Spirit	**Sfântul Duh** (m)	['sfɨntul 'duh]
the Savior	**Salvator** (m)	[salva'tor]
the Virgin Mary	**Maica Domnului** (f)	['majka 'domnuluj]
the Devil	**Diavol** (m)	['djavol]
devil's (adj)	**diavolesc**	[djavo'lesk]
Satan	**Satana** (f)	[sa'tana]
satanic (adj)	**satanic**	[sa'tanik]
angel	**înger** (m)	['ɨndʒer]
guardian angel	**înger** (m) **păzitor**	['ɨndʒer pəzi'tor]
angelic (adj)	**îngeresc**	[ɨndʒe'resk]
apostle	**apostol** (m)	[a'postol]
archangel	**arhanghel** (m)	[ar'hangel]
the Antichrist	**antihrist** (m)	[anti'hrist]
Church	**Biserică** (f)	[bi'serikə]
Bible	**Biblie** (f)	['biblie]
biblical (adj)	**biblic**	['biblik]
Old Testament	**Vechiul Testament** (n)	['vekjul testa'ment]
New Testament	**Noul testament** (n)	['noul testa'ment]
Gospel	**Evanghelie** (f)	[eva'ngelie]
Holy Scripture	**Sfânta Scriptură** (f)	['sfɨnta skrip'turə]
Heaven	**Împărăția Cerului** (f)	[ɨmpərə'ʦia 'ʧeruluj]
Commandment	**poruncă** (f)	[po'runkə]
prophet	**profet** (m)	[pro'fet]
prophecy	**profeție** (f)	[profe'ʦie]
Allah	**Allah** (m)	[al'lah]
Mohammed	**Mohamed** (m)	[moha'med]
the Koran	**Coran** (n)	[ko'ran]
mosque	**moschee** (f)	[mos'kee]
mullah	**hoge** (m)	['hodʒe]
prayer	**rugăciune** (f)	[rugə'ʧiune]
to pray (vi, vt)	**a se ruga**	[a se ru'ga]
pilgrimage	**pelerinaj** (n)	[peleri'naʒ]
pilgrim	**pelerin** (m)	[pele'rin]
Mecca	**Mecca** (f)	['meka]
church	**biserică** (f)	[bi'serikə]
temple	**templu** (n)	['templu]
cathedral	**catedrală** (f)	[kate'dralə]
Gothic (adj)	**gotic**	['gotik]
synagogue	**sinagogă** (f)	[sina'gogə]
mosque	**moschee** (f)	[mos'kee]
chapel	**capelă** (f)	[ka'pelə]

abbey	**abaţie** (f)	[a'batsie]
convent	**mănăstire** (f) **de călugăriţe**	[mənəs'tire de kə'lugəritse]
monastery	**mănăstire** (f) **de călugări**	[mənəs'tire de kə'lugərʲ]
bell (church ~s)	**clopot** (n)	['klopot]
bell tower	**clopotniţă** (f)	[klo'potnitsə]
to ring (ab. bells)	**a bate**	[a 'bate]
cross	**cruce** (f)	['krutʃe]
cupola (roof)	**boltă** (f)	['boltə]
icon	**icoană** (f)	[iko'anə]
soul	**suflet** (n)	['suflet]
fate (destiny)	**soartă** (f)	[so'artə]
evil (n)	**rău** (n)	[rəu]
good (n)	**bine** (n)	['bine]
vampire	**vampir** (m)	[vam'pir]
witch (evil ~)	**vrăjitoare** (f)	[vrəʒito'are]
demon	**demon** (m)	['demon]
spirit	**spirit** (n)	['spirit]
redemption (giving us ~)	**ispăşire** (f)	[ispə'ʃire]
to redeem (vt)	**a ispăşi**	[a ispə'ʃi]
church service, mass	**slujbă** (f)	['sluʒbə]
to say mass	**a sluji**	[a slu'ʒi]
confession	**spovedanie** (f)	[spove'danie]
to confess (vi)	**a se spovedi**	[a se spove'di]
saint (n)	**sfânt** (m)	[sfint]
sacred (holy)	**sfânt**	[sfint]
holy water	**apă** (f) **sfinţită**	['apə sfin'tsitə]
ritual (n)	**ritual** (n)	[ritu'al]
ritual (adj)	**de rit**	[de rit]
sacrifice	**jertfă** (f)	['ʒertfə]
superstition	**superstiţie** (f)	[supers'titsie]
superstitious (adj)	**superstiţios**	[superstitsi'os]
afterlife	**viaţa** (f) **de după moarte**	['vjatsa de 'dupə mo'arte]
eternal life	**viaţă** (f) **veşnică**	['vjatsə 'veʃnikə]

MISCELLANEOUS

249. Various useful words

background (green ~)	**fundal** (n)	[fun'dal]
balance (of situation)	**balanță** (f)	[ba'lantsə]
barrier (obstacle)	**barieră** (f)	[ba'rjerə]
base (basis)	**bază** (f)	['bazə]
beginning	**început** (n)	[intʃe'put]
category	**categorie** (f)	[katego'rie]
cause (reason)	**cauză** (f)	['kauzə]
choice	**alegere** (f)	[a'ledʒere]
coincidence	**coincidență** (f)	[kointʃi'dentsə]
comfortable (~ chair)	**confortabil**	[konfor'tabil]
comparison	**comparație** (f)	[kompa'ratsie]
compensation	**compensație** (f)	[kompen'satsie]
degree (extent, amount)	**grad** (n)	[grad]
development	**dezvoltare** (f)	[dezvol'tare]
difference	**deosebire** (f)	[deose'bire]
effect (e.g., of drugs)	**efect** (n)	[e'fekt]
effort (exertion)	**efort** (n)	[e'fort]
element	**element** (n)	[ele'ment]
end (finish)	**sfârşit** (n)	[sfɨr'ʃit]
example (illustration)	**exemplu** (n)	[e'gzemplu]
fact	**fapt** (n)	[fapt]
frequent (adj)	**des**	[des]
growth (development)	**creştere** (f)	['kreʃtere]
help	**ajutor** (n)	[aʒu'tor]
ideal	**ideal** (n)	[ide'al]
kind (sort, type)	**aspect** (n)	[as'pekt]
labyrinth	**labirint** (n)	[labi'rint]
mistake, error	**greşeală** (f)	[gre'ʃalə]
moment	**moment** (n)	[mo'mənt]
object (thing)	**obiect** (n)	[o'bjekt]
obstacle	**obstacol** (n)	[ob'stakol]
original (original copy)	**original** (n)	[oridʒi'nal]
part (~ of sth)	**parte** (f)	['parte]
particle, small part	**bucată** (f)	[bu'katə]
pause (break)	**pauză** (f)	['pauzə]

position	**poziție** (f)	[po'zitsie]
principle	**principiu** (n)	[prin'tʃipju]
problem	**problemă** (f)	[pro'blemə]
process	**proces** (n)	[pro'tʃes]
progress	**progres** (n)	[pro'gres]
property (quality)	**însușire** (f)	[ɨnsu'ʃire]
reaction	**reacție** (f)	[re'aktsie]
risk	**risc** (n)	[risk]
secret	**taină** (f)	['tajnə]
series	**serie** (f)	['serie]
shape (outer form)	**formă** (f)	['formə]
situation	**situație** (f)	[situ'atsie]
solution	**soluție** (f)	[so'lutsie]
standard (adj)	**standardizat**	[standardi'zat]
standard (level of quality)	**standard** (n)	[stan'dard]
stop (pause)	**pauză** (f)	['pauzə]
style	**stil** (n)	[stil]
system	**sistem** (n)	[sis'tem]
table (chart)	**tabel** (n)	[ta'bel]
tempo, rate	**ritm** (n)	[ritm]
term (word, expression)	**termen** (n)	['termen]
thing (object, item)	**obiect** (n)	[o'bjekt]
truth (e.g., moment of ~)	**adevăr** (n)	[ade'vər]
turn (please wait your ~)	**rând** (n)	[rɨnd]
type (sort, kind)	**tip** (n)	[tip]
urgent (adj)	**urgent**	[ur'dʒent]
urgently (adv)	**urgent**	[ur'dʒent]
utility (usefulness)	**folos** (n)	[fo'los]
variant (alternative)	**variantă** (f)	[vari'antə]
way (means, method)	**mod** (n)	[mod]
zone	**zonă** (f)	['zonə]

250. Modifiers. Adjectives. Part 1

additional (adj)	**suplimentar**	[suplimen'tar]
ancient (~ civilization)	**antic**	['antik]
artificial (adj)	**artificial**	[artifitʃi'al]
back, rear (adj)	**posterior**	[posteri'or]
bad (adj)	**rău**	['rəu]
beautiful (~ palace)	**minunat**	[minu'nat]
beautiful (person)	**frumos**	[fru'mos]
big (in size)	**mare**	['mare]

bitter (taste)	**amar**	[a'mar]
blind (sightless)	**orb**	[orb]
calm, quiet (adj)	**liniştit**	[liniʃ'tit]
careless (negligent)	**neglijent**	[negli'ʒent]
caring (~ father)	**grijuliu**	[griʒu'lju]
central (adj)	**central**	[ʧen'tral]
cheap (low-priced)	**ieftin**	['jeftin]
cheerful (adj)	**vesel**	['vesel]
children's (adj)	**pentru copii**	['pentru ko'pij]
civil (~ law)	**civil**	[ʧi'vil]
clandestine (secret)	**ilegal**	[ile'gal]
clean (free from dirt)	**curat**	[ku'rat]
clear (explanation, etc.)	**clar**	[klar]
clever (smart)	**deştept**	[deʃ'tept]
close (near in space)	**vecin**	[ve'ʧin]
closed (adj)	**închis**	[ɨn'kis]
cloudless (sky)	**fără nori**	['fərə 'nor^{j}]
cold (drink, weather)	**rece**	['reʧe]
compatible (adj)	**compatibil**	[kompa'tibil]
contented (satisfied)	**mulțumit**	[mulʦu'mit]
continuous (uninterrupted)	**neîntrerupt**	[neɨntre'rupt]
cool (weather)	**răcoros**	[rəko'ros]
dangerous (adj)	**periculos**	[periku'los]
dark (room)	**întunecat**	[ɨntune'kat]
dead (not alive)	**mort**	[mort]
dense (fog, smoke)	**des**	[des]
destitute (extremely poor)	**sărac**	[sə'rak]
different (not the same)	**diferit**	[dife'rit]
difficult (decision)	**greu**	['greu]
difficult (problem, task)	**complex**	[kom'pleks]
dim, faint (light)	**şters**	[ʃters]
dirty (not clean)	**murdar**	[mur'dar]
distant (in space)	**îndepărtat**	[ɨndepər'tat]
dry (clothes, etc.)	**uscat**	[us'kat]
easy (not difficult)	**simplu**	['simplu]
empty (glass, room)	**gol**	[gol]
even (e.g., ~ surface)	**neted**	['neted]
exact (amount)	**exact**	[e'gzakt]
excellent (adj)	**excelent**	[eksʧe'lent]
excessive (adj)	**excesiv**	[eksʧe'siv]
expensive (adj)	**scump**	[skump]
exterior (adj)	**exterior**	[eksteri'or]
far (the ~ East)	**îndepărtat**	[ɨndepər'tat]

fast (quick)	**rapid**	[ra'pid]
fatty (food)	**gras**	[gras]
fertile (land, soil)	**roditor**	[rodi'tor]
flat (~ panel display)	**neted**	['neted]
foreign (adj)	**străin**	[strə'in]
fragile (china, glass)	**fragil**	[fra'dʒil]
free (at no cost)	**gratis**	['gratis]
free (unrestricted)	**liber**	['liber]
fresh (~ water)	**nesărat**	[nesə'rat]
fresh (e.g., ~ bread)	**proaspăt**	[pro'aspət]
frozen (food)	**congelat**	[kondʒe'lat]
full (completely filled)	**plin**	[plin]
gloomy (house, forecast)	**întunecat**	[ɨntune'kat]
good (book, etc.)	**bun**	[bun]
good, kind (kindhearted)	**bun**	[bun]
grateful (adj)	**recunoscător**	[rekunoskə'tor]
happy (adj)	**fericit**	[feri'tʃit]
hard (not soft)	**tare**	['tare]
heavy (in weight)	**greu**	['greu]
hostile (adj)	**duşmănos**	[duʃmə'nos]
hot (adj)	**fierbinte**	[fier'binte]
huge (adj)	**uriaş**	[uri'aʃ]
humid (adj)	**umed**	['umed]
hungry (adj)	**flămând**	[flə'mɨnd]
ill (sick, unwell)	**bolnav**	[bol'nav]
immobile (adj)	**imobil**	[imo'bil]
important (adj)	**important**	[impor'tant]
impossible (adj)	**imposibil**	[impo'sibil]
incomprehensible	**neclar**	[ne'klar]
indispensable (adj)	**necesar**	[netʃe'sar]
inexperienced (adj)	**lipsit de experiență**	[lip'sit de ekspe'rjentsə]
insignificant (adj)	**neînsemnat**	[neɨnsem'nat]
interior (adj)	**interior**	[interi'or]
joint (~ decision)	**comun**	[ko'mun]
last (e.g., ~ week)	**trecut**	[tre'kut]
last (final)	**ultimul**	['ultimul]
left (e.g., ~ side)	**stâng**	[stɨng]
legal (legitimate)	**legal**	[le'gal]
light (in weight)	**uşor**	[u'ʃor]
light (pale color)	**de nuanță deschisă**	[de nu'antsə des'kisə]
limited (adj)	**limitat**	[limi'tat]
liquid (fluid)	**lichid**	[li'kid]
long (e.g., ~ hair)	**lung**	[lung]

loud (voice, etc.)	**cu voce tare**	[ku 'voʧe 'tare]
low (voice)	**încet**	[ɨn'ʧet]

251. Modifiers. Adjectives. Part 2

main (principal)	**principal**	[prinʧi'pal]
matt, matte	**mat**	[mat]
meticulous (job)	**ordonat**	[ordo'nat]
mysterious (adj)	**enigmatic**	[enig'matik]
narrow (street, etc.)	**îngust**	[ɨn'gust]
native (~ country)	**natal**	[na'tal]
nearby (adj)	**apropiat**	[apropi'jat]
nearsighted (adj)	**miop**	[mi'op]
needed (necessary)	**necesar**	[neʧe'sar]
negative (~ response)	**negativ**	[nega'tiv]
neighboring (adj)	**vecin**	[ve'ʧin]
nervous (adj)	**nervos**	[ner'vos]
new (adj)	**nou**	['nou]
next (e.g., ~ week)	**următor**	[urmə'tor]
nice (agreeable)	**simpatic**	[sim'patik]
pleasant (voice)	**plăcut**	[plə'kut]
normal (adj)	**normal**	[nor'mal]
not big (adj)	**nu prea mare**	['nu prʲa 'mare]
not difficult (adj)	**uşor**	[u'ʃor]
obligatory (adj)	**obligatoriu**	[obliga'torju]
old (house)	**bătrân**	[bə'trɨn]
open (adj)	**deschis**	[des'kis]
opposite (adj)	**opus**	[o'pus]
ordinary (usual)	**obişnuit**	[obiʃnu'it]
original (unusual)	**original**	[oriʤi'nal]
past (recent)	**trecut**	[tre'kut]
permanent (adj)	**stabil**	[sta'bil]
personal (adj)	**personal**	[perso'nal]
polite (adj)	**politicos**	[politi'kos]
poor (not rich)	**sărac**	[sə'rak]
possible (adj)	**posibil**	[po'sibil]
present (current)	**prezent**	[pre'zent]
previous (adj)	**precedent**	[preʧe'dent]
principal (main)	**fundamental**	[fundamen'tal]
private (~ jet)	**personal**	[perso'nal]
probable (adj)	**probabil**	[pro'babil]
prolonged (e.g., ~ applause)	**îndelungat**	[ɨndelu'ngat]

public (open to all)	**social**	[sotʃi'al]
punctual (person)	**punctual**	[punktu'al]
quiet (tranquil)	**liniştit**	[liniʃ'tit]
rare (adj)	**rar**	[rar]
raw (uncooked)	**crud**	[krud]
right (not left)	**drept**	[drept]
right, correct (adj)	**corect**	[ko'rekt]
ripe (fruit)	**copt**	[kopt]
risky (adj)	**riscant**	[ris'kant]
sad (~ look)	**trist**	[trist]
sad (depressing)	**trist**	[trist]
safe (not dangerous)	**neprimejdios**	[neprimeʒdi'os]
salty (food)	**sărat**	[sə'rat]
satisfied (customer)	**satisfăcut**	[satisfə'kut]
second hand (adj)	**la mâna a doua**	[la 'mɨna a 'dowa]
shallow (water)	**mărunt**	[mə'runt]
sharp (blade, etc.)	**ascuțit**	[asku'ʦit]
short (in length)	**scurt**	[skurt]
short, short-lived (adj)	**de scurtă durată**	[de 'skurtə du'ratə]
significant (notable)	**considerabil**	[konside'rabil]
similar (adj)	**asemănător**	[asemənə'tor]
simple (easy)	**simplu**	['simplu]
skinny	**slab**	[slab]
small (in size)	**mic**	[mik]
smooth (surface)	**neted**	['neted]
soft (~ toys)	**moale**	[mo'ale]
solid (~ wall)	**durabil**	[du'rabil]
sour (flavor, taste)	**acru**	['akru]
spacious (house, etc.)	**spațios**	[spaʦi'os]
special (adj)	**special**	[spetʃi'al]
straight (line, road)	**drept**	[drept]
strong (person)	**puternic**	[pu'ternik]
stupid (foolish)	**prost**	[prost]
suitable (e.g., ~ for drinking)	**folositor**	[folosi'tor]
sunny (day)	**însorit**	[ɨnso'rit]
superb, perfect (adj)	**superb**	[su'perb]
swarthy (adj)	**negricios**	[negri'tʃios]
sweet (sugary)	**dulce**	['dultʃe]
tan (adj)	**bronzat**	[bron'zat]
tasty (delicious)	**gustos**	[gus'tos]
tender (affectionate)	**gingaş**	['ʤingaʃ]
the highest (adj)	**cel mai înalt**	[tʃel maj ɨ'nalt]
the most important	**cel mai important**	[tʃel maj impor'tant]

the nearest	**cel mai apropiat**	['ʧel 'maj apropi'at]
the same, equal (adj)	**asemenea**	[a'semenʲa]
thick (e.g., ~ fog)	**des**	[des]
thick (wall, slice)	**gras**	[gras]
thin (person)	**slab**	[slab]
tight (~ shoes)	**mulat**	[mulat]
tired (exhausted)	**obosit**	[obo'sit]
tiring (adj)	**obositor**	[obosi'tor]
transparent (adj)	**transparent**	[transpa'rent]
unclear (adj)	**neclar**	[ne'klar]
unique (exceptional)	**unic**	['unik]
various (adj)	**distinct**	[dis'tinkt]
warm (moderately hot)	**cald**	[kald]
wet (e.g., ~ clothes)	**ud**	[ud]
whole (entire, complete)	**întreg**	[ɨn'treg]
wide (e.g., ~ road)	**larg**	[larg]
young (adj)	**tânăr**	['tɨnər]

MAIN 500 VERBS

252. Verbs A-C

to accompany (vt)	**a acompania**	[a akompani'ja]
to accuse (vt)	**a învinui**	[a ɨnvinu'i]
to acknowledge (admit)	**a recunoaşte**	[a rekuno'aʃte]
to act (take action)	**a acţiona**	[a aktsio'na]
to add (supplement)	**a adăuga**	[a adəu'ga]
to address (speak to)	**a se adresa**	[a se adre'sa]
to admire (vi)	**a fi încântat**	[a fi ɨnkɨn'tat]
to advertise (vt)	**a face reclamă**	[a 'fatʃe re'klamə]
to advise (vt)	**a sfătui**	[a sfətu'i]
to affirm (assert)	**a susţine**	[a sus'tsine]
to agree (say yes)	**a fi de acord**	[a fi de a'kord]
to aim (to point a weapon)	**a ţinti**	[a tsin'ti]
to allow (sb to do sth)	**a permite**	[a per'mite]
to amputate (vt)	**a amputa**	[a ampu'ta]
to answer (vi, vt)	**a răspunde**	[a rəs'punde]
to apologize (vi)	**a cere scuze**	[a 'tʃere 'skuze]
to appear (come into view)	**a apărea**	[a apə'rʲa]
to applaud (vi, vt)	**a aplauda**	[a aplau'da]
to appoint (assign)	**a numi**	[a nu'mi]
to approach (come closer)	**a se apropia**	[a se apropi'a]
to arrive (ab. train)	**a sosi**	[a so'si]
to ask (~ sb to do sth)	**a cere**	[a 'tʃere]
to aspire to ...	**a aspira**	[a aspi'ra]
to assist (help)	**a asista**	[a asis'ta]
to attack (mil.)	**a ataca**	[a ata'ka]
to attain (objectives)	**a reuşi**	[a reu'ʃi]
to avenge (get revenge)	**a răzbuna**	[a rəzbu'na]
to avoid (danger, task)	**a evita**	[a evi'ta]
to award (give medal to)	**a decora**	[a deko'ra]
to battle (vi)	**a se lupta**	[a se lup'ta]
to be (vi)	**a fi**	[a fi]
to be a cause of ...	**a cauza ...**	[a kau'za]
to be afraid	**a se teme**	[a se 'teme]
to be angry (with ...)	**a se supăra**	[a se supə'ra]

to be at war	**a lupta**	[a lup'ta]
to be based (on ...)	**a se baza pe**	[a se ba'za pe]
to be bored	**a se plictisi**	[a se plikti'si]
to be convinced	**a se convinge**	[a se kon'vindʒe]
to be enough	**a ajunge**	[a a'ʒundʒe]
to be envious	**a invidia**	[a invidi'a]
to be indignant	**a se indigna**	[a se indig'na]
to be interested in ...	**a se interesa**	[a se intere'sa]
to be lost in thought	**a cădea pe gânduri**	[a kə'dʲa pe 'gɨndurʲ]
to be lying (~ on the table)	**a sta**	[a sta]
to be needed	**a fi nevoie**	[a fi ne'voje]
to be perplexed (puzzled)	**a fi nedumerit**	[a fi nedume'rit]
to be preserved	**a se păstra**	[a se pəs'tra]
to be required	**a fi necesar**	[a fi netʃe'sar]
to be surprised	**a se mira**	[a se mi'ra]
to be worried	**a se nelinişti**	[a se nelinij'ti]
to beat (to hit)	**a bate**	[a 'bate]
to become (e.g., ~ old)	**a deveni**	[a deve'ni]
to behave (vi)	**a se comporta**	[a se kompor'ta]
to believe (think)	**a crede**	[a 'krede]
to belong to ...	**a aparține**	[a apar'tsine]
to berth (moor)	**a acosta**	[a akos'ta]
to blind (other drivers)	**a orbi**	[a or'bi]
to blow (wind)	**a sufla**	[a su'fla]
to blush (vi)	**a se înroşi**	[a se ɨnro'ʃi]
to boast (vi)	**a se lăuda**	[a se ləu'da]
to borrow (money)	**a împrumuta**	[a ɨmprumu'ta]
to break (branch, toy, etc.)	**a rupe**	[a 'rupe]
to breathe (vi)	**a respira**	[a respi'ra]
to bring (sth)	**a aduce**	[a a'dutʃe]
to burn (paper, logs)	**a arde**	[a 'arde]
to buy (purchase)	**a cumpăra**	[a kumpə'ra]
to call (~ for help)	**a chema**	[a ke'ma]
to call (yell for sb)	**a chema**	[a ke'ma]
to calm down (vt)	**a linişti**	[a linij'ti]
can (v aux)	**a putea**	[a pu'tʲa]
to cancel (call off)	**a anula**	[a anu'la]
to cast off (of a boat or ship)	**a demara**	[a dema'ra]
to catch (e.g., ~ a ball)	**a prinde**	[a 'prinde]
to change (~ one's opinion)	**a schimba**	[a skim'ba]
to change (exchange)	**a schimba**	[a skim'ba]
to charm (vt)	**a fermeca**	[a ferme'ka]
to choose (select)	**a alege**	[a a'ledʒe]

to chop off (with an ax)	**a tăia**	[a tə'ja]
to clean (e.g., kettle from scale)	**a curăța**	[a kurə'tsa]
to clean (shoes, etc.)	**a curăța**	[a kurə'tsa]
to clean up (tidy)	**a face ordine**	[a 'fatʃe 'ordine]
to close (vt)	**a închide**	[a ɨ'nkide]
to comb one's hair	**a se pieptăna**	[a se peptə'na]
to come down (the stairs)	**a coborî**	[a kobo'rɨ]
to come out (book)	**a apărea**	[a apə'rʲa]
to compare (vt)	**a compara**	[a kompa'ra]
to compensate (vt)	**a compensa**	[a kompen'sa]
to compete (vi)	**a concura**	[a konku'ra]
to compile (~ a list)	**a alcătui**	[a alkətu'i]
to complain (vi, vt)	**a se plânge**	[a se 'plɨndʒe]
to complicate (vt)	**a complica**	[a kompli'ka]
to compose (music, etc.)	**a crea**	[a 'krʲa]
to compromise (reputation)	**a compromite**	[a kompro'mite]
to concentrate (vi)	**a se concentra**	[a se kontʃen'tra]
to confess (criminal)	**a mărturisi**	[a mərturi'si]
to confuse (mix up)	**a încurca**	[a ɨnkur'ka]
to congratulate (vt)	**a felicita**	[a felitʃi'ta]
to consult (doctor, expert)	**a se consulta cu ...**	[a se konsul'ta 'ku]
to continue (~ to do sth)	**a continua**	[a kontinu'a]
to control (vt)	**a controla**	[a kontro'la]
to convince (vt)	**a convinge**	[a kon'vindʒe]
to cooperate (vi)	**a colabora**	[a kolabo'ra]
to coordinate (vt)	**a coordona**	[a koordo'na]
to correct (an error)	**a corecta**	[a korek'ta]
to cost (vt)	**a costa**	[a kos'ta]
to count (money, etc.)	**a calcula**	[a kalku'la]
to count on ...	**a conta pe ...**	[a kon'ta pe]
to crack (ceiling, wall)	**a crăpa**	[a krə'pa]
to create (vt)	**a crea**	[a 'krʲa]
to crush, to squash (~ a bug)	**a strivi**	[a stri'vi]
to cry (weep)	**a plânge**	[a 'plɨndʒe]
to cut off (with a knife)	**a tăia**	[a tə'ja]

253. Verbs D-G

to dare (~ to do sth)	**a îndrăzni**	[a ɨndrəz'ni]
to date from ...	**a data**	[a da'ta]

to deceive (vi, vt)	**a minți**	[a min'tsi]
to decide (~ to do sth)	**a hotărî**	[a hotə'rɨ]
to decorate (tree, street)	**a decora**	[a deko'ra]
to dedicate (book, etc.)	**a dedica**	[a dedi'ka]
to defend (a country, etc.)	**a apăra**	[a apə'ra]
to defend oneself	**a se apăra**	[a se apə'ra]
to demand (request firmly)	**a cere**	[a 'tʃere]
to denounce (vt)	**a denunța**	[a denun'tsa]
to deny (vt)	**a nega**	[a ne'ga]
to depend on ...	**a depinde de ...**	[a de'pinde de]
to deprive (vt)	**a priva**	[a pri'va]
to deserve (vt)	**a merita**	[a meri'ta]
to design (machine, etc.)	**a proiecta**	[a proek'ta]
to desire (want, wish)	**a dori**	[a do'ri]
to despise (vt)	**a disprețui**	[a dispretsu'i]
to destroy (documents, etc.)	**a distruge**	[a dis'trudʒe]
to differ (from sth)	**a se deosebi de ...**	[a se deose'bi de]
to dig (tunnel, etc.)	**a săpa**	[a sə'pa]
to direct (point the way)	**a îndrepta spre ...**	[a ɨndrep'ta spre]
to disappear (vi)	**a dispărea**	[a dispə'rʲa]
to discover (new land, etc.)	**a descoperi**	[a deskope'ri]
to discuss (vt)	**a discuta**	[a disku'ta]
to distribute (leaflets, etc.)	**a răspândi**	[a rəspɨn'di]
to disturb (vt)	**a deranja**	[a deran'ʒa]
to dive (vi)	**a se cufunda**	[a se kufun'da]
to divide (math)	**a împărți**	[a ɨmpər'tsi]
to do (vt)	**a face**	[a 'fatʃe]
to do the laundry	**a spăla**	[a spə'la]
to double (increase)	**a dubla**	[a dub'la]
to doubt (have doubts)	**a se îndoi**	[a se ɨndo'i]
to draw a conclusion	**a trage o concluzie**	[a 'tradʒe o kon'kluzie]
to dream (daydream)	**a visa**	[a vi'sa]
to dream (in sleep)	**a visa**	[a vi'sa]
to drink (vi, vt)	**a bea**	[a bʲa]
to drive a car	**a conduce maşina**	[a kon'dutʃe ma'ʃina]
to drive away (scare away)	**a goni**	[a go'ni]
to drop (let fall)	**a scăpa**	[a skə'pa]
to drown (ab. person)	**a se îneca**	[a se ɨne'ka]
to dry (clothes, hair)	**a usca**	[a uska]
to eat (vi, vt)	**a mânca**	[a mɨn'ka]
to eavesdrop (vi)	**a trage cu urechea**	[a 'tradʒe ku u'rekʲa]

to emit (diffuse - odor, etc.)	**a împrăştia**	[a ɨmprəʃti'a]
to enjoy oneself	**a se veseli**	[a se vese'li]
to enter (on the list)	**a înscrie**	[a ɨn'skrie]
to enter (room, house, etc.)	**a intra**	[a in'tra]
to entertain (amuse)	**a distra**	[a dis'tra]
to equip (fit out)	**a utila**	[a uti'la]
to examine (proposal)	**a analiza**	[a anali'za]
to exchange (sth)	**a face schimb**	[a 'fatʃe 'skimb]
to excuse (forgive)	**a scuza**	[a sku'za]
to exist (vi)	**a exista**	[a ekzis'ta]
to expect (anticipate)	**a aştepta**	[a aʃtep'ta]
to expect (foresee)	**a prevedea**	[a preve'dʲa]
to expel (from school, etc.)	**a exclude**	[a eks'klude]
to explain (vt)	**a explica**	[a ekspli'ka]
to express (vt)	**a exprima**	[a ekspri'ma]
to extinguish (a fire)	**a stinge**	[a 'stindʒe]
to fall in love (with ...)	**a se îndrăgosti**	[a se ɨndrəgos'ti]
to feed (provide food)	**a hrăni**	[a hrə'ni]
to fight (against the enemy)	**a lupta**	[a lup'ta]
to fight (vi)	**a se bate**	[a se 'bate]
to fill (glass, bottle)	**a umple**	[a 'umple]
to find (~ lost items)	**a găsi**	[a gə'si]
to finish (vt)	**a termina**	[a termi'na]
to fish (angle)	**a pescui**	[a pesku'i]
to fit (ab. dress, etc.)	**a plăcea**	[a plə'tʃa]
to flatter (vt)	**a flata**	[a fla'ta]
to fly (bird, plane)	**a zbura**	[a zbu'ra]
to follow ... (come after)	**a urma**	[a ur'ma]
to forbid (vt)	**a interzice**	[a inter'zitʃe]
to force (compel)	**a forța**	[a for'tsa]
to forget (vi, vt)	**a uita**	[a uj'ta]
to forgive (pardon)	**a ierta**	[a er'ta]
to form (constitute)	**a forma**	[a for'ma]
to get dirty (vi)	**a se murdări**	[a se murdə'ri]
to get infected (with ...)	**a se contamina**	[a se kontami'na]
to get irritated	**a se irita**	[a se iri'ta]
to get married	**a se căsători**	[a se kəsəto'ri]
to get rid of ...	**a scăpa**	[a skə'pa]
to get tired	**a obosi**	[a obo'si]
to get up (arise from bed)	**a se ridica**	[a se ridi'ka]

to give (vt)	**a da**	[a da]
to give a bath (to bath)	**a face baie**	[a 'fatʃe 'bae]
to give a hug, to hug (vt)	**a îmbrățișa**	[a ɨmbrətsi'ʃa]
to give in (yield to)	**a ceda**	[a tʃe'da]
to glimpse (vt)	**a vedea**	[a ve'dʲa]
to go (by car, etc.)	**a merge**	[a 'merdʒe]
to go (on foot)	**a merge**	[a 'merdʒe]
to go for a swim	**a se scălda**	[a se skəl'da]
to go out (for dinner, etc.)	**a ieşi**	[a e'ʃi]
to go to bed (go to sleep)	**a se culca**	[a se kul'ka]
to greet (vt)	**a saluta**	[a salu'ta]
to grow (plants)	**a cultiva**	[a kulti'va]
to guarantee (vt)	**a garanta**	[a garan'ta]
to guess (the answer)	**a ghici**	[a gi'tʃi]

254. Verbs H-M

to hand out (distribute)	**a distribui**	[a distribu'i]
to hang (curtains, etc.)	**a atârna**	[a atɨr'na]
to have (vt)	**a avea**	[a a'vʲa]
to have a try	**a încerca**	[a ɨntʃer'ka]
to have breakfast	**a lua micul dejun**	[a lu'a 'mikul de'ʒun]
to have dinner	**a cina**	[a tʃi'na]
to have lunch	**a lua prânzul**	[a lu'a 'prɨnzul]
to head (group, etc.)	**a conduce**	[a kon'dutʃe]
to hear (vt)	**a auzi**	[a au'zi]
to heat (vt)	**a încălzi**	[a ɨnkəl'zi]
to help (vt)	**a ajuta**	[a aʒu'ta]
to hide (vt)	**a ascunde**	[a as'kunde]
to hire (e.g., ~ a boat)	**a închiria**	[a ɨnkiri'ja]
to hire (staff)	**a angaja**	[a anga'ʒa]
to hope (vi, vt)	**a spera**	[a spe'ra]
to hunt (for food, sport)	**a vâna**	[a vɨ'na]
to hurry (vi)	**a se grăbi**	[a se grə'bi]
to imagine (to picture)	**a-şi imagina**	[aʃ imadʒi'na]
to imitate (vt)	**a imita**	[a imi'ta]
to implore (vt)	**a ruga**	[a ru'ga]
to import (vt)	**a importa**	[a impor'ta]
to increase (vi)	**a se mări**	[a se mə'ri]
to increase (vt)	**a mări**	[a mə'ri]
to infect (vt)	**a molipsi**	[a molip'si]
to influence (vt)	**a influența**	[a influen'tsa]
to inform (e.g., ~ the police about)	**a anunța**	[a anun'tsa]

to inform (vt)	**a informa**	[a infor'ma]
to inherit (vt)	**a moşteni**	[a moʃte'ni]
to inquire (about ...)	**a afla**	[a af'la]
to insert (put in)	**a pune**	[a 'pune]
to insinuate (imply)	**a face aluzie**	[a 'fatʃe a'luzie]
to insist (vi, vt)	**a insista**	[a insis'ta]
to inspire (vt)	**a stimula**	[a stimu'la]
to instruct (teach)	**a da instrucțiuni**	[a da instruktsi'unʲ]
to insult (offend)	**a jigni**	[a ʒig'ni]
to interest (vt)	**a interesa**	[a intere'sa]
to intervene (vi)	**a interveni**	[a interve'ni]
to introduce (sb to sb)	**a face cunoştință**	[a 'fatʃe kunoʃ'tintsə]
to invent (machine, etc.)	**a inventa**	[a inven'ta]
to invite (vt)	**a invita**	[a invi'ta]
to iron (clothes)	**a călca**	[a kəl'ka]
to irritate (annoy)	**a irita**	[a iri'ta]
to isolate (vt)	**a izola**	[a izo'la]
to join (political party, etc.)	**a adera**	[a ade'ra]
to joke (be kidding)	**a glumi**	[a glu'mi]
to keep (old letters, etc.)	**a păstra**	[a pəs'tra]
to keep silent, to hush	**a tăcea**	[a tə'tʃa]
to kill (vt)	**a omorî**	[a omo'rɨ]
to knock (on the door)	**a bate**	[a 'bate]
to know (sb)	**a cunoaşte**	[a kuno'aʃte]
to know (sth)	**a şti**	[a ʃti]
to laugh (vi)	**a râde**	[a 'rɨde]
to launch (start up)	**a porni**	[a por'ni]
to leave (~ for Mexico)	**a pleca**	[a ple'ka]
to leave (forget sth)	**a lăsa**	[a lə'sa]
to leave (spouse)	**a părăsi**	[a pərə'si]
to liberate (city, etc.)	**a elibera**	[a elibe'ra]
to lie (~ on the floor)	**a sta culcat**	[a sta kul'kat]
to lie (tell untruth)	**a minți**	[a min'tsi]
to light (campfire, etc.)	**a aprinde**	[a a'prinde]
to light up (illuminate)	**a lumina**	[a lumi'na]
to like (I like ...)	**a plăcea**	[a plə'tʃa]
to limit (vt)	**a limita**	[a limi'ta]
to listen (vi)	**a asculta**	[a askul'ta]
to live (~ in France)	**a trăi**	[a trə'i]
to live (exist)	**a exista**	[a ekzis'ta]
to load (gun)	**a încărca**	[a ɨnkər'ka]
to load (vehicle, etc.)	**a încărca**	[a ɨnkər'ka]
to look (I'm just ~ing)	**a privi**	[a pri'vi]
to look for ... (search)	**a căuta**	[a kəu'ta]

to look like (resemble)	**a semăna cu**	[a semə'na ku]
to lose (umbrella, etc.)	**a pierde**	[a 'pjerde]
to love (e.g., ~ dancing)	**a plăcea**	[a plə'ʧa]
to love (sb)	**a iubi**	[a ju'bi]
to lower (blind, head)	**a lăsa în jos**	[a lə'sa 'ɨn 'ʒos]
to make (~ dinner)	**a găti**	[a gə'ti]
to make a mistake	**a greşi**	[a gre'ʃi]
to make angry	**a supăra**	[a supə'ra]
to make easier	**a uşura**	[a uʃu'ra]
to make multiple copies	**a multiplica**	[a multipli'ka]
to make the acquaintance	**a face cunoştinţă**	[a 'faʧe kunoʃ'tinʦə]
to make use (of ...)	**a se folosi**	[a se folo'si]
to manage, to run	**a conduce**	[a kon'duʧe]
to mark (make a mark)	**a semnala**	[a semna'la]
to mean (signify)	**a avea sens**	[a a'vʲa sens]
to memorize (vt)	**a memora**	[a memo'ra]
to mention (talk about)	**a aminti**	[a amin'ti]
to miss (school, etc.)	**a lipsi**	[a lip'si]
to mix (combine, blend)	**a amesteca**	[a ameste'ka]
to mock (make fun of)	**a-şi bate joc**	[aʃ 'bate ʒok]
to move (to shift)	**a mişca**	[a miʃ'ka]
to multiply (math)	**a înmulţi**	[a ɨnmul'ʦi]
must (v aux)	**a fi dator**	[a fi da'tor]

255. Verbs N-R

to name, to call (vt)	**a numi**	[a nu'mi]
to negotiate (vi)	**a purta tratative**	[a pur'ta trata'tive]
to note (write down)	**a însemna**	[a ɨnsem'na]
to notice (see)	**a observa**	[a obser'va]
to obey (vi, vt)	**a se supune**	[a se su'pune]
to object (vi, vt)	**a contrazice**	[a kontra'ziʧe]
to observe (see)	**a observa**	[a obser'va]
to offend (vt)	**a jigni**	[a ʒig'ni]
to omit (word, phrase)	**a omite**	[a o'mite]
to open (vt)	**a deschide**	[a des'kide]
to order (in restaurant)	**a comanda**	[a koman'da]
to order (mil.)	**a ordona**	[a ordo'na]
to organize (concert, party)	**a organiza**	[a organi'za]
to overestimate (vt)	**a reevalua**	[a reevalu'a]
to own (possess)	**a poseda**	[a pose'da]
to participate (vi)	**a participa**	[a partiʧi'pa]
to pass through (by car, etc.)	**a trece**	[a 'treʧe]

to pay (vi, vt)	**a plăti**	[a plə'ti]
to peep, spy on	**a urmări pe furiş**	[a urmə'ri pe fu'riʃ]
to penetrate (vt)	**a pătrunde**	[a pə'trunde]
to permit (vt)	**a permite**	[a per'mite]
to pick (flowers)	**a rupe**	[a 'rupe]
to place (put, set)	**a instala**	[a insta'la]
to plan (~ to do sth)	**a planifica**	[a planifi'ka]
to play (actor)	**a juca**	[a ʒu'ka]
to play (children)	**a juca**	[a ʒu'ka]
to point (~ the way)	**a arăta**	[a arə'ta]
to pour (liquid)	**a turna**	[a tur'na]
to pray (vi, vt)	**a se ruga**	[a se ru'ga]
to prefer (vt)	**a prefera**	[a prefe'ra]
to prepare (~ a plan)	**a pregăti**	[a pregə'ti]
to present (sb to sb)	**a reprezenta**	[a reprezen'ta]
to preserve (peace, life)	**a păstra**	[a pəs'tra]
to prevail (vt)	**a predomina**	[a predomi'na]
to progress (move forward)	**a progresa**	[a progre'sa]
to promise (vt)	**a promite**	[a pro'mite]
to pronounce (vt)	**a pronunța**	[a pronun'ʦa]
to propose (vt)	**a propune**	[a pro'pune]
to protect (e.g., ~ nature)	**a apăra**	[a apə'ra]
to protest (vi)	**a protesta**	[a protes'ta]
to prove (vt)	**a dovedi**	[a dove'di]
to provoke (vt)	**a provoca**	[a provo'ka]
to pull (~ the rope)	**a trage**	[a 'traʤə]
to punish (vt)	**a pedepsi**	[a pedep'si]
to push (~ the door)	**a împinge**	[a ɨm'pinʤe]
to put away (vt)	**a ascunde**	[a as'kunde]
to put in order	**a pune în ordine**	[a 'pune ɨn 'ordine]
to put, to place	**a pune**	[a 'pune]
to quote (cite)	**a cita**	[a ʧi'ta]
to reach (arrive at)	**a atinge**	[a a'tinʤe]
to read (vi, vt)	**a citi**	[a ʧi'ti]
to realize (a dream)	**a realiza**	[a reali'za]
to recognize (identify sb)	**a recunoaşte**	[a rekuno'aʃte]
to recommend (vt)	**a recomanda**	[a rekoman'da]
to recover (~ from flu)	**a se vindeca**	[a se vinde'ka]
to redo (do again)	**a reface**	[a re'faʧe]
to reduce (speed, etc.)	**a micşora**	[a mikʃo'ra]
to refuse (~ sb)	**a refuza**	[a refu'za]
to regret (be sorry)	**a regreta**	[a regre'ta]

to reinforce (vt)	**a consolida**	[a konsoli'da]
to remember (Do you ~ me?)	**a ține minte**	[a 'tsine 'minte]
to remember (I can't ~ her name)	**a-și aminti**	['aʃ amin'ti]
to remind of ...	**a aminti**	[a amin'ti]
to remove (~ a stain)	**a scoate**	[a sko'ate]
to remove (~ an obstacle)	**a înlătura**	[a ɨnlətu'ra]
to rent (sth from sb)	**a închiria**	[a ɨnkiri'ja]
to repair (mend)	**a repara**	[a repa'ra]
to repeat (say again)	**a repeta**	[a repe'ta]
to report (make a report)	**a raporta**	[a rapor'ta]
to reproach (vt)	**a reproșa**	[a repro'ʃa]
to reserve, to book	**a rezerva**	[a rezer'va]
to restrain (hold back)	**a reține**	[a re'tsine]
to return (come back)	**a se întoarce**	[a se ɨnto'artʃe]
to risk, to take a risk	**a risca**	[a ris'ka]
to rub out (erase)	**a șterge**	[a 'ʃterdʒe]
to run (move fast)	**a alerga**	[a aler'ga]
to rush (hurry sb)	**a grăbi**	[a grə'bi]

256. Verbs S-W

to satisfy (please)	**a satisface**	[a satis'fatʃe]
to save (rescue)	**a salva**	[a sal'va]
to say (~ thank you)	**a spune**	[a 'spune]
to scold (vt)	**a certa**	[a tʃer'ta]
to scratch (with claws)	**a zgâria**	[a zgɨri'ja]
to select (to pick)	**a lua înapoi**	[a lu'a ɨna'poj]
to sell (goods)	**a vinde**	[a 'vinde]
to send (a letter)	**a trimite**	[a tri'mite]
to send back (vt)	**a expedia destinatarului**	[a ekspedi'ja destina'taruluj]
to sense (~ danger)	**a simți**	[a sim'tsʲ]
to sentence (vt)	**a condamna**	[a kondam'na]
to serve (in restaurant)	**a servi**	[a ser'vi]
to settle (a conflict)	**a aranja**	[a aran'ʒa]
to shake (vt)	**a scutura**	[a skutu'ra]
to shave (vi)	**a se bărbieri**	[a se bərbie'ri]
to shine (gleam)	**a străluci**	[a strəlu'tʃi]
to shiver (with cold)	**a tremura**	[a tremu'ra]
to shoot (vi)	**a trage**	[a 'tradʒə]

to shout (vi)	**a striga**	[a stri'ga]
to show (to display)	**a arăta**	[a arə'ta]
to shudder (vi)	**a tresări**	[a tresə'ri]
to sigh (vi)	**a ofta**	[a of'ta]
to sign (document)	**a semna**	[a sem'na]
to signify (mean)	**a însemna**	[a ɨnsem'na]
to simplify (vt)	**a simplifica**	[a simplifi'ka]
to sin (vi)	**a păcătui**	[a pəkətu'i]
to sit (be sitting)	**a şedea**	[a ʃə'dʲa]
to sit down (vi)	**a se aşeza**	[a se aʃə'za]
to smell (emit an odor)	**a mirosi**	[a miro'si]
to smell (inhale the odor)	**a mirosi**	[a miro'si]
to smile (vi)	**a zâmbi**	[a zɨm'bi]
to snap (vi, ab. rope)	**a se rupe**	[a se 'rupe]
to solve (problem)	**a rezolva**	[a rezol'va]
to sow (seed, crop)	**a semăna**	[a semə'na]
to spill (liquid)	**a vărsa**	[a vər'sa]
to spit (vi)	**a scuipa**	[a skuj'pa]
to stand (toothache, cold)	**a răbda**	[a rəb'da]
to start (begin)	**a începe**	[a ɨn'ʧepe]
to steal (money, etc.)	**a fura**	[a fu'ra]
to stop (for pause, etc.)	**a se opri**	[a se o'pri]
to stop (please ~ calling me)	**a pune capăt**	[a 'pune 'kapət]
to stop talking	**a tăcea**	[a tə'ʧa]
to stroke (caress)	**a mângâia**	[a mɨngɨ'ja]
to study (vt)	**a studia**	[a studi'a]
to suffer (feel pain)	**a suferi**	[a sufe'ri]
to support (cause, idea)	**a susține**	[a sus'ʦine]
to suppose (assume)	**a presupune**	[a presu'pune]
to surface (ab. submarine)	**a ieşi la suprafață**	[a e'ʃi la supra'faʦə]
to surprise (amaze)	**a mira**	[a mi'ra]
to suspect (vt)	**a suspecta**	[a suspek'ta]
to swim (vi)	**a înota**	[a ɨno'ta]
to take (get hold of)	**a lua**	[a lu'a]
to take a bath	**a se spăla**	[a se spə'la]
to take a rest	**a se odihni**	[a se odih'ni]
to take away (e.g., about waiter)	**a duce cu sine**	[a 'duʧe ku 'sine]
to take off (airplane)	**a decola**	[a deko'la]
to take off (painting, curtains, etc.)	**a scoate**	[a sko'ate]

to take pictures	**a fotografia**	[a fotografi'ja]
to talk to ...	**a vorbi cu ...**	[a vor'bi ku]
to teach (give lessons)	**a învăța pe cineva**	[a ɨnvə'tsa pe tʃine'va]
to tear off, to rip off (vt)	**a smulge**	[a 'smuldʒe]
to tell (story, joke)	**a povesti**	[a poves'ti]
to thank (vt)	**a mulțumi**	[a multsu'mi]
to think (believe)	**a crede**	[a 'krede]
to think (vi, vt)	**a se gândi**	[a se gɨn'di]
to threaten (vt)	**a amenința**	[a amenin'tsa]
to throw (stone, etc.)	**a arunca**	[a arun'ka]
to tie to ...	**a lega**	[a le'ga]
to tie up (prisoner)	**a lega**	[a le'ga]
to tire (make tired)	**a obosi**	[a obo'si]
to touch (one's arm, etc.)	**a se referi**	[a se refe'ri]
to tower (over ...)	**a se înălța**	[a se ɨnəl'tsa]
to train (animals)	**a dresa**	[a dre'sa]
to train (sb)	**a antrena**	[a antre'na]
to train (vi)	**a se antrena**	[a se antre'na]
to transform (vt)	**a transforma**	[a transfor'ma]
to translate (vt)	**a traduce**	[a tra'dutʃe]
to treat (illness)	**a trata**	[a tra'ta]
to trust (vt)	**a avea încredere**	[a a'vʲa ɨn'kredere]
to try (attempt)	**a se strădui**	[a se strədu'i]
to turn (e.g., ~ left)	**a întoarce**	[a ɨnto'artʃe]
to turn away (vi)	**a se întoarce**	[a se ɨnto'artʃe]
to turn off (the light)	**a stinge**	[a 'stindʒe]
to turn on (computer, etc.)	**a conecta**	[a konek'ta]
to turn over (stone, etc.)	**a întoarce**	[a ɨnto'artʃe]
to underestimate (vt)	**a subaprecia**	[a subapretʃi'a]
to underline (vt)	**a sublinia**	[a sublini'a]
to understand (vt)	**a înțelege**	[a ɨntse'ledʒe]
to undertake (vt)	**a întreprinde**	[a ɨntre'prinde]
to unite (vt)	**a uni**	[a u'ni]
to untie (vt)	**a dezlega**	[a dezle'ga]
to use (phrase, word)	**a folosi**	[a folo'si]
to vaccinate (vt)	**a vaccina**	[a vaktʃi'na]
to vote (vi)	**a vota**	[a vo'ta]
to wait (vt)	**a aştepta**	[a aʃtep'ta]
to wake (sb)	**a deştepta**	[a deʃtep'ta]
to want (wish, desire)	**a vrea**	[a vrʲa]
to warn (of the danger)	**a preveni**	[a preve'ni]
to wash (clean)	**a spăla**	[a spə'la]

to water (plants)	**a uda**	[a u'da]
to wave (the hand)	**a flutura**	[a flutu'ra]
to weigh (have weight)	**a cântări**	[a kɨntə'ri]
to work (vi)	**a lucra**	[a lu'kra]
to worry (make anxious)	**a nelinişti**	[a neliniʃ'ti]
to worry (vi)	**a se nelinişti**	[a se neliniʃ'ti]
to wrap (parcel, etc.)	**a împacheta**	[a ɨmpake'ta]
to wrestle (sport)	**a lupta**	[a lup'ta]
to write (vt)	**a scrie**	[a 'skrie]
to write down	**a nota**	[a no'ta]

Printed in Great Britain
by Amazon

70494962R00154